I0816624

POPULAR MUSIC IN EAST AND SOUTHEAST ASIA
Sonic (under)Currents and Currencies

Editor
Mayco A Santaella

Published by Sunway University Press
An imprint of Sunway University Sdn Bhd

No. 5, Jalan Universiti
Bandar Sunway
47500 Selangor Darul Ehsan
Malaysia

press.sunway.edu.my

ISBN 978-967-5492-69-3

Perpustakaan Negara Malaysia Cataloguing-in-Publication Data

POPULAR MUSIC IN EAST AND SOUTHEAST ASIA: Sonic (under) Currents and Currencies / Editor Mayco A Santaella.
ISBN 978-967-5492-69-3 (hardback)
1. Popular music--Asia.
2. Popular music--East Asia.
3. Popular music--Southeast Asia.
I. Santaella, Mayco A.
781.63095

Edited by Hani Hazman
Designed and typeset by Erin Ng
Printed and bound by CPI Group (UK) Ltd, Croydon,
CR0 4YY

CONTENTS

PREFACE

Popular Music in East and Southeast Asia: Sonic (under)Currents and Currencies serves as an introduction to genres, artists, and contemporary discourses in and of the region. The first part of the title presents two challenges: (1) the conceptualisation of popular music in this part of the world, and (2) the conceptualisation of East and Southeast Asia through popular music. This publication recognises fluid approaches to consider multiple interpretations of the field and the region(s). Global genres such as hip-hop and rock, regional genres such as Mandopop, national genres such as *dangdut*, local/provincial genres such as *campursari*, and the popularisation of traditional music forms such as *dero* present a unique scope to the conceptualisation of "popular music" in East and Southeast Asia. Simultaneously, shared genres across regions, nation states, islands, and political borders challenge the way academics conceptualise "East Asia" and "Southeast Asia". The subtitle of this publication *Sonic (under)Currents and Currencies* invites the reader to engage with alternative conceptualisations presented through an array of genres, artists, and scene-specific discourses that help build a comprehensive matrix of popular music across regions.

The post-colonial context that developed during the second half of the 20th century has encouraged a review of theoretical constructs developed in the global north. In addition to this, the post-national condition of certain genres and musical styles has led scholars to consider regional links, shared features, and popular music experiences looking at specific scenes, subcultures, and industries that create alternative spaces which, at times, challenge the conceptualisation of area studies such as "East Asia" and "Southeast Asia". Lastly, the recent decolonisation movement in academia suggests a need to re-evaluate western canons and structures recognising emic usage of etic discourses of popular music genres.

This volume covers genres, artists, and popular music issues with examples from the Philippines, Indonesia, Malaysia, and Singapore in Southeast Asia, Taiwan, Hong Kong, Japan, and South Korea in East Asia, and the United States (US) in relation to the development of specific genres, industries, and links with Asia. Genres discussed include rock, metal, punk, ballad, K-pop, Cantopop, Mandopop, R&B, hip-hop, folk songs, indie genres, *campursari*, and pop, as well as the popularisation of traditional music genres and the analysis of national anthems in relation to popular forms. The chapters consist of selected and reviewed submissions of papers delivered at the 7th Inter-Asia Popular Music Studies conference held from 3rd to 6th December 2020.

The authors discuss an array of different issues including historicity, globalisation and subcultures, masculinity, feminism, digital technology, record labels, political protests, fandom culture(s), music education, post-localisation and post-globalisation, Christianity, US influences, local music scenes, translocality, do-it-yourself cultures, cinema, choral arrangements, gender identity, heritage, nationalism, modernity, radio broadcasting, DJs, YouTube, busking, and the development of popular music styles. The breadth of topics renders the volume a useful source of contemporary popular music discourses written largely by Asian scholars, and academics working in the region.

The discussions presented in this volume cover specific genres, artists, and scenes towards the conceptualisation of the field largely from an inter-Asia positionality and experience. This contribution to the diversification of anglophone scholarship presents both challenges and new potentials. On the one hand, the authors negotiate terminology when "languaging" about specific issues and use English nomenclature for terms such as "hybridity" to discuss a topic rather than engaging indigenous alternatives such as the Malay "*kacukan*", considering its alternative signifiers. On the other hand, anglophone scholarship in Asia has provided a platform for the initial conceptualisation of East Asia and

Southeast Asia within the region, but more recently for the analysis of inter-Asia discourses beyond the confines of language, ethnicity, and nationality. The focus on popular music experiences by local scholars continues to shape canons that revisit global discourses developing local, regional, and inter-Asia alternative academic modernities.

INTER-ASIA POPULAR MUSIC STUDIES 2020

The Inter-Asia Popular Music Studies (IAPMS) Group was established in 2007 by scholars in Asia in order to establish a regional discourse on popular music. The majority of its members are from East and Southeast Asia, joined by presenters from the United States (US), Australia and the United Kingdom (UK) (among other countries) who carry out research in the region. As stated in the website interasiapop.org, IAPMS members commonly participate in the International Association for the Study of Popular Music (IASPM) both at regional and international conferences, as well as the Inter-Asia Cultural Studies Society (IACSS) which, like IAPMS, has a regional foci. Though not formally associated with an organisation, IAPMS serves as an important study group *in situ* for the investigation of popular music in Asia and has held conferences in Osaka (2008), Hong Kong (2010), Taipei (2012), Chiang Mai (2014), Melbourne (2016), Beijing (2018), and Kuala Lumpur (2020, online).

The theme for this conference and subtitle of this publication is *Sonic (under)Currents and Currencies*. As drafted by the chair of the programme committee, Kai Khiun Liew, the theme reads:

> The recent international popularity of Korean pop groups BTS and Blackpink placed Asia from passive recipients to active participants of otherwise US- and UK- dominated global pop music. However, the extent in which they represent and personify the rich undercurrent of popular music circulation in Asia remains debatable in Asia's culturally diverse landscapes. While the digital platform and social media as well as travel have intensified the flows of popular music participation, it is probably premature to idealistically suggest the levelling of more enduring historical and cultural boundaries and borders. The post-global or post-digital condition needs discussion.

In this respect, the theme of this conference, "Sonic (under) Currents and Currencies", seeks to explore the responses of popular music as local, trans-local national and transnational formations and traditions to the disruptions and changes in the region's changing techno-cultural landscape. Within such disruptions, the conference also explores the relevance and currencies of both assumptions and practices of popular music in the region. Examples range from genres and categories, cultural industries, and politics to government, fandom and activism.

Since its first conference in 2008, IAPMS has encouraged a diversity of scholarship at all levels about popular music studies in the context of Asia. The conference welcomes presentations from the academic community as well as practitioners, activists and policymakers. As the 7th conference will be held in Kuala Lumpur, Malaysia, the organising committee hopes to see greater representation of topics and presenters from ASEAN countries.

The programme committee was chaired by Kai Khiun Liew (Independent Scholar, Singapore) and included Miaoju Jian (National Chung Cheng University, Taiwan), Vicky Ho (The Open University of Hong Kong, Hong Kong), Qian Zhang (Communication University of China, China), Atchareeya Saisin (Chiang Mai University, Thailand), Jungwon Kim (Yonsei University, Korea), Kaori Fushiki (Taisho University, Japan), Kyohei Miyairi (Independent Scholar, Japan), Mayco A Santaella (Sunway University, Malaysia), and Isabella Pek (SEAMEX Institute, Malaysia).

The local arrangements committee was chaired by Mayco A Santaella (Sunway University, Malaysia) and included Azmyl Yusof (Sunway University, Malaysia), Adil Johan (Universiti Kebangsaan Malaysia, Malaysia), Christine Yong (Sunway

University, Malaysia), Rachel Ong (Sunway University, Malaysia), Frank Ong (Sunway University, Malaysia) and Isabella Pek (SEAMEX Institute, Malaysia). Last but not least, Hyunjoon Shin (Sungkonghoe University, Korea) and Jungyup Lee (University of Massachusetts, Amherst, US/Korea) were in charge of the website and public announcements.

The department of Film & Performing Arts at Sunway University hosted the 7th IAPMS conference online from 3rd to 6th December 2020. The conference featured 52 presenters from the US, Europe, Australia, and the Asia-Pacific region. The event was originally scheduled for July 2020 but was postponed due to the COVID-19 pandemic that governed all aspects of our lives at the time. Given that the situation lasted throughout the year, and with the global IASPM conference originally scheduled in Korea in July 2021, the committee decided to host the IAPMS conference online. The conference featured a keynote speech by Professor Dr Tan Sooi Beng (Figure 1) on popular music and the gramophone era in Malaya during the first half of the 20th century, which served as a good introduction to the study of Popular Music in Malaya specifically and Southeast Asia at large.

FIGURE 1 Screenshot of the keynote speech by Professor Dr Tan Sooi Beng
Source: Screenshot by author

The conference also featured a plenary session by singer, ethnomusicologist and cultural activist Grace Nono, discussing her positionality as a singer and researcher navigating coloniality, music industries, and gender struggles, towards the decolonisation of voices in academia, festivals, and the national music industry (Figure 2).

FIGURE 2 Screenshot of the plenary session with Grace Nono (left) answering a question from Professor Dr Mohd Anis Md Nor (right)
Source: Screenshot by author

Last but not least, the conference featured a live concert by Azmyl Yunor performing pieces from his recent album release, *John Bangi Blues*, along other classics from previous recordings.

FIGURE 3 Screenshot of the closing ceremony with (from left to right) Azmyl Yusof, Mayco A Santaella, Bradley Freeman, Hyunjoon Shin, Kai Khiun Liew, Aline Scott-Maxwell, Nur Lina Anuar, Mori Yoshitaka, Amane Kasai, Madoka Fukuoka, Adil Johan, Xin Ying Ch'ng, Shota Fukuoka, Storm Gloor, Miaoju Jian, Rachel Ong, Luis Zapata, Hueyuen Choong, Zhang Xiaodan, Jeremy Wallach, Nur Izzati Jamalludin and Tahsin Kuo
Source: Screenshot by author

Organising a conference of this breadth is no small task, and I would like to thank the programme committee, the local arrangements committee, the website committee and all IAPMS members who contributed to the success of this online event. At this point, we would also like to apologise for any shortcomings. Personally, I would also like to thank Donald Bowyer, Dean of the School of Arts at Sunway University, for his continuous support. *Terima kasih* to Hani Hazman for the thorough reviews and suggestions, to Carol Wong for her support, reviews and professionalism in handling this publication and to the entire production team of Sunway University Press. Last but not least, I would like to thank Graeme Wilkinson, Vice-Chancellor of Sunway University, for his perpetual dedication to the mission of this not-for-profit institution, and his support to this project specifically and to the arts at large.

Mayco A Santaella
Kuala Lumpur, Malaysia

CHAPTER 1

Rocking "Onward Singapore": The Ethnopolitics of Singing a National Anthem

Adil Johan, *Institute of Ethnic Studies (KITA), Universiti Kebangsaan Malaysia*

On August 9, 2019, Singaporeans gathered at the Padang to celebrate their 54th National Day. In the sixth act of the show, after a lively hip-hop performance, dazzling pyrotechnic display, laser show and entrance of a six-metre-tall metallic lion weighing 1000kg, the crowd fell silent to sing their national anthem. The singing was led by the veteran rock star, Ramli Sarip, fondly known throughout the Nusantara region as "Papa Rock". For the first time in their history, Singaporeans witnessed and sang along to a rendition of their anthem at a slower tempo that was infused with the raspy but seasoned Malay rock vocals of Ramli. His unique performance of "Majulah Singapura" ("Onward Singapore") proceeded to become a viral Internet hit, but it also received mixed responses.

This chapter pays particular attention to the negative and ambivalent public reactions to Ramli's version of the song and the ensuing media narrative that unfolded. I draw attention to the ethnicised politics of Singapore that emerge from the subtext of netizen comments and news headlines related to Ramli's folk-rock rendition of the anthem. These discourses are analysed in light of the nation state's geopolitical history as located within a largely Malay-speaking Nusantara region. The chapter also considers the significance of Malay popular music in revealing the complex ethnopolitics of the region. In view of Singapore's postcolonial history—the source of much of these ethnic tensions—the year 2019 was important because it marked the island state's Bicentennial; 200 years since Stamford Raffles had landed on its shores and began developing the island as a central port for the British Empire in Asia.

Situating "Majulah Singapura" in the Malay World

The island state of Singapore is separated from its neighbour Malaysia by a bridge known as the Johor-Singapore Causeway. Across from Singapore's southern and western shores are the islands of Indonesian Sumatra and Borneo, the meeting point of the three nation states of Brunei, Malaysia and Indonesia. In effect, Singapore with its majority ethnic Chinese population, who largely form the political and economic elite, is precariously surrounded by a Malay-speaking region (Rahim, 2009). Singapore was also a part of the Federation of Malaysia in 1963. Due to the unwillingness of its state leader, Lee Kuan Yew, to agree to Malaysian Prime Minister Tunku Abdul Rahman's plan for affirmative action policies (or special privileges) for ethnic Malays, Singapore seceded from the Federation in 1965 and became an independent island state. The ripples of this separation and Singapore's geopolitical precarity are evident in the erasure of Singapore's precolonial (Malay and indigenous) past in its national narrative, *The Singapore Story*, as penned by the state's founding Prime Minister, Lee Kuan Yew (2008).

However, recent government programmes during the Bicentennial have seen conscious efforts to re-script these erasures by allowing for a revision of Singapore's history of establishment. In January 2019, the once-solitary statue of Stamford Raffles erected along the north bank of the Singapore river is now accompanied—or surrounded, depending on your perspective—by four historical male figures: Tan Tock Seng, Naraina Pillai, Munshi Abdullah and Sang Nila Utama (Lim, 2019). The first three were notable individuals who arrived at the island in 1819, the same year as Raffles, but Sang Nila Utama was a Srivijayan prince from Palembang who established the Kingdom of Singapura (or Temasek) in 1299. While the erection of his statue may be related to an ahistorical or mythical account of the region's past as recorded in the *Malay Annals*, it nevertheless serves as a concrete reminder of Singapore's precolonial past and the claim of origin that people of Malay ancestry may have on Singapore. Along with an appointment of the state's first Malay President in 47 years (and first-ever female to hold the post) in 2017, the visible initiatives that led to and coincided with the Bicentennial are seen as a move by the Singaporean state to reconcile its differences with the Malay world and its Malay citizens.

Prior to this in 2012, a series of state-sponsored events in recognition of the national anthem's composer, Zubir Said, marked a shift towards greater visibility of the state's Malay minority population. Elsewhere, I have analysed ethnographically how such events empower Singapore-Malays by recognising their community's role in nation making, but such events also brought to the surface the affective tensions that were experienced by Malays as marginalised actors in the state's formation (Adil, 2021). Importantly, "Majulah Singapura" as the national anthem of Singapore (barring a constitutional amendment), has and always will be sung in Malay, one of the four official national languages. However, this is complicated by observing that the anthem is "not understood by most Singaporeans owing to their lack of familiarity with the national language" (Rahim, 2009, p. 2). All these ethnopolitical currents underscore Ramli Sarip's Malay-rock aesthetic in singing Singapore's national anthem, and the political tensions of Chinese-Malay race relations in the region further elucidate some of the negative responses to his rendition.

Ramli Sarip, "Papa Rock" of the Nusantara

From the 1970s until the 1990s, rock and eventually heavy metal were part of a major popular music culture expressed across the Singapore-Malaysia-Indonesia border (Wallach, 2011; Ferrarese, 2016; Adil & Santaella, 2021). Ramli was the frontman of the Singaporean-based band Sweet Charity, who articulated this tripartite Nusantara network of rock in the Malay language. The group's hit song "Kamelia" released in the album *Pelarian* was a rendition of an Indonesian singer-songwriter's song "Camelia 2" (Sweet Charity, 1980). However, the band recorded the song with the "heavier" aesthetic of a guitar-keyboard-bass-drums rock band ensemble. They also introduced the song with an extended section much alike the introduction of Dee Dee Bridgewater's version of Elton John's "Sorry Seems to be the Hardest Word" (Bridgewater, 1978). Sweet Charity is considered among the pioneers of the burgeoning Malay rock scene in the Malay Peninsula, consequently imparting a huge influence on Malaysian rock bands popular in the 1990s such as Wings, Lefthanded and Search.

Ramli's career as a rock singer who performed in pubs and proceeded to record hit albums for the Nusantara market is also tied to the history of moral policing of youth subcultures in 1970s Singapore (Adil, 2014). His social circle of mostly Malay rockers would have been subject to the policing of hippie culture in Singapore during this period. The public's state of moral panic viewed with suspicion Malay youths who sported "long hair and tight jeans", participated in rock music culture, and thereby associated such "youths as having a propensity to consume drugs, which was commonly believed to be related to … the hedonism of a rock and roll lifestyle" (Liew & Fu 2006, p. 103). It is perhaps this historical association of Ramli's long-haired rock persona that has elicited both excitement and anxiety over his performance of the national anthem. The following pages highlight a chronology of headlines that cover the public reactions to his performance of "Majulah Singapura". I also extract some comments and commentary from these news articles for analysis (see Table 1).

Reactions to Ramli Sarip's Rock Rendition

In light of the geopolitical relationship between Singapore and its neighbour across the causeway, it is telling that the first headline in the chronology, with a focus on "racist" reactions, was sourced in Malaysian press (Tan, 2019). The second headline, from a non-establishment news website, was quick to acknowledge (within the same day, no less) the Malaysian press coverage, albeit with a more critical spin on the accusations of racism (Lay, 2019). Both articles, however, cited negative reactions in the online technology forum HardwareZone, which included comments from user darkseidluv who wrote "if you are singing it this way, we might as well half-mast the flag", and users that suggested that the singer's "funeral-like" adaptation could be a violation of the National Anthem Act (Lay, 2019; Tan, 2019). However, *The Malay Mail* focused more on the racist remarks in the forum, in particular, a comment by user testart who wrote that Ramli was "singing like it's some praying song in the mosque" (Tan, 2019). This particular comment raised some interesting religious, cultural and musical issues. The reference to a "praying song" hints at the Islamic or Middle Eastern aesthetic inferred by Ramli's singing style, which includes melodic turns and embellishments that use a *maqam*-like or melodic/harmonic minor-like modality. This vocal approach is characteristic of the Nusantara rock vocal style that employs Malay *asli* melodic motifs that draw connections with Quranic recitation styles and Malay *syair* performances (Tan, 1993; Adil, 2014). However, the xenophobia is evident in the comment's implication that such an aesthetic approach is undesirable for a rendition of the national anthem, a *sacred* symbol of the state's sovereignty.

TABLE 1 *Headlines on Ramli Sarip's National Day Parade 2019 rendition of "Majulah Singapura"*

No.	Headline	Date	Source
1	Singer Ramli Sarip the target of racist comments for "funeral" version of Singapore's national anthem "Majulah Singapura"	07/08/2019	*The Malay Mail*
2	M'sia media labels as "racist" comments criticising Ramli Sarip's NDP rendition of 'Majulah Singapura'	07/08/2019	*Mothership*
3	Ramli Sarip's emotional NDP rendition of Majulah Singapura stirs souls and debate	08/08/2019	*The Straits Times*
4	Much dignity and passion in Ramli Sarip's stirring rendition of Majulah Singapura	08/08/2019	*The Straits Times*
5	Rocker's emotional take on national anthem stirs debate	09/08/2019	*The Straits Times*

All the first four articles listed in Table 1 were reporting on the National Day Parade rehearsals that occurred days before the official event. Ramli's rendition was already making waves through a Facebook post from Ng Eng Hen, Singapore's Defence Minister, who attended a preview performance on August 1, 2019. He posted that the rendition was "soul-stirring to hear, even moving some in the audience during the rehearsals to tears" (Wong, 2019a, 2019b). The state-controlled news outlet *The Straits Times* attempted to provide less sensational coverage of the topic, citing less flippant reactions to the song. The most negative comment cited was from a Facebook user who opined that Ramli's rendition was suited to a funeral that was "sad, depressing and lonely" (Peter, as cited in Wong, 2019a, 2019b). Wong's articles, replicated across two days with differing headlines, cited comments from two 13-year-olds who represented an ambivalent view towards the anthem's rendition; Neo Rui Heng said "I was confused at first, as I had not heard the song sung this way before … But it was creative and I liked it", while his classmate Ikhwan Faqif opined that he "didn't like the part when he (Ramli Sarip) sang the words 'Majulah Singapura' but (overall) it was very nice and heart-warming to hear him sing" (Wong, 2019a, 2019b). The articles in *The Straits Times* therefore frame the issue around musical taste as opposed to racism, eliding the vitriolic and xenophobic viewpoints that could threaten interethnic relations in the country, focusing instead on nuanced comments that are supportive (at best) and ambivalent (at worst) of Ramli's rock rendition of the anthem.

The Straits Times coverage of Ramli effectively worked to subdue the "brickbats" and "sectarian commentators" to his "funeral-like" version of the anthem with a commentary piece by the paper's music correspondent, Eddino Abdul Hadi (2019). Abdul Hadi (2019) highlighted Ramli's illustrious musical contributions and acclaim within the region: "one of the most accomplished artistes of the Merdeka (post-war independence) Generation". Further, his commentary highlighted how Ramli's approach to the national anthem, "accompanied by acoustic guitar and choir, is meditative and solemn—a paean to the country's spirit of progress, to 'maju' [*sic*], to always move forward toward better days". However, the fact remains that any progressive attempt to reinterpret the fixed symbols of Singapore's nation state will always face a regressive public discourse of cynicism and anxiety. Such acts of revisioning, if not just updating, the national narrative are further complicated by the ethnicised geopolitics of the nation state and its popular artistes, like Ramli, who transcend national borders.

Rocking Onwards

This chapter has presented preliminary research on how examining popular music in media discourses has the potential of unravelling the currents of ethnopolitical tension and reconciliation in Singapore and its surrounding Nusantara region. This chapter is a preamble to deeper rooted issues of structural racism in Singapore that have been revealed by mass media events in popular culture.

There are two directions in which this study can be further developed. The first is to move forward with the issue covered; Ramli Sarip proceeded to release a music video of his "Majulah Singapura" rendition in December 2019, around the same time that an updated official version of the anthem was released. This caused some confusion and even anger among citizens, who mistook his version to be the new official anthem.

The second direction required for this study is to move back to a month before the National Day celebrations. In July 2019, the media broadcaster Mediacorp launched an advertising campaign for an electronic payment application that featured the actor and DJ Dennis Chew. The campaign displayed images of Chew playing roles of different everyday Singaporeans, which included him cross-dressing as a Malay woman wearing a *tudung* (headscarf) and representing a supposedly ethnic Indian man, in brownface makeup (Lee, 2019). This brownface controversy prompted comedienne and rap artiste Preetipls, or Preeti Nair, to release a rap music video in condemnation of the advertising campaign (Ng, 2019). The video was a viral hit, but also offended many citizens, thereby prompting the state authorities to ban the circulation of the video (Ang, 2019; Ng, 2019). A future study requires a wider reading of racism reportage in Singaporean media, and how popular music expressions provide a means to rock the foundations of the state's ethnopolitics.

References

Abdul Hadi, E. (2019, August 8). Much dignity and passion in Ramli Sarip's stirring rendition of Majulah Singapura. *The Straits Times.*

Adil, J. (2014). Disquieting degeneracy: Policing Malaysian and Singaporean popular music culture from the mid-1960s to early-1970s. In B. Barendregt (Ed.), *Sonic modernities in the Malay World: A history of popular music, social distinction and novel lifestyles (1930s–2000s).* Brill.

Adil, J. (2021). Singapore arts icon or Malay nationalist?: Mobilising Zubir Said across the Causeway. In A. Johan, & M. A. Santaella (Eds.), *Made in Nusantara: Global studies in popular music.* Routledge.

Adil, J., & Santaella, M. A. (Eds.). (2021). *Made in Nusantara: Global studies in popular music.* Routledge.

Ang, P. (2019, July 31). Public should refrain from circulating and sharing Preetipls video: Police, IMDA. *The Straits Times.*

Bridgewater, D. D. (1978). Sorry seems to be the hardest word [Song]. On *Just Family* [33⅓ RPM Vinyl Disc]. Elektra 6E-119. https://www.discogs.com/Dee-Dee-Bridgewater-Just-Family/release/759938

Ferrarese, M. (2016). Southeast Asian glamour: The strange case of rock kapak in Malaysia. In I. Chapman, & H. Johnson (Eds.), *Global glam and popular music: Style and spectacle from the 1970s to the 2000s* (pp. 232–44). Routledge.

Lay, B. (2019, August 7). M'sia media labels as "racist" comments criticising Ramli Sarip's NDP rendition of "Majulah Singapura". *Mothership.* https://mothership.sg/2019/08/ramli-sarip-national-anthem-criticise/

Lee, K. Y. (1998). *The Singapore Story: Memoirs of Lee Kuan Yew.* Prentice Hall.

Lee, V. (2019, July 28). Mediacorp apologises after ad stirs debate about depictions of race. *The Straits Times.*

Liew, K. K., & Fu, K. (2006). Conjuring the tropical spectres: Heavy metal, cultural politics in Singapore and Malaysia. *Inter-Asia Cultural Studies*, 7(1), 99–112.

Lim, J. (2019, January 4). Four new statues unveiled alongside Sir Stamford Raffles. *Today.* https://www.todayonline.com/singapore/four-new-statues-unveiled-alongside-sir-stamford-raffles.

Ng, H. W. (2019, July 30). Police looking into rap video by local YouTube star Preetipls allegedly containing offensive content. *The Straits Times.*

Rahim, L. Z. (2009). *Singapore in the Malay world: Building and breaching regional bridges.* Routledge.

Sweet Charity. (1980). Kamelia [Song]. On *Pelarian* [Audio Cassette]. WEA Q40 93223. (Courtesy of Asia Culture Centre, Gwangju, South Korea)

Tan, M. Z. (2019, August 7). Singer Ramli Sarip the target of racist comments for "funeral" version of Singapore's national anthem "Majulah Singapura". *The Malay Mail Online.* https://www.malaymail.com/news/showbiz/2019/08/07/singer-ramli-sarip-the-target-of-racist-comments-for-funeral-version-of-sin/1778524

Tan, S. B. (1993). *Bangsawan: A social and stylistic history of popular Malay opera.* Oxford University Press.

Wallach, J. (2011). Unleashed in the East: Metal music, masculinity, and "Malayness" in Indonesia, Malaysia and Singapore. In J. Wallach, H. M. Berger, & P. D. Greene (Eds.), *Metal rules the globe: Heavy metal music around the world* (pp. 86–107). Duke University Press.

Wong, L. (2019a, August 8). Ramli Sarip's emotional NDP rendition of Majulah Singapura stirs souls and debate. *The Straits Times.*

Wong, L. (2019b, August 9). Rocker's emotional take on national anthem stirs debate. *The Straits Times.*

CHAPTER 2

Defenders of the Faith: How Internet Bulletin Boards Gave Rise to the Taiwanese Extreme Metal Community

Bartosz Czerwiński, *National Taiwan Normal University*

Once a niche created by and for outsiders, now a resource available for everyone. There is no doubt that extreme genres of metal music, such as black, death or thrash metal, have already reached nearly every corner of the world, earning themselves a global fan base. With Internet platforms and streaming services like Bandcamp, Spotify and Last.fm so readily accessible, reaching any metal band from any country across the globe now seems effortless. However, taking a step back to 20 years ago, to a world where VHS tapes were the norm and the Internet was not yet ubiquitous, we would be clueless as to where to look for anything flying under the mainstream radar. Through the tape-trading subculture, underground magazines and university bulletin board systems, however, extreme metal managed to reach far-flung corners of the world, from its birthplace in the West to remote countries like Taiwan. Growing like a giant snowball, picking up local cultures and trends, extreme metal music has quickly turned into a platform for expressing uniqueness, and a complex system of cultural codes and references.

Through interviews with two representatives of the Taiwanese extreme metal scene, Derek Sleazy (grindcore[1] drummer and owner of an extreme metal music label) and Fog (leader of an underground black metal band, Inferno Requiem), I analyse how, despite the relatively few official information distribution channels, extreme metal music had managed to gain a small but devoted fan base in Taiwan in the 1990s.

Taiwanese Metal: Mainstream and Underground

With the appearance of music channels like MTV, VH1 and their local counterparts, heavy metal music quickly managed to grow itself into a firm subculture in the 1990s, especially in countries craving for new, western trends, such as in the states of the former Eastern Bloc. Numerous radio and television programmes were produced in tandem with the burgeoning tape-trading and piracy cultures, quickly expanding the popularity of extreme metal. Although heavy metal music in newly liberated European states like Poland gave metal fans a lot more to identify with, the fans were arguably less passionate about metal music itself, with many of them considering the enthusiasm for the music being merely a phase in life.

Extreme metal never earned itself a firm place in the Taiwanese mass media. As far as I know, there was never any TV show or radio programme that played strictly extreme metal music or metal video clips. Back in the day, extreme metal music was viewed by the Taiwanese mass media as an odd curiosity, rather than a form of art that their fans would like to win respect for. This also became a point of concern for Taiwanese die-hard metal fans. Musicians had to admit that people who approached extreme metal in Taiwan were usually those seeking an outlet in their daily life, perceiving aggressive metal singers screaming their lungs out on stage as the perfect way to escape everyday corporate identity or fulfil their need of being different from others (Fog, personal communication, April 2019).

Since the inflow of extreme metal music to Taiwan had to take the alternative or more limited route, it was natural that it reached a smaller audience. However, one could argue that this route led to the music having a much firmer and more devoted fan base, winning with quality over quantity (if there is any way of measuring faithfulness towards metal).

The Taiwanese extreme metal scene, by all means, should be considered small. Taking its size into consideration, it is particularly difficult to distinguish between *mainstream* and *underground* metal, as the acts from both worlds often blend into one another. What perfectly reflects this is the frequent listing of bands like Chthonic and Inferno Requiem together in articles on Taiwanese metal, usually written by independent bloggers or indie music services (Lin, 2016). The first of the two bands is currently one of the hottest metal acts in Taiwan, attracting crowds of angry youngsters during regional festivals, while the other despises clean record production and actively self-sabotages its popularity.

International Flow of Information

Some of the most radical extreme metal genres, such as grindcore, never witnessed major commercial success, although they were meant to remain underground as a form of alternative music. Grindcore or death metal music, due to its radical, abrasive sound that is certainly not for everyone, frequently had to go through alternative ways of distribution to reach fans around the world. Releasing their debut album *Scum* through Earache Records in 1987, English grindcore pioneers Napalm Death even earned themselves a mainstream television appearance in their home country. At the time, such an appearance was just the tip of the iceberg of popularity (societysghoul, 2009). The lack of official distribution in many countries outside of England however, pushed many extreme metal bands (including Napalm Death) to find alternative ways of reaching their fans abroad (Overell, 2014). In Taiwan, it was online record trading.

Rapid computerisation in Taiwan could be the crucial factor in enabling the flow of extreme metal music into the island. This very factor is frequently mentioned in research papers dealing with the arrival of foreign trends or the spread of domestic pop cultural trends in Taiwan. The achievement of economic prosperity in the early 2000s and the establishment of a firm hardware/software infrastructure on the island quickly led to the wiring up of most houses in Taiwan. In the article *Music and Cultural Politics in Taiwan*, Wai-Chung Ho noted that: "According to the recent 'Household Online in Taiwan Survey' during September and October 2005, 76% of 4,072 interviewed households in Taiwan owned computers, which was up from 73% in 2004" (Ho, 2007, p. 473).

Following the arrival of online music platforms like Yahoo-Kimo Music, foreign and domestic trends started becoming available for nearly everyone (Ho, 2007). Since extreme metal music never reached mainstream status in Taiwan, its arrival to the island had to take a slightly different route.

Golden Era of Internet Discussion Boards

How BBS Gave Rise to the Taiwanese Extreme Metal Subculture

Although tape and record trading is a phenomenon existing all around the world, it took a slightly different turn in Taiwan during the late 1990s and early 2000s. Unlike the Balinese tape trading events in the 1990s which were organised at certain locations (Baulch, 2003), the Taiwanese extreme metal tape and record trading culture revolved mostly around university bulletin board systems (BBS). Tape trading and the related transactions took place mostly online, with fresh heavy metal releases being imported from the United States, Europe or Japan by self-appointed metal promoters. Derek Sleazy, owner of the underground Taiwanese grindcore record label Rotten Pyosis, eagerly participated in the BBS online tape trading culture in the late 1990s and early 2000s. "Due to the obvious limits of an early Internet era, most of the transactions were finalised without prior *playing* of the actual record" (D. Sleazy, personal communication, May 2018). Each record was introduced to a growing group of BBS users just through its band name, title, track list and a description provided by the seller. Lists of records for sale or exchange and subtopics about particular albums slowly started evolving into an early metal discussion forum, with users exchanging their opinions about bands they listened to and CDs they bought.

At first, BBSs functioned as separate identities affiliated with the biggest Taiwanese universities. Therefore, heavy metal subforums could exist in many different BBSs, among many different Taiwanese universities. According to Sleazy, the turning point or start of the golden era of Taiwanese Internet discussion boards was the integration of the systems into one BBS. The integration eventually provided unlimited flow and exchange of information among students of all Taiwanese universities, and direct access to extreme metal resources for anyone curious (D. Sleazy, personal communication, May 2018). A huge number of the current Taiwanese extreme metal fans, now reaching their mid-30s or 40s, bought their first metal record through the tape trading system established on the BBS.

In 1990s Taiwan, rock and metal music witnessed a rapid growth in popularity. The lack of official distribution channels for rock and metal records eventually gave rise to the culture of piracy, followed by the establishment of live music venues showcasing rock and metal acts. However, all these activities centering around Taipei involved a relatively small amount of actual extreme genres (black, death, thrash and grindcore); thus, the bars and record stores could not reach their target audience scattered around the island (Lee, 2007). Reflecting upon his first contact with extreme metal music, Sleazy mentioned that for someone like him, while growing up in Yilan, getting in touch with metal communities or buying a metal record would have been impossible without the

BBS. That was where he first heard about extreme metal genres such as black metal or grindcore (D. Sleazy, personal communication, May 2018).

Quickly, the BBS became a home for the *lost and lonely* among Taiwanese metal fans and those who sought something more than just Iron Maiden or Black Sabbath records. Subtopics that narrowed down to the rarest metal microgenres were revealing a truly globalised picture, with users exchanging band names and record titles from all around the world. During our interview, Sleazy proudly admits that one of the biggest influences in his life as a metal musician was the Polish grindcore band, Dead Infection (D. Sleazy, personal communication, May 2018). The narrower and more unorthodox the genre, the more globalised and international its audience is, as die-hard metal fans would go to great lengths to lay their hands on anything connected to their favourite bands.

The leader of the Taiwanese black metal band Inferno Requiem, who goes by the alias of Fog, also admits that the legendary DBS Holy Land (one of the most prominent Internet extreme metal record trading spaces and discussion forums available on the BBS in Taiwan) was the place where he first encountered black metal culture, and eventually bought his first black metal record in the mid-1990s (Fog, personal communication, April 2019).

A very detailed insight into the early years (1995–2001) of Chthonic, a widely recognised Taiwanese melodic black metal band frequently referred to as the "Black Sabbath of Asia", was provided in Chu Meng-Tze's (2001) master's thesis *The Musical Practices of Taipei Rock Bands—A Case Study of Chthonic.* A transparent portrait of Taipei rock and metal culture during the second half of the 1990s provided by Chu proves that Freddy Lim, founder and leader of Chthonic, was also actively participating in online record trading and acquired most of his extreme metal records either through friends residing outside of Taiwan or through extreme metal discussion forums on a local BBS. The story of Lim encountering heavy metal and eventually engaging in its popularisation and development could serve as a Taiwanese heavy metal coming-of-age tale, which ends with the establishment of Taiwan's biggest metal band, Chthonic. Chu also mentions all of the factors which played a major role in the process of establishing the Taiwanese extreme metal scene. In all likelihood, many Taiwanese metal musicians in the 1990s had to travel down the same road as Lim and his bandmates: From being illuminated by metal music in one of the live show venues, meeting like-minded individuals in university music clubs, and polishing their music tastes through university BBS, to establishing their own band and slowly crystalising their own style.

Conclusion

Although the BBS is still widely used in Taiwan, metal subforums met with a natural decline after Facebook, Last.fm and other social media platforms started dominating the global Internet market. With access to records on eBay or in-chain stores, metalheads lost interest in online record trading. What has laid to rest and turned to digital ash of Internet tape trading was the massive data loss which occurred to the BBS somewhere around the end of the previous decade. My interviewees have a vague memory of when this happened exactly, but they all sadly agree that on that day, the Taiwanese metal community irretrievably lost its biggest local metal catalogue (D. Sleazy, personal communication, May 2018).

Notes

[1] Grindcore is a fusion of heavy metal and hardcore punk, characterised by heavily distorted bass and electric guitars, fast blast drumbeats, growled vocals, and a straightforward song structure rarely exceeding two minutes in length. Grindcore scene emerged in Europe and the United States in mid-1980s, spearheaded by acts such as Napalm Death, Repulsion and Brutal Truth.

References

Baulch, E. (2003). Gesturing elsewhere: The identity politics of the Balinese death/thrash metal scene. *Popular Music, 22*(2), 195–215.

Chu, M. (2001). *Taibei chuangzuo yuetuan zhi yinyue shijian yu meixue: yi shan ling yuetuan wei li 台北創作樂團之音樂實踐與美學-以「閃靈」樂團為例* [The musical practice and aesthetics of Taipei rock bands: A case study of Chthonic] [Master's thesis, National Taiwan University]. https://ndltd.ncl.edu.tw/cgi-bin/gs32/gsweb.cgi/ccd=QhhV2u/record?r1=1&h1=3

Ho, W. C. (2007). Music and Cultural Politics in Taiwan. *International Journal of Cultural Studies, 10*(4), 463–483.

Lee, S. (2007). *Yaogun Taiwan: Taiwan zhonjinshu yue mi de wenhua rentong yu shuijian 搖滾台灣：台灣重金屬樂迷的文化認同與實踐* [Rock Taiwan: Cultural identities and practices of heavy metal music fans in Taiwan] [Master's thesis, Shih Hsin University]. https://ndltd.ncl.edu.tw/cgi-bin/gs32/gsweb.cgi/ccd=QhhV2u/record?r1=1&h1=2

Lin, S. (2016, December 12). *Pandian Taiwan zhongjinshu yuetuan shi zhang jingdian zhuanji 盤點台灣重金屬樂團十張經典專輯* [Taiwan's ten classic heavy metal records]. https://solomo.xinmedia.com/music/104607-M

Overell, R. (2014). *Affective intensities in extreme music scenes: Cases of Australia and Japan*. Palgrave Macmillan.

societysghoul. (2009, February 7). *Napalm Death Rare Lee and Bill 1989 What's That Noise BBC Pt 1.* [Video]. https://www.youtube.com/watch?v=zsytdmYtcf8

CHAPTER 3

Subversive, Still in the Middle Ground: CHAI's Assertions and Male Discourse of Authenticity

Chiharu Chujo, *Université Jean Moulin Lyon III*

In the Japanese popular music scene, the hyper-gendered norm has dominated female representation for decades. This norm has palpable implications: to the general public, many female singers in Japan such as female idols have been assumed to embody naive immaturity and vulnerability, or a certain magnanimity based on motherhood. The majority of female Japanese singers have seemed to avoid speaking explicitly about either gender issues of women's representation or their social gendered positions.

However, feminist movements such as #MeToo have had a growing impact on Japanese society over the last few years. In this context, a female punk rock band called CHAI caused a sensation. Their provocative standpoint, which rejects the aesthetic norm anchored in Japanese society and proposes an alternative perspective to the stereotypical style, seems to popularise the notion of gender equality in the Japanese popular music milieu. However, CHAI's popularity can be attributed not only to their subversive personality but also to their musical authenticity which is, as musicologist

Marion Leonard pointed out, often based on and in favour of androcentric discourse (Leonard, 2007). To what extent, then, did their positionality or subjectivity as a female band put them at an advantage in this scene? By analysing their performances and the discourse of their critics, I examine the process by which this group was recognised as a female band in the Japanese popular music scene.

CHAI, A Japanese Female Punk Band Hitting the Charts

CHAI is composed of four young women and became active in 2012. Formed as an independent rock band in Japan, CHAI has attracted fans from around the world since their appearance on the popular music scene: in 2016, they started streaming their EP, from which one song ranked number 36 on Spotify's UK Top 50 chart. Their debut album *Pink*, released in October 2017, reached number 41 on the Oricon Albums chart (a Japanese music chart equivalent to the *Billboard* charts) and it was subsequently released in the United States (US) in 2018. Today, with their growing popularity in the Japanese pop music scene, the band continues to tour and perform in Europe, Asia and the US.

Through their psychedelic and melodic punk music, CHAI uses a unique concept that they call "neo-*kawaii*". The term "*kawaii*" is originally used to describe the affection for something cute and puerile. The notion of *kawaii*—considered a feminine virtue by the majority of Japanese women—is a device that women use not only to seduce men, but also to enhance their identities (Yomota, 2010). Today, the term is often used in the context of some specific aesthetic standard of a material article, a style, a character or a person, especially in Japanese beauty culture. In terms of gendered beauty norms, it principally refers to features such as big eyes, white skin and slender bodies (Tanimoto, 2008). In the sphere of Japanese popular music, the *kawaii* standard is associated with the figures of female idols (Stalker, 2018). CHAI deconstructs and questions the concept of *kawaii* in order to propose an alternative perspective to an aesthetic standard entrenched in Japanese society.

CHAI's Advocacy

CHAI's arguments about aesthetic norms are tangibly highlighted in their song lyrics. In constantly questioning "Where's the personality?" (CHAI, 2018), CHAI declares to their audience that "Cute is motivation" but "merely being cute is boring" (CHAI, 2017). For them, being selfish, meaning privileging one's self and one's wants and needs, is the only way to establish an aesthetic notion that could encourage self-recognition for each individual. This standpoint is also illustrated in their music videos. In the video for "N.E.O.", for instance, they caricature particular physical characteristics with which many people in Japan are uncomfortable, such as single eyelids or obesity. CHAI considers such bodily features *artistic*; for instance, single eyelids are called "cool eyes" (*kûru ai*) and obesity is described as "a body well-padded like a cushion" (*kusshon bodi*). It is worth noting that CHAI does not merely replace negative notions of appearance with positive ones, but they incorporate a parodic perspective into such replacements. When referring to physical characteristics that are incompatible with aesthetic norms, CHAI qualifies such beauty features with positive, albeit ridiculous, expressions. We can see here CHAI's satirical attempt to denounce the categorisation of appearance based on social aesthetic norms. CHAI's concept of neo-*kawaii*, thus, proposes an alternative to the conventional *kawaii* norms of bodily representation which, in a gender critical perspective, are reminiscent of vulnerable women.

Performances that Show the Body

Gender critiques of visual representations, such as Laura Mulvey's studies, point out that female bodies are constantly subjected to a male gaze (1975). Other scholars argue this point, revealing an attempt to build the aspects and experiences of the female body in different and alternative ways (Robinson, 2015). CHAI's performances can be used as an example in such a counterargument. Indeed, female Japanese singers such as Kumi Koda have mesmerised with their bodies and sex appeal time and time again. However, much of this is just a *showing*, which relies on the premise that women are *objects to be seen* within a framework of body representation based on gender norms, even if they seem to be showing their bodies in a provocative way. CHAI's showing, which seems to be aimed at breaking such norms, is visibly distinguishable from that of those female singers. We can see in CHAI's showing, an agency-like subjectivity through which a subject can manipulate his or her own body without succumbing to the gaze of male domination, or more specifically, phallic domination (phallocentrism).

Public Reception of CHAI's Standpoint

Thanks to their subversive position against Japanese beauty norms, CHAI—already well received by critics—has been hailed in discourses on women's advocacy in diverse countries (Delhaye, 2019). The band was recently invited on a TV programme featuring bodily complexes on NHK, a national Japanese TV channel, as a model of women who have overcome the beauty complex. Music critic, Hiroshi Takaoka, analyses the reasons for which CHAI has such a big impact in Japan:

> The word *kawaii* has become too prevalent … , especially as a term to assess a woman's appearance, and it has consequently acted in an oppressive way for them. Obviously, evaluation by others does not work the way you want it to. Evaluations are directly and indirectly thrown at people, and forced them into a *kawaii* competition. If "I want to be *kawaii*" is transformed into "I have to

> be *kawaii*" by social oppression, then people may say to themselves "I'm no good if I'm not cute" or "It's the end of the world if I'm not *kawaii* anymore". I would like to call this mechanism "curse of *kawaii*". (Takaoka, 2020)[1]

Takaoka's analysis reveals that CHAI's sarcastic standpoint towards the "curse of *kawaii*" empowers their audience to kick back against such a restrictive aesthetic concept (Takaoka, 2020).

CHAI as Third-Wave Feminism?

There may be an analogy drawn between CHAI's position and that of some female punk groups of the Riot Grrrl movement which spread through the US in the 1990s. Riot Grrrl was started by young female punk groups such as Bikini Kill and Bratmobile, who advocated for women's rights through events and other activities, arguing that "the loud music, moshing, music production, labelling around and distributing sound sources, and social movements that men do, can be done by girls too" (Labry, 2010).[2] It is worth highlighting that the actors involved in Riot Grrrl put a positive value on girlhood in their activities. These protagonists of Riot Grrrl accepted and supported the notion of cuteness, which was used as a representation of girls and criticised by other American female rock singers such as Gwen Stefani in the 1990s. While some musicians and feminists see this notion as consumerism of the female body, as Wald puts it, the representation of cuteness in Riot Grrrl is a "self-consciously idealising representation" (1998), a strategy of alternative resistance. One can see such interpretation of cuteness in a central discourse of third-wave feminism.

CHAI's position of denouncing women's beauty norms through their own concept of cuteness thus, seems quite similar to this third-wave feminist discourse which the actors in the Riot Grrrl movement used as a catalyst to empower themselves. Despite this analogy, though, there are a few points that distinguish CHAI from Riot Grrrl. First, while CHAI is critical of the beauty norms, they actually follow them in some ways. Although they seem to oppose the concept of *kawaii*, CHAI members are photogenic in their own bodily representations in commodified images. The girl group retains, to some extent, the aspect of *kawaii* that refers to idols. Their frontal image is reminiscent of idols, who are generally not required to be highly skilled as musicians (Murayama, 2011). A number of critics of this female band have highlighted this contrast between their musicality and image, arguing that "they do not have only a singular concept but a high level of musical performance". At first glance, this appears to be a purely positive assessment of their quality as musicians, which seems fair. However, it is worth noting that their appearance plays a key role in emphasising their high level of musicality. Their concept of defying social beauty norms is, in fact, commodified by the disparity between their musicianship and ideas. As they promote their concept of neo-*kawaii* with their image, they compromise with the objectification of the female body. Leonard pointed out the male dominance in the music industry's standards of evaluation for musicians:

> Because of the commercial nature of music production, the industry continually seeks to present music products as understandable (placing all new releases within recognisable genres and categories) and accessible. … Popular music canons are formed through aesthetic judgement made by musicians and critics such as biographers, journalists and historians, who are informed by, often tacitly agreed, notions of value, taste and worth. … Through this process a large number of musical texts that have been variously promoted by record labels and music journalists over the past few decades can be given an aura of stability by the selection of particular performers as "greats". (Leonard, 2007, p. 27)

Praises of CHAI's musical ability by critics, who use terms such as "groovy" and "high musical performance", are indeed based on this canonical standard revealed by Leonard (2007). With this point in mind, can we then say that the fact that CHAI has become popular because of the gap between their musicality and concept, is a paradoxical representation of the male-dominated structure of the music world, or more specifically, of Japanese society? This, of course, requires an analysis of the music production and market system surrounding CHAI. Nevertheless, it is to be noted that CHAI's standpoint is still quite ambivalent in terms of gender issues.

CHAI and Third-Wave Feminism in the Japanese Social Context

According to Tanaka (2016), a third-wave feminist perspective finally appeared in Japanese society in the 2010s, two decades later than in occidental societies. This third-wave feminism is also related to neoliberal concepts in terms of the socio-economic structure. In neoliberalism, the autonomy of individual effort is highly esteemed and generally represented by financial independence. To assert one's subjectivity, it is necessary to show that one is financially autonomous. In this context, the feminist concept, which aims to defend women's rights and highlight women's subjectivity, is actively promoted in the market economy: feminism is caught up in a market economy system and ends up becoming, as suggested by McRobbie (2008), "commodity feminism" (p. 532). Such ambivalence is seen in CHAI's image, which is adjustable enough to be promoted in the music market. Tanaka (2020) also analysed that, particularly in the socio-historical context of Japanese society, a strong backlash against feminism has significantly influenced feminist discourse since the 1990s, and advocates are unconsciously compelled to be pleasant for the public. Using Banet-Weiser's concept of "accommodating feminism" (2018), Tanaka (2020) argued that women in Japan are forced to masquerade as women who are not aggressive, as accommodative women, in order to survive in a society that is extremely hostile towards the image of subversive feminist assertions. Thus, to make their standpoint more understandable or convincing to the public, one has to be fashionable, stylish and pleasant. Although CHAI does not pretend to be a feminist group, its standpoint and position in Japan may well describe this intrinsic contradiction.

Conclusion

Through this chapter, I have tried to analyse the features that make CHAI popular as a female protest band in the Japanese popular music scene. CHAI's amicable assertions, even feminist-like ones, accommodate the dominant male discourse of musical canons as well as those of most of the Japanese population, unaccustomed to facing radical and critical discourse about gender issues. CHAI's ambivalent positionality thus reflects that of the majority of women in Japan who face situations subordinate to those of their male peers. Still, since the 2010s, there have been various female musicians denouncing gender issues in different ways, such as Seiko Ōmori and Akko Gorilla. Even some female idols such as Ayaka Wada have started showing their gender critical standpoint. Other comparative analyses of the new female pop music scene is necessary in the future.

Notes

1 Translated by author.

2 Riot Grrrl is a feminist punk movement that emerged and gradually spread in the United States in the 1990s, in which fanzines and event-based activities were embraced by young women who had never been socially committed before (Labry, 2010).

References

Banet-Weiser, S. (2018). *Empowered: Popular feminism and popular misogyny*. Duke University Press.

CHAI. (2017, April 28). Sayonara Complex. [Video]. https://www.youtube.com/watch?v=AkiSZ076vOc

CHAI. (2018, September 7). N.E.O. [Video]. https://www.youtube.com/watch?v=GXsCb-cClz8

Delhaye, E. (2019). *Les rockeuses japonaises qui dynamitent les diktats du kawaii* [The Japanese rockers who blast the diktats of the kawaii]. Télérama. https://www.telerama.fr/sortir/chai,-les-rockeuses-japonaises-qui-dynamitent-les-diktats-du-kawaii,n6266754.php

Labry, M. (2010). Riot Grrrls américaines et réseaux féministes «underground» français [American Riot Grrrls and French "underground" feminist networks]. *Multitudes, 42*(3), 60–66. doi:10.3917/mult.042.0060.

Leonard, M. (2007). *Gender in the music industry: Rock, discourse, and girl power (Ashgate popular and folk music series)*. Routledge.

McRobbie, A. (2008). *The aftermath of feminism: Gender, culture and social change*. SAGE Publications.

Mulvey, L. (1975). Visual pleasure and narrative cinema. *Screen, 16*(3), 6–18.

Murayama, R. (2011). *AKB 48 ga hitto shita itsutsu no himitsu: Burēku genshô wo māketingu senryaku kara saguru* [The five secrets of AKB48's success: an exploration of breakthrough phenomena from a marketing strategy perspective]. Kadokawa Shoten.

NHK. (2019, January 9). *Kurôzu appu gendai* [Close up gendai]. https://www.nhk.or.jp/gendai/articles/4229/index.html

Robinson, H. (2015). *Feminism-art-theory: An anthology 1968–2014*. Wiley Blackwell.

Stalker, N. (2018). "Cool" Japan as cultural superpower: 1980s–2010s. In *Japan: History and culture from classical to cool* (pp. 362-400). University of California Press. www.jstor.org/stable/10.1525/j.ctv2n7fgm.15

Takaoka, H. (2020). "Neo kawaii" tte nani? Gāruzubando CHAI ga shiji sa reru riyū [What is "neo-kawaii"? Why the girl band CHAI is so supportive]. *Diamond Online*. https://diamond.jp/articles/-/226703.

Tanaka, T. (2016). Going beyond the body of girls who play sports: From the perspective of third-wave feminism. *Japan Journal of Sport Sociology, 24*(1). https://www.jstage.jst.go.jp/article/jjsss/24/1/24_51/_pdf

Tanaka, T. (2020). Kanji no ii feminizumu?: Popyurāna mono o meguru, watashi-tachi no ryōgi-sei [Pleasant feminism?: Our ambivalence about something popular]. In *Gendai shisô, 48*(4), 26–33.

Tanimoto, N. (2008). *Biyô seikei to keshô no shakai gaku* [Sociology of cosmetic surgery and make-up]. Shinyōsha.

Yomota, I. (2010). *Kawaii ron* [Theory of kawaii]. Chikuma Shobō.

Wald, G. (1998). Just a girl? Rock music, feminism, and the cultural construction of female youth. *Signs, 23*(3), 585–610.

CHAPTER 4

How Digital Technology Contributes to the Growth of Small Independent Record Companies in Hong Kong

Edmond Tsang, ***Technological and Higher Education Institute of Hong Kong***

Technological development is a fundamental driver of economic growth. Short-term disruptions, however, are always a side effect of technological advancement (Broughel & Thierer, 2019). Due to the availability of music downloading, sales of CDs—the dominant medium for popular music sales since the 1990s—fell from 2.5 billion units in 2000 to 1.8 billion in 2006 globally (Janssens et al., 2009). Such decline reflects the pathetic situation of the music industry as CD sales used to form an essential part of recorded music sales (Daniel, 2019). The Cantopop market has been facing the same situation since the new millennium. Owing to the shrinkage of the market, big record companies have become increasingly conservative by mainly publishing traditionally well-received karaoke songs. Such tactic, unfortunately, has caused Cantopop to become more homogeneous, accelerating its decline.

Since the late 2000s, a number of independent music labels have gradually been established and have started making significant contributions to the development of Cantopop. These independent music labels include Hummingbird, 3721 Production, Redline Music, Frenzi Music, JC Music, Private Zoo, Strawberry Fields, Kingdom C, Goomusic, FreeUp Music, Silly Thing, Sunny Ideas, and Chance Music. They all share some similarities: (a) they were founded with minimal start-up costs compared to traditional record companies; (b) the founders are usually musicians who are often involved in music productions; (c) only a few singers get signed to the label; and (d) they cooperate with big record companies to help them distribute their music. These independent music labels can be further divided into two categories: (a) those that focus only on the production and management of their artists, and (b) those that would also handle marketing matters. This chapter discusses the nature of small independent record companies through three case studies and describes how technology contributes to the development of these companies.

Case One

Kingdom C

Kingdom C, founded in 2007, is a typical successful case of the first category of music labels and focuses mainly on music production and management of their artists. Shortly after its establishment, Kingdom C signed four singers, King Wu, On Chan, Andy Leung and Jase Ho, in 2009 who later formed the group, C AllStar. Thanks to the release of the hit song "Sky Ladder" in 2010, the all-male group won numerous awards from local TV and radio channels. Their music was surprisingly so well received that their CD album was awarded the IFPI Hong Kong Top Sales Music Award in 2012. In 2014, C AllStar successfully organised a concert in the Hong Kong Coliseum, which was considered "the venue for Cantopop stars to prove their popularity" (Chu, 2017). Although the group disbanded in 2017, the four singers have become solo artists under the Kingdom C label.

Case Two

Frenzi Music

Another similar independent music label is Frenzi Music. Established in 2011, Frenzi Music was founded by two renowned musicians in Hong Kong, Vicky Fung and Victor Tse. Their first artist was Michael Lai, who showed his talent by winning various singing competitions. After successfully creating a buzz for Lai, Frenzi Music signed a female singer Tang Siu Hau in 2016. Prior to working under the Frenzi Music label, Tang participated in *The Voice*, a singing contest in a reality-show format broadcasted by Television Broadcasts Limited (TVB), the dominant broadcaster in Hong Kong. Winners of *The Voice* are usually signed to the Voice Entertainment Group Ltd, a record label and talent agency founded by TVB in 2013. This record company has the advantage of monopolising the promotion and distribution of TVB drama theme songs and soundtracks. Nonetheless, this also becomes a disadvantage as it leads to the homogeneity of song style—the standard Cantonese karaoke song. Dissatisfied with the factory-like production style, Tang chose to work with Frenzi Music, which allowed her the freedom to try different genres. Tang's musical talent has earned her numerous annual music awards, including the Silver Award for Commercial Radio's Ultimate Best Female Singer. Aside from Lai and Tang, Frenzi Music also signed Jing Wong, Nowhere Boys (a band of five members), and per se (a group of two members). A typical characteristic of independent music labels in Hong Kong is that they welcome a diverse range of musical styles. It is therefore not surprising that the music produced under Frenzi Music does not mainly consist of karaoke songs, but include genres such as British rock, indie rock, folk music, and ballad, with lyrics that are not only confined to Cantonese, but also in English.

Case Three

Strawberry Fields

Both Kingdom C and Frenzi Music are music labels that focus on music production and artists management. They have their own recording studios for their productions and have arranged for some of their artists to sign marketing and distribution contracts with Media Asia Entertainment Group, a large distribution and record company in Hong Kong. Nevertheless, there are other independent music labels that handle both music production and marketing, while only leaving the distribution to record companies. Strawberry Fields, established in 2010, is one example. This label had only signed one artist, Charmaine Fong, during the early days of its establishment. Prior to joining Strawberry Fields, Charmaine Fong had a rather unsuccessful career under Universal Music, one of the largest international record companies, and her music was not well received in Hong Kong. Upon joining Strawberry Fields, which gives her the freedom to compose and sing her own music, her songs were embraced by the younger generation. This helps explain why only within eight years, Charmaine Fong was crowned Most Popular Female Singer in the Commercial Radio Hong Kong Annual Awards Ceremony in 2017 and 2019, and three of her songs were voted the Best 100 Songs of the Decade from 2010 to 2019 on the Cool Music Forum.

Owing to the significance and success of these independent music labels, it is worthwhile to understand why they have been established since the new millennium and the reasons contributing to their growth.

Impact of Technological Advancement on Production

The impact of technological advancement has contributed to a reduction in the production and distribution costs of musical works. The oligopolistic market before the new millennium was created largely due to the expensive music production equipment and the limited means of promotion channels. The digitalisation technology of music production led to something called "creative destruction", a term coined by Joseph Schumpeter (1942). Before the birth of the Digital Audio Workstation (DAW), music production could only be done in professional studios with reel tape machines and large analogue consoles, contributing to high production costs due to the large investment in the equipment. The development of the DAW enables the creation, recording, mixing, and mastering of sonically high-quality songs on a computer (Vaughn, 2014). Installing core DAW software such as ProTools or Logic Pro, coupled with various audio plug-ins, the musical outputs can sound identical, if not better, to those produced by large consoles with different expensive outboards.

Moreover, not only can the latest audio plug-ins imitate the sounds of expensive outboards including compressors, equalisers, reverberation machines, and finalisers, they can also function as audio editors, such as for the purpose of noise cancellation or tuning. With the assistance of such powerful audio plug-ins, singers can record their vocal tracks even in small rooms without acoustic treatment. With the assistance of noise cancellation, de-click, and reverberation plug-ins, vocal tracks can sound very similar to one produced at a large world-class studio. Before the new millennium, almost all Cantopop songs were recorded and produced in large local recording studios, such as Dragon Studio, Avon Recording Studios, Tang Lou Studio, D&M Studio, and Q-Sound Studio, which were equipped with professional outboards. As a result of the advancement of recording technology, smaller scale or even home studios have become increasingly significant in Cantopop productions since 2000. They have gradually replaced the role of the larger studios of the 1980s and 1990s. Aside from a cheaper rental cost, a remarkable advantage of these musician-owned studios is that producers can test and experiment various music ideas and styles with singers at their own studios without additional rental costs. This supports the growth of small independent labels. The advancement of the DAW technology has completely transformed the Cantopop production industry.

Impact of Technological Advancement on Music Selling and Marketing

In addition to music production, the impact of technological advancement has drastically changed the way music is sold. The traditional big record companies have always had some sort of monopoly over the distribution of music to customers. Before music streaming became popular, record companies dominated the entire supply chain from building recording studios to music selling and marketing. They were the giant players in the market as they centralised the control of music supply. Digital technology, however, has seriously weakened the power of large record companies, and empowered musicians and consumers (Ko, 2016).

Pop music listeners in Hong Kong were flooded by karaoke songs during the 1990s and early 2000s. However, in recent years, with the growth of the Internet, these standardised melodic and lyric styles could no longer satisfy local music lovers. In the heydays of Cantopop, when Internet browsing was not commonplace, musical works were only broadcasted on TV or radio channels. Listeners were passively fed with plug-songs chosen by the record companies. In addition, Cantopop songs before the new millennium were published in the form of CDs. If someone wanted to buy a particular song of a singer, he or she would have to purchase the entire music album which contains around 10 songs. This model gave record companies a strong controlling power because the production cost of a whole album (such as CD printing) and the marketing cost during the days without Internet was huge. Nonetheless, the development of online music purchase has changed the scenario. Since Apple's iTunes Music

Store started selling legalised digital music in 2003, listeners have been able to buy any single song online without having to bundle purchase the less preferable songs. Nowadays, music streaming has become increasingly popular and music can be enjoyed through music streaming providers including Spotify, Apple Music, YouTube Music, Moov, KKBox, and Joox, by paying a monthly subscription fee.

A research on the musical preference of Hong Kong people was conducted in 2015. Over 1,600 Hong Kong music lovers between the ages of 12 and 64 were interviewed. The results show that 64% of them listen to music through music streaming services whereas only 24% would buy CDs (Joox, 2015). Moreover, rather than passively receiving marketing information from record companies on television or radio channels, music lovers could browse and have access to a plethora of information about their favourite songs through various media on the Internet. With big data technology, music streaming providers would even know someone's musical preferences through their search habits and recommend songs they might like. This further erodes the significance of the marketing powers of the big record companies.

The Flexibility of Independent Music Labels

Owing to their structural and organisational inertia, major record companies were reluctant to handle the market changes (Silver, 2013; Morris, 2015; Mulligan, 2015). This explains why the sales of recorded music have dropped tremendously since the digitalisation of music and the availability of peer-to-peer technologies (Peitz & Waelbroeck, 2004; Liebowitz, 2005; Zentner, 2006). As large structured organisations, traditional record companies have standard procedures for their music productions. For instance, they would have decided the financial budgets for all their artists at the beginning of the financial year. Once the budget has been decided, it would be difficult to amend even if it is necessary to do so. The independent music labels, however, do not have such restrictions. They can adjust their productions in response to any social development. Thus, independent music labels have the advantage of plugging songs that fit the ever-changing tastes of listeners. In the Ultimate Song Chart Awards from Commercial Radio Hong Kong 2010, all the songs which won the Ultimate Top Ten Songs Awards were produced by international and local big record companies. By 2019, only five songs (50%) were produced by them. This reveals the growing significance of independent music labels.

Conclusion

The revered lyricist, James Wong, once said "Cantopop is dying" but Wang (2020) refuted the comment and suggested that Cantopop is developing vibrantly. I would argue that the main reason for the dynamic development of Cantopop is the growth of independent music labels because they are more flexible—for instance, in terms of musical styles and budgeting— compared with the traditional record companies. The independent labels are also more willing to promote different genres of Cantopop, catering to different tastes of a wider audience. Such growth, however, would not be possible without technological advancement, which has significantly reduced production cost, and transformed the selling and consumption patterns that have lowered the entry barrier into the music industry. It is envisaged that the contribution and significance of independent music labels will continue, if not increase, with the development of Cantopop in the near future.

References

Broughel, J., & Thierer, A. (2019). *Technological innovation and economic growth: A brief report on the evidence.* Mercatus Research, Mercatus Center at George Mason University.

Chu, Y. W. (2017). *Hong Kong cantopop: A concise history.* Hong Kong University Press.

Daniel, R. (2019). Digital disruption in the music industry: The case of the compact disc. *Creative Industries Journal, 12*(2), 159–166.

Janssens, J., Van Daele, S., & Vander Beken, T. (2009). The music industry on (the) line? Surviving music piracy in a digital era. *European Journal of Crime, Criminal Law and Criminal Justice, 17*, 77–96.

Joox. (2015). *Joox Music Census 2015.* https://digitaltalker.blogspot.com/2015/10/joox-2015.html

Ko, H. (2016). *An integrated brand-led business model for the music industry.* [Doctoral dissertation]. The University of Hong Kong.

Liebowitz, S. (2005). Pitfalls in measuring the impact of file-sharing. *CESIFO Economic Studies, 51*, 435–473.

Morris, J. W. (2015). *Selling digital music, formatting culture.* University of California Press.

Mulligan, M. (2015). *Awakening: The music industry in the digital age.* MIDiA Research.

Peitz, M., & Waelbroeck, P. (2004). The effect of Internet piracy on CD sales—Cross section evidence. *Review of the Economic Research on Copyright Issues, 1*, 71–79.

Schumpeter, J. A. (1942). *Capitalism, socialism and democracy.* Routledge.

Silver, J. (2013). *Digital medieval: The first twenty years of music on the web ... and the next twenty*. Xstorical Publications Media.

Vaughn, M. (2014). *History of DAW*. https://logitunes.com/blog/history-of-daw/

Wang, K. J. (2020). *Hong Kong popular culture: Worlding film, television, and pop music*. Palgrave Macmillan.

Zentner, A. (2006). Measuring the effect of file sharing on music purchases. *Journal of Law and Economics, 49*, 63–90.

CHAPTER 5

Hitback: The Ballad as Venue for Political Protest in the Philippines

Florentino A Iniego, Jr,
University of the Philippines Diliman

I grew up with ballads that were part of the music repertoire played on radio programmes and television commercials in my youth. Coupled with songs that were played over and over through public music platforms, the lyrics of these songs could be found in chord book magazines, oftentimes with corresponding chords such as the *Jingle Chordbook Magazine*. As a form of popular music, thus, these ballads are etched in my memory:

> "Listen, while I'll tell you a story / The tale of the Marlboro brand," goes the Marlboro Radio Commercial. (Arnold, 1968)

> "Christ you know it ain't easy / You know how hard it can be / The way things are going / They're gonna crucify me," is the message from John and Yoko's wedding. (Lennon & McCartney, 1969)

Through these popular songs and with the aid of chord book guides on how to accompany oneself on a musical instrument, I learnt how to play the guitar and sing with guitar accompaniment.

Singing and playing the guitar became my passport to socialising with friends and acquaintances. In comparison, perhaps I was like the poet Balagtas (Francisco Baltazar, 1788–1862) who grew up reciting the *awit* (song) and *korido* (corrido), or writer Plaridel (Marcelo H. Del Pilar, 1850–1896) who solemnly mumbled *dasal* (prayers) and sang the *pasyon* (passion). I was a Tagalog youth serenading Jocelyna with the melody of a *kundiman* (love song).[1]

Over the years, these music forms have developed to contain subversive undertones. In the late 1800s, the *awit* became an "allegory of protest" in the book *Florante at Laura* (Lumbera & Lumbera, 1982, pp. 40–41), the *dasal* and *pasyon* became a fervent, teasing parody against the prayers of the Spanish friars in the book *Dasalan at Tocsohan (Prayers and Temptations)* (Lumbera & Lumbera, 1982, p. 44) and the *kundiman* "Jocelynang Baliuag" is none other than a revolutionary song of the Katipunan, the organisation of Filipino revolutionaries founded in 1896 which aimed to topple down the Spanish regime (Maceda, 1994).

In the 1950–1960s, the folk ballads by Pete Seeger, Bob Dylan, Joan Baez, and Peter, Paul and Mary became a vehicle of social protest against civil rights abuse and the United States' (US) involvement in the Vietnam War (Schall, 1977). As cited by Santos (1994), Filipino musicians not only absorbed the American style of protest music but also integrated it into the local expression of nationalist ideas in songs that encouraged listeners to rebel against authority and convention.[2]

More than the lyrics and tune of the songs, this chapter discusses the ballads of Filipino poet Bienvenido Lumbera for his prose on the struggle for freedom and democracy.

The Protest Ballads of Lumbera

Bienvenido Lumbera's (Figure 1) poems valiantly highlight the nationalist struggle of the Filipino people against the dictatorial regime of Ferdinand Marcos. Though imprisoned during the martial law period, Lumbera never wavered in his stand on national freedom and democracy. Aside from his radical writings, Lumbera's dedication and significant contribution to academic research on art, literature and culture garnered him the Ramon Magsaysay Award for Journalism, Literature, and Creative Communication (1993) and he was hailed as the National Artist for Literature (2006).

The goals and limitations of Lumbera's ballads are clear: (a) As recited/sung poetry, the audience is made aware of themes that embolden, urge and attract political consciousness; and (b) while narrative poetry does not discuss themes comprehensively, it touches upon issues that can inspire deeper discourse (Lumbera, 2008). Lumbera's three ballads from 1973, 1990 and 1991 as compiled in his anthology *Likhang Dila, Likhang Diwa* (1993) are political testimonies written during the nation's turbulent stages of struggle against the US-Marcos Dictatorship and the US-Aquino Regime.

FIGURE 1 Bienvenido Lumbera, a Filipino poet, librettist, critic and dramatist, often performed his poems during rallies and other political gatherings
Source: Lumbera (1993). Used with permission.

"Ballad of Freedom" (1973)

Written on Independence Day (June 12), this ballad is an optimistic reflection on the "arrival of morning" from a "whole night of darkness". The ballad is divided into four parts of short poems which, according to the poet, "... can be separated as small songs with a single tune". Each part of the poem has four stanzas: the first three have three lines per stanza, where each line has a regular metre and eight syllables (typical in the *korido* and *pasyon* form) and an irregular rhyme.

The first Lumbera ballad in the period of "white horror" sown by dictator Ferdinand Marcos adheres to the strategic line of the nationalist movement as written in the fundamental documents of the people's movement. This ballad is serious, deep and solemn. It dismisses the belief that "fate" brings about the nation's misery (stanza 2). It is anchored in the principle that the dynamic movement of the people is decisive: "because man welded, the chain breaks" (stanza 2), "the movement will live, because the masses hold the line" (stanza 5). It has faith in the lessons from history that someday the "oppressed will rise up," "the despised will go up" and "be exalted as lord" (stanza 3). It knows the fundamental alliance that will dismantle the class enemy: "workers and farmers ... bonded, united, refused enslavement by foreigners and the bourgeoisie" (stanza 13). While "the sky may be gloomy" and "each wail is nurtured, the revolution flourishes" (stanzas 7–8).

The dismissal of fate, decisive masses, lessons from past history, class struggles, and revolutionary solutions: these are the ballad's declarations which will rouse comrades to march, exclaim and sing in unison, advocating social change.

Every poet and writer during the 1970s strived to carry the movement's political line while honing their skills in their literary work. As the chair of an organisation of writers and artists espousing radical social changes called the Panulat para sa Kaunlaran ng Sambayanan (PAKSA) in 1970,[3] Lumbera and cadres in the cultural field led workshops to achieve dialectical bonding of art and politics. One of the creative calls of PAKSA was the development of existing forms of native or foreign literature. Cultural activists were tasked to apply revolutionary ideals in the practice and popularisation of literary forms (Lumbera & Lumbera, 1982).

The fusion of form and structure of the *korido* and *pasyon* and the application of the national-democratic line were some of the devices utilised by the piece "Ballad of Freedom" during this period of darkness.

"Ballad of Cory's Emergency Powers" (1990)

After four years of Cory Aquino as President, with the blessing of *people's* power in February 1986, the ruling class went back to their old ways. As the saying goes, "the song remains the same", with Aquino replacing Marcos and the country remaining beholden to the US.

During her first year in power, Aquino, familiarly known as "Tita (Aunt) Cory" already had blood on her hands: the Mendiola massacre in January 1987 was immediately followed by the massacre in Lupao, Nueva Ecija in February 1987. Bullets, not land, became the response of Hacienda Luisita's landlord. Instead of abrogating external debts of the country which had supposedly gone through a revolution, Aquino quickly signed a letter of intent and oath of allegiance to the International Monetary Fund and World Bank. The "Cory Magic" disappeared and the symbolic yellow colour of the 1986 People Power Revolution faded.[4]

Meanwhile, the liberation movement which was allegedly "left behind" and rendered rudderless after the People Power uprising (also known as the EDSA uprising) once again corrected this observation and launched a new wave of advancement. It exposed the fascist nature of the US-Aquino regime and repelled the lunge of *total war*. For Aquino, however, the immediate political threat to her reign did not come from the left, but instead the ultra-right military forces.

The theme of Lumbera's second ballad is Aquino's request for emergency powers to quell threats to her regime by a series of coup d'etats by the military's Reform the Armed Forces Movement (RAM). The ballad, composed of 25 stanzas patterned after the rhyme and metre of *awit*, was recited in a rally in front of the Senate in 1990. If the first ballad is serious, direct and gallant, the second is a melodramatic plea for the Aquino regime to take cognisance of the welfare of the common folks.

In this ballad, Lumbera borrowed the popular folk song "Doon Po sa Amin" ("In Our Town") to express that justice in the country has remained blind, mute, deaf and lame following the EDSA uprising. From stanzas 1–8, the source of "militaritis", a term coined by critics of the regime to mean the use of military to suppress dissent, is stated. The following are stanzas 4 and 5:

<table>
<tr><td>Dito po sa atin, krisis ay sandamak
Utang sa dayuha'y pataas na lagnat,
Presyo ng bilihi'y pantog na humilab,
Sa malubhang lagay, baya'y naghihirap</td><td>Here in our town, crises abound,
Foreign debt is a rising fever,
Prices of commodities bladderful,
In severe situation, the nation suffers.</td></tr>
<tr><td>At doon po naman sa ating batasan,
Ang bait at muni ay kulang at kulang,
Ang imbestigasyo'y larong bata lamang,
Patintero ngayon bukas ay lutuan.</td><td>And in our congress,
Sanity and wisdom are lacking,
Investigation is but child's play,
Patintero now cooking game tomorrow.</td></tr>
</table>

The people doubted the authenticity of the bombing and exchange of fire by government and rebel soldiers. The popular notion was that the skirmishes between government and rebel forces were but a prelude to the declaration of emergency powers. Thus: "How about us ... often regarded as the majority? / Our situation is like a chopping board, / If emergency powers become guns, we certainly are dead again." (stanzas 19–21). In the conflict between the ruling class and RAM under the guise of the people's soldiers, this was what lay ahead for the people (stanza 14):

Ganyan ba talaga ang palad	Is the fate of the oppressed really
ng api?	like that?
Sa away ng elit,	In the squabble of the elite,
napapasantabi,	step aside,
Kapag nadisgrasya ng bala	If accidentally hit by an Uzi
ng Uzi,	bullet,
Lalaitin ka pa't	You will be mocked
"Usisero kasi."	"Curious that is why."

It may be noted that most of the characters involved in this melodrama were made to be spoken by Lumbera himself. The characters can be summarised as people who were wary that Aquino intended to resurrect fascist rule (stanza 23):

Ang emergency rule tugon	Emergency rule is a response
sa kudeta,	to coup d'etat,
Hindi ito sagot sa aming	It is not an answer to our
problema,	problems,
Unang hakbang ito	It is the first step to
tungong diktadura	dictatorship,
Emergency ngayon,	Emergency now,
bukas martial law	martial law tomorrow.

"Ballad of the Dismantling of the Military Bases" (1991)

Continuing to highlight the traditional structure of *awit* and the tune of witty poetry against the policy of the US-Aquino regime, Lumbera recited again a ballad to celebrate another victory of the people against imperialist control in the Philippines—the dismantling of the US military bases in the Philippines—in front of the Senate on September 16, 1991.

After World War II, US imperialism ensured the certainty of their military bases in the country. Patronised by puppet regimes of the republic, the US-RP (Republic of the Philippines) Military Bases Treaty was signed in 1947, giving the US extraterritorial and perpetual rights for its military bases to remain for 99 years and cover more than 20 strategic areas in the country (Guerrero, 1979). While the US fully benefited from the military bases, the troubles these wrought in the nation became acute. The bases seemingly became a haven for prostitution, the human rights of citizens living around the bases were allegedly violated, and most of all, the US military presence was seen as a big slap to the sovereignty and independence of the Philippines.

For the Filipinos who were aware and hateful of centuries of foreign exploitation, the most physical manifestation of this travesty—the military bases—had to end. Lumbera's ballad fiercely exposes Aunt Cory's explicit endorsement of "Bushtang" or US President George Bush (stanzas 4–5):

Itong kaharian ng Reynang Dilawan,	This queendom of Queen Yellow,
Ay suking kolonya ng Haring si Bushtang,	Is client colony of King Bushtang,
Ang ekonomiya't ang pamahalaan,	The economy and government,
Kunwari'y sa Pinoy, ay kapit-Merikan.	Pretending for Pinoy, is pro-American.

Ngunit panahon man ng	But though the season of
kolonyal kontrol,	colonial control,
Hindi napipigilang bayan	The people cannot be prevented
ay tumutol,	from refusing,
Dominasyong Kano'y dapat	American domination must
nang maputol,	be ended,
Soberanya nati'y angkinin	Our sovereignty should be
na ngayon.	claimed now.

The ballad showcases three decisive factors that pushed the people's fight to a favourable situation. First, the decision by a majority of Senators to "refuse to surrender to the queen's wrath ... / Let us sow in our hearts / Nationalist fervour drenched in blood" (stanza 15). Second, the eruption of Mount Pinatubo which produced lahar flooding, ash fall, and tremors that damaged the facilities of Clark Air Base and Subic Naval Base (stanza 14). Third, the people's wrath which could deliver a final blow to imperialist control in the country (stanza 19–21).

In line with the significant date of the declaration of the Philippine Independence, Lumbera's ballad celebrates the victory of the Filipino people (stanza 24):

Bayan, araw ngayong	People, this day is
napakadakila—	very great—
Batiin ng sigaw, ng awit,	Greet with a shout, a song,
ng tula	a poem
Ang piglas sa langit ng	Our flag's flutter
ating bandila,	in the sky,
Bagong Hunyo 12, ganap	New June 12, complete
na paglaya!	independence!

Conclusion

From the sources of tradition in *kundiman*, *dasal*, *pasyon*, *awit* and *korido*, the ballad as a form of narrative poetry-song (with its Spanish-American influence) finds its roots in the development of indigenous and popular music in the Philippines. It concretely reflects the vision, experiences, and aspirations of the people. Consciously or not, the writer, poet and composer's creative imagination does not remain patterned after or subservient to the dominant flow of romanticism, sentimentalism, as well as commercialism.

Historically, as liberating transformations were applied to traditional literary forms, the period of Lumbera's ballads dealt a counter-hegemonic blow against the fascist dictatorship and imperialism in the country. Armed with subversive intervention, these ballads served as words recited and lyrics sung by the Filipino people to achieve justice, freedom and democracy.

Notes

[1] The *kundiman* is a love song popular among the Tagalogs in the central and southern part (Luzon) of the Philippines. Religious forms (*dasal, pasyon*) and metrical romances (*awit, korido*) were introduced through Spanish colonialism to hasten the spread of Catholicism and Hispanisation in the entire Philippine islands from 1593 till the mid-1800s.

[2] Protest song ballads composed by Peter Seeger ("Where Have All the Flowers Gone", "We Shall Overcome") and Bob Dylan ("The Times They Are A-Changin'", "Blowing in the Wind") and sung by Joan Baez and Peter, Paul, and Mary have become the theme songs of protest movements in the United States and the Philippines (Schall, 1977; Santos, 1994).

[3] Panulat para sa Kaunlaran ng Sambayanan (PAKSA or Writers for the Advancement of the People) is a national organisation of activist writers established in July 1970. Its objective was to create a body of literature infused with the national-democratic line and ideology which will help develop the political consciousness of the masses. PAKSA would be outlawed upon the declaration of martial law in 1972 (Ordonez, 1996).

[4] On January 22, 1987, some 20,000 farmers and members of various progressive groups marched to Mendiola Bridge (now Chino Roces Bridge) in Manila calling on then-President Corazon Aquino to implement genuine agrarian reform. However, soldiers fired at the marching farmers. Thirteen died as a result and many more were injured. Two weeks later in February 1987 in Lupao, Nueva Ecija, 17 farmers were reportedly massacred by government troops after they were accused as members of the New People's Army. In addition, instead of making a clean break with Marcos' past policies, Aquino adopted the same economic policies so closely identified with IMF-World Bank prescriptions (Clarin, 2019).

References

Clarin, A. M. A. (January 22, 2019). 32 years after Mendiola massacre, farmers still demand justice. *Bulatlat*. https://www.bulatlat.com/2019/01/22/32-years-after-mendiola-massacre-farmers-still-demand-justice

Arnold, E. (1968). City ballad. In *Marlboro Radio Commercial* [Audio file]. https://archive.org/details/tobacco_oeo23e00

Guerrero, A. (1979). *Philippine society and revolution* (3rd ed.). Central Publishing House.

Lennon, J., & McCartney, P. (1969). The ballad of John and Yoko. [Lyrics]. https://www.beatlesbible.com/songs/the-ballad-of-john-and-yoko

Lumbera, B. (2008). *Poetika/Politika: Tinipong mga tula* [Poetics/Politics: Selected poems]. University of the Philippines Press.

Lumbera, B., & Lumbera, C. N. (1982). *Philippine literature: A history and anthology*. Anvil Publications, Inc.

Lumbera, B. (1993). *Likhang dila, likhang diwa* [Created by the tongue, created by the mind] [Photograph]. Anvil Publications, Inc.

Maceda, T. G. (1994). Protest songs. In *Cultural center of the Philippines: Encyclopedia of Philippine art* (Vol. VI, pp. 114–122). Cultural Center of the Philippines.

Ordonez, E. A. (Ed.). (1996). *Nationalist literature: A centennial forum*. Philippine Writers Academy (Panulat) and University of the Philippines Press.

Santos, R. (1994). Songs and ballads. In *Cultural center of the Philippines: Encyclopedia of Philippine art* (Vol. VI, pp. 59–67). Cultural Center of the Philippines.

Schall, L. M. (1977). The ballad as vehicle for social protest. *Studies in Popular Culture, 1*(1, Winter 1977), 26–35. https://www.jstor.org/stable/i23412969

CHAPTER 6

Persona of A-Mei in Transition: Fan Identity and Identification

Gui Ren, *Communication University of China*

With the development of online social networks, music fans now have a stronger sense of community within which they shape their online and real-life identities. An idol's persona plays an important role in constructing the identity of his or her fans. Different personas allow fans to construct different identifications and identities. In this chapter, I use the popular Chinese singer Zhang Huimei, better known as A-Mei, as a key example of an idol whose persona resonates with the young and rebellious. Hailing from an ethnic group native to Taiwan, A-Mei has gone from singing in pubs and bars to becoming the "Queen of Mandopop". Her music has not only provided a figure for the textual identification of several generations of young people, but also struck a chord with people who identify with her persona as a "rebel", "feminist", and "gay godmother". I use the case of A-Mei as an example to explore the fan-celebrity connection, and the relationship between an idol's persona and fan identity and identification to understand how and why fans identify with their idol.

Based on the theory that fan identity and communities are mediated by texts, different identities, politics and other perspectives, this chapter discusses the relationship between

A-Mei's transitional persona and fan identity and identification, and analyses the following questions: How do fans build their identity and identification through the idol's persona? Do different personas provide fans with different imaginary spaces? Will a fixed idol persona attract a fixed fan base? What are the other factors that affect the identity and identification of fans in addition to the idol's persona?

A-Mei's Persona in Transition

Before China's economic reform and opening-up policies, people listened to songs that were predominantly filled with heavy metaphors and political nuances. With the reform and opening-up, mainland Chinese society entered a new historical period. Audiovisual and multimedia materials began entering the market and permeating everyday life, and popular music from Hong Kong and Taiwan rapidly became popular in mainland China. In the 1990s, most of the popular female singers in China reflected the sentimental temperament of urban women; it was the trend of conveying a woman's vulnerability and expressing her yearning for romantic love. Against this backdrop, A-Mei with the persona of a Taiwanese aboriginal singer, appeared unique and wild in the eyes of the public.

A-Mei, born Zhang Huimei, is a popular aboriginal Taiwanese Mandopop singer. She is the first ever Taiwanese singer to receive an exclusive interview with CNN in the United States and has appeared on the cover of the Asian edition of *Time Magazine*. From singing in bars and pubs, she has become known as one of the best Mandarin female singers, earning numerous music awards and accolades in the Mandarin-speaking world. People from all walks of life in Taiwan and the mainland were excited to hear this fresh and exciting voice emerge from one of the indigenous tribes in Taitung. She had a wild yet charming allure that made her different from other female singers. When she debuted, instead of keeping to the persona of a traditional and meek Chinese woman, A-Mei's music and performances reflected her independent and wild side. Her first album, *Sisters*, was a huge hit and uniquely resonated with many women. She portrayed an independent aboriginal woman standing under the blue sky, singing her story naturally and powerfully. In her second album, *Bad Boy*, she created the persona of a rebellious woman, encouraging women to live life to the fullest, challenging the status quo and the traditional characteristics of female pop singers. The feminist undertones of this album were carried through in all her subsequent albums, with A-Mei using her music to validate female self-worth and independence. Over the years, A-Mei has undergone several changes to her image and musical style, but in 2009, she created an alter-ego under her native name, Amit, and with her music, explored themes such as gender politics, gender norms, and LGBT issues. In the eyes of the public, A-Mei has showcased different images and identities at different stages of her career, and the period between each transition gives people a chance to think and reflect on her persona and influence. With labels such "rebel", "feminist" and "gay godmother" attached to her persona and music, A-Mei has contributed greatly to the Chinese music scene and the community. She has been championing LGBT rights for many years and reacted with joy when Taiwan's same-sex marriage bill was passed.

Richard Dyer, a professor of film studies at the University of London, first proposed the concept of "star studies" in his book, *Stars*, published by the British Film Institute in 1979 (Dyer, 1979). Star studies integrate sociological semiotics and other methodologies to establish a new research method for the celebrity-star image. They reveal the *constructed* identities of celebrities, covering both the public and private lives. Dyer believed that the star image is a collection of all textually constructed images, including screen roles and supervised public images (such as the images in pin-ups and press releases, and public appearances in real places and occasions). Each element is complex and contradictory, and a star is all of it taken together (Dyer, 1979). As public figures, celebrities focus on society and their celebrity capital or recognisibility shaped by media presentations. The separation between the foreground and the background of a celebrity's identity is no longer clear, as it exists in the dual space of real society and network society. In other words, audiences can see a star's stage persona as he or she appears in real life as well as the star's real persona in his or her daily life via social media.

The identity construction of a star subject is complicated. The "body" of a star is displayed as a visual image, and has become the most beautiful consumer product in contemporary society. Being in the public eye means a star's private space is constantly publicised. The superposition of various complex factors constructs a corresponding identity in the mind of the public. A-Mei's own personality is chic and casual. On stage, she is flashy and sexy, stepping out confidently in her high heels. However, behind the scenes, she is a vulnerable woman who has suffered career setbacks and personal losses including the sudden death of her music producer, the man who had helped her the most in her career. After each trial, however, she would emerge stronger and undeterred by negativity. A-Mei's persona is not just the image that the media paints in their coverage and reports to the public, but also the image that she actively conveys to the public through public appearances and social media. A-Mei fearlessly conveys her views on social platforms to champion the rights of women and the LGBT community. The look and poses in her photographs are avant-garde and bold, and her engagement with her fans has earned her a large and loyal following.

How Do Fans Gain Identity From the Persona of A-Mei

The word "fan" comes from the Latin "fanaticus", a word which has a strong religious nuance. It was around 1889 when fanaticus first appeared in the English language in the abbreviated form "fan" to mean fanatical people. In his book, Text Poacher: TV Fans and Participatory Culture, Henry Jenkins defined a fan as someone who displays "fanatic involvement in ball games, commercial or entertainment activities, infatuation, admiration or worship of people who are singers or sports stars" (Jenkins, 2013). Therefore, the psychology of fans can be described as fanatical and obsessive, and every move of an idol may influence the views and behaviour of fans.

Since her debut in 1996, A-Mei has rapidly achieved commercial success and is extremely popular in the Mandarin-speaking world, often being referred to as a diva of the Mandarin pop music scene and a style icon. Her fans are enamoured of her charm and style, and often replicate her outfits and looks. Fans who share the same identity and idol tend to gather together because they are connected with a sense of identity and belonging. According to Liu (2006), the renowned French psychoanalyst Jacques Lacan proposed the theory of the "mirror stage", believing that human cognition originated from people's fascination with images, which is a projection of the "ideal self" and an illusory existence. While pursuing self-identification, each individual hopes to perfectly present their own image in order to achieve an ideal state. When they are unable to present their "ideal self", people will project their emotions onto others. (Liu, 2006, pp. 24–27). Fans' projection of idols supports the "mirror stage" theory. Fans find their ideal self through idols and use *transitional objects* to complete their identity. The persona of a celebrity constantly changes in the media, and A-Mei's multiple personas have attracted a large and loyal following that includes both feminists and traditional women, as well as the LGBT community. Everyone can use A-Mei's music and personas as a basis for connecting in groups and from which they can address their own individual struggles related to gender norms, heteropatriarchy or LGBT issues; her different personas influence fans in their behaviour and psychology. In the same way, Li Yuchun, winner of the Chinese televised singing contest *Super Girl* in 2005, started the trend of gender-neutral dressing. In the process of fans following their idols and even developing imaginary relationships with them, they may incorporate the idols' values and attitudes into their own behaviour, resulting in personal transformation. Not only can they find their ideal self, they are also able to interact and communicate within the fan community to construct a new self. In the process, the sense of group identity is strengthened.

However, in the age of the Internet, idol worship has undergone essential changes compared to the 1990s. Fandom has gradually become a product of people's self-consciousness, and idol worship has become increasingly emotional and life-oriented. Due to accessibility to information, ease of communication, and sharing of resources on the Internet, celebrities can easily publicise their work or connect with fans. The interactions between idols, fans and the public, between fans and fans, and between fans and the public, have also become more convenient and frequent. The virtual space created on the Internet now provides more possibilities for subcultural groups to construct ideal identities. The collection of fans' virtual identities and network groups has provided fans with various opportunities to express themselves. As a nonconformist Chinese singer who frequently speaks out for the LGBT community, A-Mei would always use the song "Rainbow" from her album as a standing track for her concerts. The track includes the lyrics "our love is very similar, because men hurt"; such obvious lyrics often appear in A-Mei's songs to draw people's attention to issues that matter to her. At her concerts, she would often recreate a rainbow ocean on stage or wave a rainbow flag in support of gay couples. Her concert videos are continuously reposted or re-created by her fans on social networks, attracting the psychological attention of LGBT groups. Psychological identity emphasises the subject's spiritual sense of belonging; that is, paying attention to the psychological level of identity and sense of belonging, and studying the relationship between the process of identity achievement, and the individual's psychological experience (Song, 2016). Fan identification refers to the psychological connection that individuals have with their idols. Through her engagement with fans and her intervention in gender norms, A-Mei encourages people to reflect on themselves and recognise changes in their self-perception. A-Mei amasses many fans as a result, all of whom identify with her ideals and incorporate her values into their own behaviour and thinking. Projection forms a unique psychological experience, thereby helping fans gain a sense of identity.

Conclusion

With the advent of new media and network technologies, the public personas of stars are becoming more vivid and real. The persona of a star is not only a product of the stage, it can also reflect the changes in the social environment, and even express the ideal self-image of fans or the public image of the star. The public can reinterpret the persona of the star through the media, and assign different meanings to the persona symbols in their minds. Fans tend to exist in a group; they can connect with each other because of their appreciation of a star's persona and form their own community, in which self-identity or group identification is achieved. When their own feelings and the ideal self that the fan wishes to develop are projected into the image of a star, the persona of the star will not only be reshaped by the fan, giving fans a broader space for imagination, the image of the star may also fall in line with fans' expectations. Under the influence of these factors, the star's persona becomes more meaningful.

References

Dyer, R. (1979). *Star*. British Film Institute.

Jenkins, H. (2013). *Textual poachers: TV fans and participatory culture* (X. Zheng, Trans.). Peking University Press.

Liu, W. (2006). Lacan's mirror image theory and self-construction. *Academic Communication*, 24–27.

Song, S. I. (2016). *Research on gay identity under social media: Take social media Blued as an example* [Master's thesis, Jinan University].

Zhang, H. M. [aMEI_feat_A-Mit]. (2013, January 16). *撐同志, 反歧視!* [Supporting gay people, against discrimination]. Weibo. https://m.weibo.cn/1777924625/3535129534740755

CHAPTER 7

Seiko Matsuda's Concert and the AI Singing of Hibari Misora

Hiroshi Ogawa, *Kansai University*

Popular music trends are generally short-lived. However, once a song is loved by people, it becomes a hit and continues to be loved as time passes. In this chapter, I consider new meanings of hit songs over the decades, acquired through live performances from the same singer. The subject of my consideration is the pre-40th anniversary concert of Seiko Matsuda's debut held in 2019. As a contrasting phenomenon, I refer to the artificial intelligence (AI)-powered singing of the late Hibari Misora, a legendary Japanese vocalist, which was experimentally created in 2019.

The Iceberg Model

In 1980, the NHK Public Opinion Survey conducted a nationwide survey on music behaviour and consciousness, and presented an iceberg model to understand the correlation between music and course of life (NHK Public Opinion Survey Office, 1982). In that model, it was assumed that people are enthusiastic about the music they listen to in their late teens and early 20s. The findings showed that people continue to love the music they enjoyed or were exposed to when they were young. Music that is supported by the younger generation will sweep the market and become a phenomenon. In the iceberg analogy, the tip of the iceberg on the surface of the water represents the music that the present younger generation supports. It is, so to speak, the flow of music. Eventually, the boom of the music will decline. However, while it is no longer a phenomenon, it remains a favourite among a generation of people who became enamoured with it when they were in their youth. The tip of the iceberg now sinks below the surface of the water and becomes part of the iceberg below. Over time, a generation's favourite music sinks deeper, reaching the very bottom of the iceberg. An underwater iceberg is layered by generations. It is a stock of music that is invisible, but remains alive through being sung in the media, karaoke bars and live performances. This model is still useful in considering the meaning of music in today's media society.

Seiko Matsuda
Singing Idol of a Consumer Society

The 1980s was an era in which Japan enjoyed a consumer society, when its people thrived on buying and using goods. Seiko Matsuda, who made her record debut in 1980 and released many hit songs in succession, was an idol of that particular generation. This is due to a couple of reasons.

First, she successfully used TV commercials to sell her music. She released a new song every three months, and from the debut single up to the fifth single, her songs were continually tied in with TV commercials in which she herself appeared.

Second, she created songs that evoked an atmospheric "holiday mood" which were suited to be played in resorts. Takashi Matsumoto, a member of the band Happy End, had been providing the lyrics to Matsuda's songs since 1992 and he often wrote about events set against seaside and mountain resorts.

Matsuda was also a new type of idol in that she won the admiration of many modern young women. She continued singing after her marriage in 1985 and the birth of a daughter in 1986. In 1989, she became an independent artist and established her own office. From 1992, she began self-producing her albums and writing the lyrics to many songs herself. Almost every year until 2018, she released an album and held a concert based on the theme of the album.

The songs from a new album would be sung in the first half of the concert. She would dress in a way that projected an image of a mature and sophisticated woman. During this half, the audience was mostly quiet. The second half of the concert consisted of the performance of a medley of her 1980s hits that the audience had been waiting for. Matsuda would appear wearing an idol costume just as she did in the 1980s and sang her hit songs. The audience would be on their feet, clapping their hands, applauding happily and exuberantly.

Pre-40th Anniversary Concert of Seiko Matsuda's Debut in 2019

The 2019 concert was positioned as a pre-40th anniversary concert of Matsuda's debut and was different from all the other concerts that had been held to date. Only single hits from the 1980s and 1990s were sung at the show. Until then, there had not been any instance where the same singer sang hit songs from her 20s, which was over 30 years ago. That was only possible for Matsuda, who released many hit songs in the 1980s and continued to hold live concerts ever since. The songs that were sung at the concert were written for her by well-known musicians such as Takashi Matsumoto, Haruomi Hosono, Eiichi Ohtaki, Yumi Matsutoya, Motoharu Sano and Ami Ozaki.

Hibari Misora

Bringing Hibari Misora Back With AI

After Seiko Matsuda's nationwide tour ended, a special feature called "Hibari Misora Revived by AI" was televised on the Japanese broadcaster NHK's documentary programme *NHK Special* on September 29, 2019 (NHK Special, 2019). Hibari Misora was a legendary Japanese singer who died in 1989 at the age of 52, and the year 2019 marked the 30th anniversary of her death. In the programme, Misora's singing was brought back to life using the latest AI singing synthesis technology based on the recordings and images that remain in the archives of NHK and record companies.

The programme presented the process of reproducing Misora's voice, singing, and movements, and the process by which a new song "Arekara" ("Since Then") was created for the AI Misora. After the programme was aired, a lot of debate was generated. Some said the tribute was very touching, while others felt it was an act of disrespect to the late singer. Nevertheless, the AI Misora made a special appearance in the popular programme NHK *Kohaku Uta Gassen* (Red and White Singing Contest) on New Year's Eve and sang "Arekara" again.

The lyrics of the song were written by Yasushi Akimoto, who also wrote Misora's final single. In the song, the AI Misora sang: "What have you been doing since then? I'm getting old, too." In the middle of the song, she spoke to the audience: "It's been a long time, I've been watching you for a long time, You have been working hard. Please do your best to my part." It was a moment in which the long-gone Misora addressed the audience.

Conclusion

Both the singing of the AI Hibari Misora and the pre-40th anniversary concert of Seiko Matsuda's debut bring one to reflect on the meaning of music of the past three decades. The AI Hibari was a created ghost. While Misora had passed away in 1989, the created 3-D image was of her still in her prime. Misora's fans were impressed by the realistic reproduction of her voice and singing ability. While they would not feel old with her, the AI image would have reaffirmed their age and sparked them to reflect on the meaning of the past 30 years.

On the contrary, the concert held by the 57-year-old Seiko Matsuda brought fans a completely different meaning to the past 30 years. Two contrasting perspectives were presented by Matsuda. On one hand, the concert gave a feeling of nostalgia to audience members who were about the same age as Matsuda. On the other hand, it presented an "alternate reality" of sorts where the world which emerged from the Matsuda concert was one that would have been if the consumer society of the 1980s had continued to this day. In reality, however, the economic bubble burst in the early 1990s, the Japanese economic growth stagnated, neoliberal policies were introduced, and economic disparity widened. The music sung at Matsuda's concert was provided to her by Japanese city pop artists. The significance of the concert could be a clue as to why city pop as a genre has been receiving a lot of public attention recently.

References

NHK Special. (2019): Hibari Misora revived by AI. *NHK Archives*. https://www2.nhk.or.jp/archives/tv60bin/detail/index.cgi?das_id=D0009051109_00000

NHK Public Opinion Survey Office. (1982). *Gendai-jin to ongaku* [Modern people and music]. Nihon Hoso Shuppan Kyokai.

CHAPTER 8

K-Pop in Malaysian Popular Music Education: Yea or Nay?

Hueyuen Choong, *University of Westminster*

Popular music education in Malaysia is dominated by the study of Western popular music (henceforth, to be referred to as W-pop), predominantly those from the United States (US) and the United Kingdom (UK). This hegemony was never questioned as there is a commonly accepted understanding that the term *popular music* refers to W-pop, whereas music from other regions that display W-pop characteristics have their own distinct labels, such as Latin pop, J-pop, Cantopop and of course, K-pop. These derivative labels can be argued as efforts to not only denote W-pop as its own unique entity, distinct from the variety of popular music existing in other regions of the world, but also connote its relative cultural primacy over its offshoot variations.

The hegemony is evident in popular music-based instrumental tuitions in Malaysia. While there is no doubt of the inclusion of non-W-pop content in lessons given the unique social and cultural make-up of the society, there is an unarguable predominance of W-pop within those contexts due to the global influence of W-pop culture. This notion is further supported by the fact that popular music examination boards in Malaysia mainly derive from the UK and assess knowledge of W-pop.

A quick examination of published descriptions of some university programmes in Malaysia also reveals this hegemony to some extent, with some clearly stating a focus on Western modern music (National Academy of Arts, Culture & Heritage or ASWARA) and popular or contemporary music (UCSI University and Sunway University), while others on the skills and expertise to be acquired through the programme (University Malaya and University Teknologi MARA). The programme descriptions are not conclusive, but research may yield an indication of hegemony, as the history of W-pop's induction into Europe's higher educational institutions signifies that the point of entrance of popular music into formal music study was through liberal studies.

In the UK, this began in the 1970s and early 1980s when literature put forth notions that popular music was an entity that needed to be examined through sociological and cultural lenses to expose its meanings (Parkinson & Smith, 2015; Warner, 2017). In other words, it was scholarly literature that legitimised the academic study of popular culture in the UK, and it placed the field's origins within many pre-existing liberal disciplines. Vocationally inclined programmes which ranged from recording to music performance, however, only began emerging in the 1990s (Warner, 2017). In Norway, popular music had already begun wiggling its way into institutions prior to the establishment of its first non-Western classical music higher education programme in 1979. Specifically, the introduction of popular music to music academia took place when a thesis on modern/contemporary jazz was written in 1974. Since then, there has been rapid growth of theses exploring various popular music styles (Dyndahl et al., 2016).

In both instances, preceding the formal study of W-pop practices was the liberal study of the subject, rendering research interest a credible indicator of the current and forthcoming academisation of music. Searching through Google Scholar with the keywords "Malaysia AND Western popular music" returned 13,500 results, while "Malaysia AND (K-pop OR "Korean popular music")" returned 881. While this is not indicative of the curriculum content of the Malaysian courses, it undoubtedly illustrates W-pop's predominance in Malaysian academia. However, it also shows that K-pop is making its way into learning institutions, akin to the development of popular music studies in the UK and Norway.

K-Pop in Malaysia

Beyond institutional walls, it is impossible to ignore the popularity of K-pop, since its exponential international growth over the last 20 years has been "threatening the established music and media supremacy of Europe, America and Japan" (Howard, 2015, p.298). K-pop's most recent prominent global success came in the form of a group called BTS, who by 2018, topped the US *Billboard* charts, were awarded the Billboard Music Award for Top Social Artist twice in a row, acquired a portfolio that includes collaborative acts with internationally renowned artists, and were invited to address a General Assembly of the United Nations (Howard, 2015; Doré & Pugsley, 2019).

Within the context of Malaysia, K-pop as part of the wider phenomenon known as the Korean Wave or Hallyu, has infiltrated the lives of the Malaysian youth, with K-pop radio programmes receiving higher ratings than others. Its popularity and presence can also be translated into the influence it wields. This is evident in the increased emulation of South Korean styles and fashions, and the ever-growing consumption of Korean dramas, music, skincare products, and interest in the Korean language. In a 2019 study on the attitude and behaviour of Malaysian consumers towards Korean products, it was concluded that the Korean Wave was an influential factor (Arifin et al., 2013; Gan, 2019).

K-pop has had a very prominent presence in the lives of many all around the world, and Malaysia is clearly not spared of its *invasion*, yet it has barely made its way into the realms of institutionalised popular music learning. While the instinctive response would be to divert attention to the factors that led to this situation, the question that this chapter focuses on is whether K-pop has a place in those institutions. The issue is complex in and of itself, but this chapter grounds the examination in three questions: (1) Does K-pop fall under the jurisdiction of these institutions? (2) Will there be resistance? (3) Is there a need for inclusion?

Does K-pop Belong to the Category of Music that Popular Music Programmes are Teaching?

What are the criteria for music to be subsumed under the label of popular music? The term "popular music" has been used inconsistently to represent a wide range of music; refer to Bennett (1980, p. 3), and Jones and Rahn (1977, pp. 82–85). While the various definitions drafted by popular music scholars do overlap with each other, they are not always in one accord as each author characterised the music from a variety of normative, negative, sociological and technological-economic angles (Birrer, 1985, as cited in Middleton, 1990). Needless to say, this resulted in popular music eluding a unanimous definition as there is no consensus on how to define popular music and all attempts are plagued by their own imperfections. However, be that as it may, where would K-pop be situated when examined with those definitional boundaries?

K-pop has largely been characterised as music that is primarily known for "highly produced, sugary boy- and girl-bands" known as idol groups which are a dominant form of K-pop ensembles. Donning "fashionable, colourful outfits", they perform "slick dance routines and catchy tunes" that are best described as a "fusion of synthesised music" that "[combined] bubblegum pop with the musical elements of electro, disco, rock, R&B, and hip-hop". Furthermore, the music relies heavily on "the audiovisual marketing strategy of using music videos" (Howard, 2014, p. 404; Kim, 2017, pp. 4–6; Gan, 2019, p. 7). It is precisely this calculated formula, rooted in accessibility, that propelled its global dominance; the using, not mere copying, of Western styles paired with other "attractive [visual] attributes in a non-threatening, pleasant package" (Kim, 2017, p. 20; Lie, 2012, p. 356). Lie (2012) continued to write that K-pop is "uniformly diatonic, lyrics peppered with English phrases, the singing style is resolutely syllabic or 'Western' Pop, and dance is an integral element of the performance". Therefore, it is "trivially Korean in the sense that singers and producers are almost exclusively ethnic Korean ... yet as a matter of traditional culture, there is almost nothing 'Korean' about K-pop" (pp. 359–360).

As can be seen from the characterisation above, the aural elements of K-pop appear to be mere peripheral cogs in the K-pop machine. However, if the examination is concentrated solely on the aural details, it is evident that K-pop not only contains elements of W-pop, but it can be argued that it is entirely built on W-pop. Even when considering the non-aural characteristics, overlaps can still be observed; the marrying of singing and dancing is evident in post-MTV W-pop and the "manufacturing [of] K-pop artists and sound invite[s] comparisons to the production practices of Motown" (Lie, 2012, p. 350; Kweon, 2018, p. 56).

When juxtaposing the characterisation of K-pop with the variety of boundaries of popular music that were enacted to differentiate one music from another, to include/exclude a music into/from a category, how would K-pop fair against those criteria?

Will There be Resistance from Music Education?

It may be too early to postulate that there will be resistance from formal institutions, but a prediction can always be informed by the past. The developments that led to the academisation of Western jazz and popular music in the UK and the US provide insightful inferences particularly because their formalisation narratives bear striking resemblances.

As explained earlier, the academisation of popular music in the UK largely began from liberal disciplines. In the US, however, it primarily emerged out of the industrial demand for professional musicians, and the need for the education of musicians yearning for a professional career (Powell et al., 2015; Krikun, 2017). However, both jazz and popular music faced academic discrimination as they were perceived to "lack complexity and intellectual content" (Alper, 2007, p. 160).

Even when finally making an entrance into formal realms, jazz and popular music were subjected to the mercy of "the powerful dominating presence of the Western Art music tradition" (Warner, 2017, p. 131). This domination not only shaped the way subsequent music was taught in formal environments but was also the driving force behind the resistance to the induction of jazz and popular music into academia. In other words, the earliest instances of popular music content in academia were allowed at the discretion of the regulating forces: music professors and other academic employees (Dyndahl et al., 2016). Commonly observed practices in today's formal popular music education can be informed by the ways its advocators responded to the need to promote its legitimacy: packaging popular (and jazz) music into a pedagogic model that made sense to the gatekeepers (Gatien, 2009).

It is not too far-fetched to speculate that K-pop will eventually go through the same process, as its beginnings are already looking quite familiar. However, in this case, the dominating presence is not occupied by the Western Art music tradition, but W-pop, and the incumbent gatekeepers are now scholars of W-pop, instigating one to wonder if K-pop will be subjected to a similar fate.

Is There a Need for Inclusion?

As demonstrated through the Google Scholar search exercise, K-pop has already begun attracting academic interest from liberal disciplines including those from Malaysia, but is there an industrial need for the formalised study of Korean popular music? Becher and Trowler (2001, p. 171), as cited by Parkinson and Smith (2015, p. 101), suggested that a discipline's establishment is dependent on its *mode of genesis*: internal genesis, external genesis and external stimulation. The first comprises disciplines that "emerge from specialist interests in other disciplines", the second "where disciplines are created in response to societal demand for certain types of knowledge" and the third describes "existing disciplines [that were] reconfigured towards societal demand" (p. 102).

Is there an industrial demand for local production of musicians well-versed with the practices of K-pop? Would these graduates be prepared for local careers or for one in South Korea? There is a well-established and organised route to K-pop stardom, and the industry is very much in the control of entertainment companies who regulate and govern every aspect of the business, from scouting and training talents to the backend business of creating and producing the music (Howard, 2014). Also, the Korean music industry is filled with songwriters, lyricists, arrangers, music producers, and musicians trained in foreign institutions (Lie, 2012). This means these agents entered the industry equipped with knowledge and skills of Western art and/or popular music, as opposed to being specifically trained (like the scouted talents) for their roles in the K-pop industry.

Therefore, is there a societal demand to create new or to reconfigure existing disciplines in Malaysia to accommodate K-pop? Is there a gap that can be filled by the local training of K-pop music practices? If there is, do current provisions adequately prepare students to meet that demand? If there is not, how then should popular music education in Malaysia respond to K-pop?

Conclusion

This chapter did not set out to seek an explanation behind K-pop's scant presence in institutionalised learning, but rather provide food for thought for agents within the field moving forward. It has been 20 years since the global invasion of K-pop; it is even plausible to argue that it is the current dominant music culture in Malaysia, and it is knocking on the doors of our learning institutions right now. How should we answer?

References

Alper, G. (2007). Towards the acceptance of a bachelor of music degree in popular music studies. *College Music Symposium, 47*, 156–166.

Ariffin, Z. Z., Othman, K., & Abdullah, R. T. (2014, August). *Analyzing the dimension of Korean popular culture among Malaysian adolescent.* 5th International Conference on Humanities and Social Sciences, Songkla, Thailand.

Becher, T., & Trowler, P. (2001). *Academic tribes and territories: Intellectual enquiry and the cultures of discipline.* Open University Press.

Bennett, H. S. (1980). *On becoming a rock musician.* University of Massachusetts Press.

Doré, P., & Pugsley, P. C. (2019). Genre conventions in K-pop: BTS's 'Dope' music video. *Continuum, 33*(5), 580–589.

Dyndahl, P., Karlsen, S., Nielsen, S. G., & Skårberg, O. (2017). The academisation of popular music in higher music education: The case of Norway. *Music Education Research, 19*(4), 438–454.

Gan, X. N. (2019). *Soft power of Korean popular culture on consumer behaviour in Malaysia* [Doctoral dissertation, UTAR].

Gatien, G. (2009). Categories and music transmission. *Action, Criticism, and Theory for Music Education, 8*(2), 94–119.

Howard, K. (2014). Mapping K-pop past and present: Shifting the modes of exchange. *Korea Observer, 45*(3), 389.

Howard, K. (2015). K-pop: The international rise of the Korean music industry. *Ethnomusicology Forum, 24*(2), 298–300.

Jones, G., & Rahn, J. (1977). Definitions of popular music: Recycled. *Journal of Aesthetic Education, 11*(4), 79–92.

Kim, A. (2017). *Korean popular music (K-pop), youth fan culture, and art education curriculum* (Order No. 10606250) (Publication No. 2022418255) [Doctoral dissertation, University of South Carolina].

Krikun, A. (2017). The historical foundations of popular music education in the United States. In G. D. Smith, Z. Moir, M. Brennan, S. Rambarran, & P. Kirkman (Eds.), *The Routledge research companion to popular music education* (pp. 33–45). Routledge.

Kweon, G. (2018). *School of K-pop: Teaching a nation through idol survival programs* [MA thesis, University of North Carolina at Chapel Hill Graduate School]. Carolina Digital Repository. https://doi.org/10.17615/vhah-9f32

Lie, J. (2012). What is the K in K-pop? South Korean popular music, the culture industry, and national identity. *Korea Observer, 43*(3), 339–363.

Middleton, R. (1990). *Studying popular music*. McGraw-Hill Education.

Parkinson, T., & Smith, G. D. (2015). Towards an epistemology of authenticity in higher popular music education. *Action, Criticism and Theory for Music Education, 14*(1), 93–127.

Powell, B., Krikun, A., & Pignato, J. M. (2015). "Something's happening here!": Popular music education in the United States. *IASPM@ Journal, 5*(1), 4–22.

Warner, S. (2017). Where to now? The current condition and future trajectory of popular music studies in British universities. In G. D. Smith, Z. Moir, M. Brennan, S. Rambarran, & P. Kirkman (Eds.), *The Routledge research companion to popular music education* (pp. 127–139). Routledge.

CHAPTER 9

Post-Local Pop in the Post-Global Condition?: The Case of Korean Indie Rock from 2007 to 2019

Hyunjoon Shin, ***Sungkonghoe University***

The "global-local" binary has long served as a key conceptual framework to examine popular music in the globalised world. However, the meanings of the couplet and the relationships between the pair have been highly contested. In particular, the term "local" has been and is still uncertain in this framework. If it is not fashionable to associate the local with cohesion, organicity, community and roots due the rampant processes of globalisation, should we discard the term altogether or redefine it profoundly?

In order to answer the question, I draw some cases from local indie music in South Korea from the last two decades. What is interesting is that some of the indie bands and musicians have incorporated the "roots", consciously or unconsciously, since the late 2000s. The roots include not only the canons of local popular music in the near past, but also the legacies of music that originated from an older past. I do not want to equate the roots with "tradition" because they are not the object of the handing down of authentic historical heritages, but instead that of utilising past sources in a rather random way for creative blending.

Yet, in one way or another, a number of indie bands and musicians began incorporating, constructing and creating "Koreanness" in their creativity as well as performativity.

Paradoxically or not, the tendency of showing the "local" roots has closely been associated with "global" exposures. These strands of repertories and genres of indie music have been to put at a grid-type space where the disparate temporal forces are constantly at work (and rework) without linear arrangements. Actually, a number of these local bands have performed their own versions of globalisation without getting sufficient fame and recognition in their home country. As far as I know, it is also the case in other parts of the region. Thus, the binary of global-local is problematised in this music genre which has gone beyond the emulation of international styles and sounds. As I said elsewhere (Shin & Lee, 2020), concepts like indigenisation, domestication, glocalisation and hybridisation have become outdated in explaining the configurations of popular music in general, particularly indie music in Korea and beyond.

In this chapter, I trace the evolution of the process, practice and arrangement of Korean indie music, particularly the rock genre, from the mid-2000s to the late 2010s. 2013 was the year in which rock band Jambinai, having successfully blended avant-garde jazz, post-rock, and *gugak* (national music), made a breakthrough in the national scene as well as in the international one. The use of the "pre-modern" roots as a source of creativity was not so explicit before that breakthrough. The later period will be dealt with in a later research.

2007–2012: Making the Genealogy of Korean Rock

Chang Kiha and the Faces

The starting point of Chang Kiha's retro sound was his reflection on the use of Korean language in popular music. He said in our interview, "When I made the first album, I was convinced that Song

Ch'ang-sik, Pae Ch'ŏl-su, and Kim Ch'ang-wan [rock or folk-rock stars in the 1970s] provided the answer to the question of how to sing in Korean" (C. Kiha, personal communication). Korean pop, including rock, is greatly influenced by American pop. Particularly since the 1990s when Korean musicians set to adopt hip-hop in earnest, it has become a norm in certain genres—including rock—for Korean language to be bent and chopped to sound like English. In so doing, the language is conformed to the flow and rhythm of the music but sounds far from the way ordinary Korean people speak. This concern led Chang to appreciate Korean rock from the 1970s and to emulate its style.

Chang's induction to old Korean rock was owing to the fact that he was a drummer of the eccentric band Nunttŭgo K'obein led by Kkamakkwi who had a significant amount of knowledge on 1970s Korean rock. This led to the production of his hit debut album *Pyŏl il ŏpsi sanda* (I'm Doing Okay), the album that wore its influences on its sleeve. For the second album, Chang hired Yohei Hasegawa, who is originally from Japan and relocated to Korea as a guitarist in numerous bands. Hasegawa introduced Chang to a lot of music that the latter had never heard of, including Japanese bands such as The Sparks and Hikashu. It appears that Chang was impressed by the depth and breadth of Hasegawa's musical knowledge.

He co-produced the eponymous second album with Hasegawa. The result was quite different from its predecessor. Although the unmistakable Chang imprints were still there, such as the characteristic "loser" sentiment and unique vocal delivery, references were no longer as obvious. It sounded a lot like late-1970s Korean funk-inflected bands such as Saranggwa P'yŏnghwa and The Devils, complete with the conspicuous use of the organ, but it was impossible to pinpoint exactly who they used as references. The speculation was partially vindicated when the band scored a hit with a cover version of the late-1970s funk song "P'ungmunŭro tŭrŏsso" ("I Heard It through a Rumour") by The Yankees from the film soundtrack of *Nameless Gangster* (Pŏmjoewa ŭi chŏnjaeng).

This could be seen as a clue as to what they were listening to and studying at the time.

Chang Kiha and the Faces have been so successful that they were rapidly outgrowing the local indie circuit. Since 2010, they have finished four Japanese tours and held concerts in the United States (US) and the United Kingdom (UK). In Japan, they shared the stage with Japanese indie luminaries such as Zazen Boys and Tokumaru Shugo, and signed a deal for the official Japanese release of their two albums. In 2011, the music video for the single "Nŏrang narangŭn" ("You and I") from their second album was shown on a large LED screen on a skyscraper in central Tokyo.

Despite the strong marketing initiative, the public response to their music in Japan has so far been rather underwhelming. What is interesting is that Japanese *otaku* fans of 1970s Korean rock have rarely been translated into fans of Chang, despite the fact that his music is as close as it gets to a contemporary reincarnation of the music they love. It shows that vintage rock and contemporary indie music are two separate microcosms. Even though Chang's music represents a happy occasion in which these two worlds have come together to create something new, it has not been enough to bridge the gap between these two different cultures. It would be interesting to see how the relationship between them might unfold after the 2010s.

Galaxy Express

Unlike Chang Kiha and the Faces who arrived at vintage Korean rock aesthetics from lyrical concerns, Galaxy Express adopted the aesthetics while they were searching for their musical identity. They had their start in the Hongdae punk community. Park Jong-hyun, guitarist and vocalist, was then playing in Mowgli, the band he formed with a few Japanese friends. The band regularly performed at the tiny punk venue Skunk Hell. One night, Lee Ju-hyun, who would later become the bassist and vocalist of Galaxy Express, saw Park's band perform "Pisok ŭi yŏin", the canon of Korean rock performed by Shin Joong Hyun. At the time, in clubs like Skunk Hell, bands were expected to emulate foreign—American, European and Japanese—bands, and be entirely indifferent to any other kind of music. Park and Lee shared discontent with this blind allegiance to a genre and the pressure to have a generic style and sound.

Galaxy Express mentioned Nirvana and Motörhead as influences, and said they liked The Hives and The Vines among contemporary bands. For a Korean punk band, these are rather common references. The band also dug pro-punk bands from the 1960s and 1970s like MC5 and The Stooges. Absorbing these diverse influences, they were growing out of the punk straitjacket. However, they claimed that what made their music truly original was the experience of accidentally making a "strange" sound during practice sessions. Lee explained:

> While jamming, when we were not consciously trying to sound like a foreign band, we found this strange archaic sound … that was completely different from what we were doing at the time. We were so surprised [at] how it came out so naturally. At first, we did not like it and tried to get rid of it because it sounded so uncool. Later, however, we were gradually drawn into its charm and came to accept it. (L. Ju-hyun, personal communication)

They characterised this unfashionable sound and the feelings attached to it as Korean, which sounded similar to what they heard in old Korean rock and pop songs. This experience made them believe that "Koreanness" is not something created by design but a spontaneous expression of bodily habitus. It was materialised in early songs such as "Maeil Maeil" ("Everyday") and "Saebyŏk" ("Dawn"), and then the entire second CD of their double CD full-length debut album, *Noise on Fire*.

Since 2009, Galaxy Express has been increasingly engaged in performing abroad. They have carried out club tours in Japan, Hong Kong, Taiwan, France, the UK and the US, and participated in numerous festivals. In March 2012, in particular, *The New York Times* selected their live show at the annual South by Southwest Festival as one of ten highlights of the event (Pareles, 2012). What is interesting is that, in contrast to Chang Kiha and the Faces who see no difference between performing locally and abroad, the members of Galaxy Express find their experience abroad to be reinforcing their identity as a Korean band.

Lee commented, "We found that we had better show what [foreign bands] do not have than trying to sound similar to them. We get a better response from the audience that way" (L. Ju-hyun, personal communication). At the start of this research, I thought that Galaxy Express would be the most western-sounding of the three bands I was researching. However, it turned out that they had the strongest identity as a Korean band. It is still unclear whether their Korean identity is more of an ideology or has any substance in their music. However, it is clear that they use old Korean rock music with a view to articulate and claim their Korean band identity. The music of Galaxy Express shows an intriguing blend of their punk background and the influence from largely psychedelic old Korean rock. It has attracted comments like "punk but psychedelic" and "supercharged psychedelic rock" from the foreign audience.

In the narrative of Galaxy Express, words like "bodily habitus", "naturalness" and "Koreanness" loom large. While Chang Kiha and the Faces chose old Korean rock in a conscious and calculative fashion, Galaxy Express had already inscribed rock deeply in their bodies. This narrative of inevitability produced their affective engagement in old Korean rock as a source of their identity. What is interesting here, however, is that their friendship with Japanese expatriates and the experiences in international festivals played crucial roles in forming and consolidating this engagement. The former deepened their affective association with old Korean rock and the latter was mobilised to strengthen their Korean identity, which called for a heavier use of Korean rock references. In this respect, their Korean identity and their attachment to old Korean rock could be seen to have a translocal dimension.

Goonam

Goonam is different from both Chang Kiha and the Faces and Galaxy Express in that they were not as well versed in old Korean rock as either of those two bands. For them, Japanese music is closer to the heart since they started out as fans of Fishmans, the Japanese dub reggae band from the 1980s. The band has had a small but devoted following in Korea since the 1990s. The Fishmans fan club started in 2001 as an online community and extended itself to offline in 2003 by opening a live club in Hongdae called Kuchu Camp, named after a Fishmans song. The club organises various events including memorial festivals for the late Sato Shinji, the leader of the band, and holds live shows of Fishmans-related artists from Japan under the banner *Subarashikute Nice Choice.*[1]

The Goonam members originally belonged to this community as fans. After they formed the band and released an album, they were invited by Kuchu Camp and gave several live concerts there. However, they were not enthusiastic fans of Fishmans; they were just obsessed with one song by that band called "Ikareta Baby" ("Distrait Baby") which is rather exceptional and unrepresentative of Fishmans' music. It is not difficult to see the influence of the song on Goonam's music as the relaxed groove and dreamy melodies of the song became the template for all of Goonam's songs.

Goonam is the kind of band who does not listen to a lot of music but assembles their influences from discrete pieces of everyday experience such as a nameless Mongolian song from a documentary film on television or *ppongtchak* music sung collectively on chopstick beats at Korean traditional wine bars. Among old Korean rock, they quote Tshe Devils and Pŏnnimdŭl as their influences. These are definitely left-field choices that show their lack of concern for established cultural prestige. While old Korean rock is often represented by the canons of Shin Joong Hyun and Sanulrim, they do not mention these names and their music does not show any trace of their influence. What is more, the "influence" from The Devils and Pŏnnimdŭl hardly stretches beyond one or two songs. Perhaps, this is due to the fact that they came from a dance music background where different rules and conventions govern.

Goonam's music is immediately recognisable from its winding grooves that somehow evoke Koreanness, specifically the country's traditional dance rhythms. Particularly abroad, Goonam is often considered the most unique Korean band. As Kaori Matsuda, an organiser of the cross-border music festival Seoul-Tokyo Sound Bridge, put it, "While other Korean bands have similar sounding bands in Japan, Goonam does not have an equivalent. They are a unique export from Korea" (K. Matsuda, personal communication). On the other hand, Aya Hamada, a Japanese staff who accompanied a group of Hongdae bands in their collective UK tour, said that "Goonam received the best reaction. The audience was crazy about the groove" (A. Hamada, personal communication).

Unlike Galaxy Express and, to a lesser degree, Chang Kiha and the Faces, Goonam does not have a strong identity as a Korean band. Instead, they identify themselves as an Asian band when performing abroad. This is probably based on an honest assessment of their influences, which include not only old Korean rock but also Mongolian folk music, the music of Fishmans, and Okinawan folk music. It is quite interesting that this multicultural amalgam sounds so Korean. In this respect, Goonam's retro rock could be seen as another form of translocal construct in which cultural elements from various localities were put together to produce a *local* style.

Conclusion

Since 2016, there has been emerging discourse that the world is entering a "post-global" condition. Even though I do not uncritically adopt the neologism, it cannot be denied that the operation of hegemony during globalisation has been under question. It means that the so-called "(Anglo-)American hegemony" in popular music is challenged, though not yet confirmed.

When I started writing this chapter, I threw out a crude question in a rather mechanical way: "If the global has turned into the post-global, has the local evolved into the post-local too?". But the question was not totally futile when I tried conceptualising the practices of a number of Asian indie, sometimes nameless, bands who have performed their own versions of international tours.

The term "translocal" used before shows that emerging networks of musical practices have become widely dispersed but closely encountered under the mobile, uncertain, and ever-changing conditions even after globalisation as we know it. The translocal has become one way of constructing authenticity for the artists and cultural intermediaries in the highly networked community.

Yet, the translocal, by definition, is not so much about the musical works, products and forms (or the dubious word "contents") as flows, routes and circuits.[2] How should we define cultural products that are neither interested in national fame nor international breakthrough? The post-local is the term for "temporarily", "hypothetically" and "suggestively", adopted by me only in this chapter for the Inter-Asia Popular Music Studies conference. Does it make sense or is it just another redundant category?

Acknowledgements

Parts of this chapter were co-written by Keewoong Lee.

Notes

1 The artists include Keiichi Sokabe, Hanaregumi, Bonobos, Kisell, Otouta, Hicksville and Spencer. For Sokabe Keiichi and his involvement in Japanese indie music in general, see Mōri (2009).

2 Bennett and Peterson (2004) applied the term to the concept of "scene".

References

Bennett, A., & Peterson, Richard A. (Eds.). (2004). *Music scenes: Local, translocal, and virtual.* Vanderbilt University Press.

Mōri, Y. (2009). J-pop: From the ideology of creativity to DIY music culture. *Inter-Asia Cultural Studies, 10*, 498–512.

Pareles, J. (2012, March 18). A fan base without borders. *The New York Times.* http://www.nytimes.com/2012/03/19/arts/music/springsteen-gives-keynote-at-sxsw-festival.html?pagewanted=all&_r=0

Shin, H, & Lee, K. (2020). The question of geographic scale in Asian popular music: Global, local, regional, and translocal. *Korean Journal of Popular Music, 25*, 181–213.

Shin, H. (2011). The success of hopelessness: The evolution of Korean indie music. *Perfect Beat 12*(2), 147–165.

CHAPTER 10

The Introduction of American Folk Songs in South Korea and Japan: Focusing on YMCA and Rōon (Workers' Music Association)

Janghee Son, ***Osaka University***

As 30 years have passed since the end of the Cold War, many historians are conducting studies on various aspects of the Cold War period. Every part of the world has its own account of "Cold War history" since the war was a global phenomenon. The Cold War itself never escalated into a direct conflict, but East Asia—unlike Europe—experienced several "hot wars" related to the Cold War (such as the Chinese Civil War, the Korean War and the Vietnam War). These resulted in heavy casualties and extreme political hostility that still exists to this day (leading to inter-Korean tensions and conflicts between China and Taiwan). These events changed world history and the importance of studies on the Cold War and its aftermath in East Asia cannot be overstated.

Although Cold War studies have, for a long time, focused primarily on political and diplomatic history, there has been a gradual shift towards cultural history since the 2000s. Extensive research on the films, literature and television dramas produced during the Cold War period has been conducted. In addition, it should also be noted that the number of comparative studies and joint research is increasing. Historical assessment and positioning of one country's Cold War history can be accomplished by comparing with that of adjacent countries.

This chapter conducts a comparative study of popular music in South Korea and Japan. In detail, I compare two institutions, namely Korean YMCA and Rōon (労音 Workers' Music Association), which respectively played a crucial role in disseminating American folk songs in South Korea and Japan. Comparing the social background of these institutions as footholds of American folk songs might provide us with new insights into how the geopolitics of East Asia influenced popular music in South Korea and Japan.

Christianity in Korea and "Singalong Y" of YMCA

Before taking a look at the connection between American folk songs and the Korean YMCA, it is necessary to understand the position of Christianity in Korean modern history. Western missionaries started being dispatched to the Korean peninsula from the late 19th century. Among them, the United States (US) missionaries had the highest proportion. Nearly 90% of the Protestant missionaries dispatched to Korea from 1893 to 1983 were Americans. Under the Japanese colonial rule from 1910 to 1945, Christian churches functioned as "symbols of modernity" because they provided Koreans with opportunities of secondary and higher education (including going to the US), which the Japanese authorities did not provide. In addition, the high proportion of American missionaries made Christian churches a sort of "shelter" from the oppression of the Japanese colonial rule.

Korean Christian churches were largely concentrated in the northern region during the colonial period. Pyongyang, now the capital of North Korea, was even called the "Jerusalem of Asia". After the liberation and division of the Korean peninsula in 1945, Christian churches in the northern area fled to South

Korea. This escape from the Northern communist regime and the ensuing Korean War (1950–1953) inspired extreme anti-communism among Korean Christians. At the same time, a lot of economic support and relief goods from the US were concentrated in Christian churches, which made them the largest civilian institution in South Korea (Kim, 2012).

During the period of military dictatorship from 1961 to 1987, Christian churches in South Korea were still largely subordinate to American churches. Ironically, this subordination provided Christian churches with exceptional autonomy, since the South Korean authoritarian regime was politically and economically dependent on America and thus, could not ignore the influence of American churches (Kang, 2013).

The Korean YMCA was first established in Seoul in 1903. During the colonial period, the YMCA's main function was introducing Western culture to Korea. Although the YMCA building in Seoul was devastated in the Korean War, its reconstruction was completed in the 1960s. From 1965, the YMCA embarked on a "Singalong Y" campaign, in which university students gathered in the Seoul YMCA main hall every Saturday and learnt to sing several songs accompanied by an electric organ and an acoustic guitar. In October 1965, the Singalong Y Chorus was formed and made appearances at various events. From 1966, Singalong Y started growing and spreading with the support of radio music programmes (Kim, 2015). In 1970, five years after Singalong Y started, the first folk song festival took place in the Seoul YMCA main hall. The folk festival was reported in a newspaper article:

> YMCA, which inspired the folk song boom through programmes such as *Singalong Y* and has been leading a virtual national choral movement for five years, is supposed to host Y Folk Festival at 7 p.m. September 2 in Seoul YMCA main hall, which is the first domestic large-scale folk song festival. (Daily Sports, August 27, 1970)

Another article by the same newspaper, published two days after the folk festival, highly rated the festival:

> The aim of the organisers, which is to accomplish a boom of sound, Korean modern folk songs, was successfully reflected. It has demonstrated a bright prospect of the domestic folk song movement from now on. (Daily Sports, September 4, 1970)

According to the articles, the folk festival was recognised as an extension of Singalong Y and the national choral movement. It was also considered as a starting point of the folk song movement. It is also important to note that the aim of the festival was to create "sound, Korean modern folk songs", although what makes a folk song *Korean* is unclear.

Japanese Cultural Party's Cultural Movement and Rōon

Rōon, an organisation which was first established in 1949 and reached its peak in the early 1960s, basically aimed to provide workers with opportunities of listening to "sound music". The organisation was a result of a "democratic cultural movement" after World War II (Takaoka, 2011, p. 321). The Japanese Communist Party (JCP), which was decimated during the 1930s due to political suppression, was re-established soon after the end of the war and the imprisoned leaders of JCP were emancipated. Since they were the only group who had not surrendered to the militarism during the Asia-Pacific War, JCP wielded tremendous influence in post-war Japan, especially among intellectuals. As a result of the democratic cultural movement mainly led by JCP, various cultural movement organisations including Rōon were established. Although the Red Purge in the early 1950s severely curtailed its political power, JCP's cultural policy still greatly determined the musical orientation of Rōon in the 1960s. JCP insisted that Japan was being dominated by American imperialism, and a cultural movement should become part of any revolutionary movement in order to realise Japan's national independence. In 1965, Rōon adopted a resolution to create national and democratic popular music (Takaoka, 2011).

The so-called "sound music" which Rōon sought to propagate was a notion contrary to "vulgar music", which mostly referred to popular music. The criticism against popular music by intellectuals, the political spectrum which varied from the Left to the Right, which had already started in the pre-war period, remained intense after 1945 (Wajima, 2018). Rōon also excluded popular music from its concerts in its early stage. However, since classical music could not satisfy the musical needs of the young post-war generation, most local organisations of Rōon started establishing popular music sectors in the late 1950s. The proportion of popular music continued increasing throughout the 1960s. For example, in 1965, popular music and classical music respectively took up 63% and 28% of Rōon's regular meetings (例会 *reikai*). In 1968, the proportion of popular music exceeded 70%, while that of classical music decreased to less than 20% (Takaoka, 2011).

In 1965, American singer Odetta Holmes visited Japan for the first time and made an appearance at a regular Rōon meeting. From then on, Rōon started incorporating American folk songs in its programmes. Japanese folk singers such as Takaishi Tomoya also held concerts at regular meetings of Rōon (Nagasaki, 2013). Okabayashi Nobuyasu, who was called the "Bob Dylan of Japan", recalled that he had over 100 concerts at Rōon within a year in the late 1960s (Okabayashi, 2011). From 1969 to 1971, a large-scale folk festival named All Japan Folk Jamboree was held in the city of Nakatsugawa by the local Rōon organisation.

Conclusion

American folk songs were introduced in the mid-1960s both in South Korea and Japan. In the former, Christian organisations which had been greatly "American" since the colonial period and extremely anti-communist since the Korean War, played an important role in the proliferation of American folk songs in the country. In the latter, the left-wing cultural movement which was greatly influenced by JCP functioned as a base for folk music. Although their ideological positions might have been polar opposites, they shared the aim of disseminating "sound music" and creating "national music". How the "soundness" of music was defined respectively in the cultural politics of South Korea and Japan and how Korean YMCA and Rōon dealt with the contradiction between pursuing national music and introducing American songs, remain to be answered in future research.

References

Kang, I. C. (2013). *Resistance and surrender: Military regimes and religion.* Hanshin University Publishing Institute. (*강인철*. 2013. *저항과 투항 - 군사정권들과 종교. 서울: 한신대학교 출판부.*)

Kim, H. C. (2015). *Walking through the history of Korean popular music.* Alma. (*김형찬*. 2015. *한국대중음악사산책. 서울: 알마.*)

Kim, J. H. (2012). *Citizen K, leaves the church: The sociology of the success, failure and desire of Korean Protestantism.* HyunAmSa. (*김진호*. 2012. *시민 K, 교회를 나가다 - 한국 개신교의 성공과 실패, 그 욕망의 사회학. 서울: 현암사.*)

Nagasaki, R. (2013). *Postwar cultural history of connection: Rōon, and Takarazuka, Banpaku.* Kawade Shobō Shinsha. (長崎励朗. 2013. *「つながり」の戦後文化誌* -労音, そして宝塚, 万博. 東京: 河出書房新社.)

Okabayashi, N. (2011). *Okabayashi, talks about Nobuyasu.* DU BOOKS. (*岡林信康*. 2011. *岡林, 信康を語る. 東京*: DU BOOKS.)

Takaoka, H. (2011). High growth and cultural movement: The development and decline of Rōon movement. In Ōkado Masakatsu (Ed.), *Questions on growth and the Cold War* (pp. 319–364). Ōtsuki Shoten. *(高岡裕之*. 2011. *高度成長と文化運動 -労音運動の発展と衰退. 大門正克 編. 成長と冷戦への問い. 東京: 大月書店.*)

Wajima, Y. (2018). *Creating enka: The "Soul of Japan" in the postwar era.* Public Bath Press.

CHAPTER 11

Burgerkill Plays Dayton: The Arrival of Indonesian Metal in Ohio

Jeremy Wallach & Esther Clinton,
Bowling Green State University

Asia is home to millions of metalheads. Massive, long-established metal scenes in nations such as Japan, Indonesia, Malaysia, Singapore, and Nepal exert influence on the rapidly expanding scenes in India, China, Mainland Southeast Asia, and Central Asia. As social disruptions of neoliberal capitalist development and the concomitant proletarianisation of non-affluent classes take place in Asian nations, metal's appeal increases, whilst the most successful of Asia's metal bands such as Taiwan's Chthonic and Japan's Babymetal have begun to attract global attention.[1]

This essay spins a tale of two metal cities, Dayton, Ohio in the United States (US) and Bandung, West Java in Indonesia, and their surprising points of connection despite considerable cultural and geographical distances between them. On October 19, 2019, Indonesian metal stalwarts Burgerkill played at Jimmie's Ladder 11, an unassuming bar-restaurant in Dayton, Ohio, on a bill with three other bands, the New York-based thrashers Suaka and two local groups, crossover thrash outfit Act of God and the headliner, doom/sludge trio Maharaja (Figure 1). Accustomed to playing before tens of thousands of fans at teeming outdoor concert events, the members of Burgerkill viewed their do-it-yourself or DIY two-week-long US tour with Indonesian-American group Suaka as a "return to [their] roots" of playing in small venues (Dethnomusicology 2019).[2] Burgerkill had certainly come a long way from their beginnings as a raucous local hardcore band in the underground rock scene of 1990s Bandung, and their intense, arena-scaled performance had a normally apathetic Ohio rock club audience standing up from their bar stools, eyes riveted to the stage.

FIGURE 1 Commemorative sticker for the Indonesian Invasion USA 2019 tour featuring Burgerkill and Suaka. The sticker combines the mascots for both bands.
Source: Authors' collection (Wallach & Clinton, 2019)

Bandung Roots

The city of Bandung has played a central role in Indonesia's enormous metal scene for the last 30 years (Baulch, 2007; James & Walsh, 2015; Wallach, 2008, 2012, Wallach et al., 2011). Burgerkill is Bandung's proudest metal export, and its imprint is analogous to Metallica's outsize presence in the 1980s San Francisco Bay Area metal scene. Burgerkill emerged from the local underground scene to first achieve rock star status in its home country and then played giant festivals in Australia and Europe (including Germany's Wacken Open Air in 2015, the most prestigious gig in the metal world), all while staying connected to their subcultural roots (Luvaas, 2012, p. 53; Hutabarat & Kusumah, 2015). Bandung remains one of the most fertile cities in the world for metal bands, a distinction it shares with several cities in Ohio, including Dayton. But the similarities between West Java and Ohio do not end there: the presence of heavy industrial labour, the preponderance of male performers and audience members, and the tendency of scene participants to be in their 30s and 40s are three additional features they have in common. Are these factors sufficient to explain the remarkable durability and wide appeal of metal music and culture around the globe? Perhaps a more productive inquiry would begin by looking into the forms of sociability present at the Burgerkill event, whereby gregarious interactions between Indonesian and American metalheads emphasised their shared enthusiasm for the music and ability to "talk metal" (Clinton & Wallach, 2016).

One Night in Ohio

We arrived at Jimmie's Ladder 11 before the bands started and were enthusiastically welcomed with warm hugs and the typical Indonesian greeting "*Sudah makan*?" (Have you eaten yet?). We had not but found it difficult to disengage (one of us had met both bands years ago) to take advantage of the bar-restaurant's food.

The two Indonesian bands set up merch tables run by members and band friends—we bought Suaka shirts, one of which shows the members of the band riding a *barong* (Balinese mythical being that looks like a monster but is actually supposed to scare away demons) through the Capitol Building in Washington DC. We laughed and talked with the band members until the first of the local bands, Act of God, started playing. A hardcore crossover group with a dynamic singer, Act of God played a strong set and, after the show, we bought a CD from the guitarist. Next up was Suaka, performing an updated thrash metal style reminiscent of the Californian band Death Angel. The audience had been respectfully quiet and enthusiastically watched the first couple of bands, even participating in performer-audience banter, and many members of the audience were milling around the room, drinking assorted microbrews and mixed drinks, and talking quietly to people they knew.

Burgerkill was the third band to play. While it seemed like the first two bands had good nights, the atmosphere changed drastically once Burgerkill started playing. The patrons' respectful quiet became pin-drop silence as everyone's attention turned to the makeshift stage, even alcohol was largely forgotten. Burgerkill's strong presence and enthusiastic, skilful playing drew everyone at the bar up to the stage. People who had previously stood idly watching other bands now began moving to the loudly complex music and crowding the stage. Burgerkill's lead singer, a tall thin man with a powerful voice, carefully watched the crowd, making eye contact and drawing in even people who had probably come to the venue primarily to drink, not to see bands (Figure 2).

FIGURE 2 Burgerkill performing at Jimmie's Ladder 11, October 19, 2019
Source: Author's own (Wallach, 2019)

Even though they were used to playing to massive crowds, Burgerkill's members took this small venue seriously, establishing a strong rapport with audience members. The music seemed to come easily to them, though given how complex the music was, it must have required a lot of attention and teamwork. But the band was careful not to show how hard they were working; part of being a great performer is making difficult material look effortless. Ethnomusicologist and fellow Indonesian metal specialist Dennis W. Lee[3] saw Burgerkill perform a week later in Detroit, and described a similar scene:

> Even in the midst of all these killer bands [with whom they shared the stage], Burgerkill were able to almost immediately assert themselves as a next-level act. They set up quietly on the dark stage, and as the lights and their intro soundscape came up, they stood with their backs to the audience, building drama as only seasoned acts can. They started into "Darah Hitam Kebencian" ("Black Blood of Hatred") from their 2006 album *Beyond Coma and Despair*, with a dramatic opening riff leading into a vicious blasting section during which vocalist Vicky leaned into the audience and screamed, "Come on motherfuckers!" People moved up right away. You could sense the vibe in the room starting to shift; people's eyes widened with surprise as they realised they were experiencing something special. It's not every night that you get to watch a world-class band destroy a tiny club. (Dethnomusicology, 2019)

As is customary for metal bands the world over, Burgerkill's set consisted mostly of original songs from their previous recordings. We, however, would like to discuss the two cover songs they chose to perform, "Air Mata Api" ("Tears of Fire"), a 1989 song by Indonesian singer-songwriter Iwan Fals, as well as "Atur Aku" ("Regulate Me") by the 1990s Bandung underground fixture Puppen, the song the band played last.

Performing Indonesian Rock History

The Indonesian folk-rock singer known as Iwan Fals was born Virgiawan Listianto on September 3, 1961 in the capital city of Jakarta. His father was a colonel in the Indonesian armed forces. According to some commentators, his father's military connections may be the main reason why Fals was never severely punished by the autocratic Suharto government for his socially conscious and critical songs.[4] To Fals' die-hard fans, he is known simply as *Bang* Iwan—Bang is the Jakartanese honorific for "older brother", considered less formal than the standard Indonesian "*Pak*". With a recording career that spans five decades, Iwan is one of the few figures in Indonesian popular music regarded as a "legend" and he is considered the greatest recording artist in Indonesian history.

Puppen was a seminal Bandung underground group whose 1997 song "Atur Aku" is a defiant declaration of individual autonomy and holds the distinction of being one of the first underground rock songs in Indonesia to contain obscenities *in Indonesian*—quite daring for the time.[5] Like Burgerkill, the band's music straddles the line between punk and metal. Puppen's two founding members, guitarist Robin Malau and vocalist Arian Tigabelas, were friends with members of Burgerkill when both groups were starting out. The pair followed different paths after Puppen disbanded in 2002; Robin is a successful web designer in San Jose, California while Arian is currently the frontman of the Indonesian stoner metal supergroup Seringai. There was really no mystery why Burgerkill included these covers in the Dayton show—the band had previously recorded versions of them and often performed both live—but it was certainly fortuitous that the first Indonesian heavy metal band ever to play in Ohio performed songs by its country's greatest mainstream rock artist and its foremost underground metal pioneer.

Conclusion

We believe we were the only members of the audience in Dayton who knew the current whereabouts of the founding members of Puppen. In fact, we were probably the only ones who recognised two of Burgerkill's songs as covers of other Indonesian artists. What was significant was that for the rest of the audience, it did not matter. That night, a historic exchange had taken place: from the time we started researching heavy metal in Indonesia, there had been an unmistakable desire among musicians and fans for the direction of influence to be a *two-way* street, that one day Americans might hear the best rock that *Indonesia* had produced. After six decades of Indonesian rock music and four decades of Indonesian metal, Americans finally had that opportunity, and the extreme metal that arose in heartland American cities like Dayton had at last come full circle, in Burgerkill's compelling performance of rock music's global triumph.[6]

Notes

[1] For more on the global economic and social dimensions of heavy metal music fandom, see Kahn-Harris (2007) and Wallach et al. (2011). See Wallach and Clinton (2017) for a theory of why metal appeals to members of proletarianised, medially positioned social groups.

[2] The 16-day US tour was put together on a shoestring after several rounds of visa paperwork. The American spouse of Suaka's Indonesian singer/guitarist was invaluable in helping navigate the bureaucratic maze to allow Burgerkill into the country.

[3] See Lee (2018).

[4] See Ibrahim (2011) for a comprehensive history of Iwan Fals' work and cultural impact. Ibrahim classifies "Air Mata Api" as a song with "*Tema Religius* dan *Refleksi Kehidupan*" (Religious Themes and Reflections on Life) rather than a message on social criticism (p. 272). The lyrics of the song are poetic and somewhat obscure; their dark, foreboding imagery might be what appealed to the members of Burgerkill.

[5] A more in-depth discussion of Puppen and "Atur Aku" can be found in Wallach (2003).

[6] On rock's transformative global impact, see Wallach (2020).

References

Dunn, L. C. & Jones, N. A. (Eds.). (1994). *Embodied voices: representing female vocality in Western culture.* Cambridge University Press.

Baulch, E. (2007). *Making scenes: Reggae, punk, and death metal in 1990s Bali.* Duke University Press.

Clinton, E., & Wallach, J. (2016). Talking metal: A social phenomenology of hanging out in metal culture. In N. Varas-Díaz and N. W. R. Scott (Eds.), *Heavy metal music and the communal experience* (pp. 37–55). Lexington Books.

Dethnomusicology [Lee, D. W.]. (2019, November 5). Burgerkill in America. *Medium.* https://medium.com/@dethnomusicology

Hutabarat, F., & Kusumah, I. R. A. [Kimung]. (2015). Market development using community shared values: The story of Burgerkill. In T. M. Karjalainen & K. Kärki (Eds.), *Modern heavy metal: Markets, practices and cultures* (pp. 532–543). Aalto University School of Business.

Ibrahim, I. S. (2011). *Aku bernyanyi, menjadi saksi: Hidup, gitar, dan perlawanan dalam balada musik Iwan Fals* [I sing, become a witness: Life, guitar, and resistance in the music of Iwan Fals]. Fiskontak.

Kahn-Harris, K. (2007). *Extreme metal: Music and culture on the edge.* Berg.

James, K., & Walsh, R. (2015). Bandung rocks, Cibinong shakes: Economics and applied ethics within the Indonesian death-metal community. *Musicology Australia, 37*(1), 28–46.

Lee, D. W. (2018). 'Negeri seribu bangsa': Musical hybridization in contemporary Indonesian death metal." *Metal Music Studies, 4*(3), 531–548.

Luvaas, B. (2012). *DIY style: Fashion, music and global digital cultures.* Berg.

Wallach, J. (2008). *Modern noise, fluid genres: Popular music in Indonesia, 1997–2001.* (2008). University of Wisconsin Press.

Wallach, J. (2003). 'Goodbye my blind majesty': Music, language, and politics in the Indonesian underground. In H. M. Berger & M. T. Carroll (Eds.), *Global pop, local language* (pp. 53–86). University Press of Mississippi.

Wallach, J. (2011). Unleashed in the East: Metal music, masculinity, and 'Malayness' in Indonesia, Malaysia and Singapore. In J. Wallach, H. M. Berger & P. D. Greene (Eds.), *Metal rules the globe: Heavy metal music around the world* (pp. 86–105). Duke University Press.

Wallach, J. (2012). Distortion-drenched dystopias: Metal in island Southeast Asia. In N.W.R. Scott (Ed.), *Reflections in the metal void* (pp. 101–119). Inter-Disciplinary Press.

Wallach, J. (2020). Global rock as postcolonial soundtrack. In A. Moore & P. Carr (Eds.), *Bloomsbury handbook for rock music research* (pp. 469–485). Bloomsbury.

Wallach, J. (2019, October 19). Burgerkill performing at Jimmie's Ladder 11, October 19, 2019. [Photograph].

Wallach, J., Berger, H. M., & Greene, P. D. (Eds.). (2011). *Metal rules the globe: Heavy metal music around the world.* Duke University Press.

Wallach, J. & Clinton, E. (2017). The horror and the allure: Metal, power, gothic literature, and multisubjectivity. In B. Bardine & M. Elovaara (Eds.), *Connecting metal to culture: Unity in disparity* (pp. 99–118). Lexington Books.

Wallach, J., & Clinton, E. (2019). Commemorative sticker for the Indonesian Invasion USA 2019 tour featuring Burgerkill and Suaka. The sticker combines the mascots for both bands. [Photograph].

CHAPTER 12

Creating a Local Music Scene and Translocal Network: Taking DIY Label Qiii Snacks Records in Guangzhou, China as an Example

Jianzhe Chen, *Osaka University*

The concept of "music scene" has been extended with the development and proliferation of Internet technology. Bennett and Peterson identified three general types of music scene:

> The first, local scene, corresponds most closely with the original notion of a scene as clustered around a specific geographic focus. The second, translocal scene, refers to widely scattered local scenes drawn into regular communication around a distinctive form of music and lifestyle. The third, virtual scene, is a newly emergent formation in which people scattered across great physical spaces create the sense of scene via fanzines and, increasingly, through the Internet. (Bennett & Peterson, 2004, p. 6)

The indie music scene in China, while influenced by those in Europe and the United States (US), is characterised by depoliticisation, low localisation and low industrialisation

(Motoaki, 2011). Despite these characteristics, the Chinese indie music scene is seeing a gradual change. This chapter considers the significance of the Chinese indie music scene construction and the social interaction it encourages. Using Quangzhou's record label Qiii Snacks Records (QSR) as a case study, this chapter discusses the local and translocal network connections built by Chinese do-it-yourself (DIY) indie music labels, such as QSR, and the roles they have played in forging those connections.

QSR's predecessor was Full Label, a record label that was active in Guangzhou from 2006 to 2016. At that time, Full Label guaranteed certain popularity for the Guangzhou underground music acts due to its drive in organising small live gigs at unconventional venues. In 2016, the founder Xiao Zhao pulled out from Full Label for personal reasons, and the remaining core members established QSR. While inheriting the Full Label's style of holding DIY performances at small venues, QSR also began helping indie bands in releasing their work systematically.

QSR's core members are the members of three local bands, all of whom have full-time day jobs outside of the label. After work, they devote themselves entirely to the routine matters of QSR. With amazing efficiency, QSR has put out 29 physical music releases (as of April 2020) in a span of four years. Strictly speaking, QSR is not a commercial entity but a loose group of like-minded people. Apart from the core members, their close friends occasionally help conduct the label's businesses. When speaking on the original intention for creating the label, QSR's manager and daily business operator Xiao Ji said, "In Guangzhou, we do not have a label and music group that we particularly like, so we want to make one ourselves" (X. Ji, personal communication, May 2020).

On the QSR's homepage, it is stated that the label is "a Guangzhou-based local hobby group with around 500 members" which aims to spice up the local music scene and distribute various music products. The reference to "500 members" is, of course, an exaggeration. There were only six core members when QSR was first established, and there has never been more than 20 people involved in the running of the business.

The Process of Building a Local Scene

Releases

In releasing the work of local bands, QSR helps spread and distribute music containing regional and cultural attributes (such as Cantonese indie music) and the work of non-local bands in Guangzhou. QSR has helped release the work of six local bands from Guangzhou and three bands from Guangdong, and put out six releases with Cantonese songs (see Appendix for the catalogue).

Events

Bennett and Peterson described "local scene" as a "focused social activity that takes place in a delimited space and over a specific span of time in which clusters of producers, musicians, and fans realise their common musical taste, collectively distinguishing themselves from others by using music and cultural signs often appropriated from other places" (2004, p. 8).

One of the most important objectives of QSR in Guangzhou is to invite and host shows for touring bands who come to the city. These moves make QSR an important link in the translocal scene connection, which will be explained in more detail later. QSR' DIY activities based in Guangzhou primarily cover four types of shows.

The first type is **Eat Yourself DJ Party (食自己放听会 *Shi Ziji Fang Ting Hui*)**. Vinyl DJ sets are played at such shows. Fuji Yosuke, a Japanese musician living in Guangzhou and a member of the participating DJ group Diggy Boys,[1] said: "Of course, now vinyl has become popular again. But back in 2016, vinyl record DJs were a rare breed as lugging around crates of vinyl records was cumbersome and inconvenient; so, the Eat Yourself DJ Party at the time was a very innovative activity. And through music and such events, I got to know many friends who share the same interest in vinyl, thus the Diggy Boys group was formed. It gave me a sense of belonging when I live outside of Japan" (F. Yosuke, personal communication, May 2020) The Eat Yourself DJ Party events are arranged and hosted at unconventional venues such as Daily Craft,[2] Vinylhouse Cafe[3] and Rozz-Tox at Loft345.[4]

Through such events, QSR manages to establish an extensive, cooperative network within the Guangzhou music scene and maintain the scene's social activities.

The second is **Slam Dunk with the Ball Under Your Balls (胯下入樽 *Kua Xia Ru Zun*)**. To connect non-local bands with those from Guangzhou's indie music scene, QSR would host a series of live shows and invite both types of bands to participate. These shows are emblematic of the passion and straightforwardness of the bands and of QSR's orientation or attitude towards music. The Slam Dunk with the Ball Under Your Balls Vol.04 show in 2017 was one of the most representative of the whole series of live shows. Four bands including Forests (Singapore), Wellsaid (Hong Kong), David Boring (Hong Kong), and Nein or Gas Mus (Guangzhou) played together at a secret venue in Guangzhou. Recalling the scene of that night, Xiao Ji was too excited to complete his sentence: "People sang along and bumped around, guitar cables broke in the chaos ..." (X. Ji, personal communication, May 2020). For such a rousing show, however, there were no more than 30 people in the audience. Ji continued, "For a show, I don't need four or five hundred people to come. My goal is one hundred people. Once we can pay the cost and pay the bands, we can continue to do the next one. We are not about making this big. Each of us has a job, and the reason that we started all this is not to make money" (Lu, 2017).

The third is **jAM ROOM**. This series of live shows by local and non-local bands started in 2016 as a no-stage, ultra-small event taking place in rehearsal rooms. The difference between the jAM ROOM and Slam Dunk shows is that the latter is usually held in proper venues. The size of the audience at the jAM ROOM shows is generally limited to 10 to 15 people, with no tickets issued and the location undisclosed. Attendees first need to make an appointment with QSR by email to know the venue and are required to prepare and bring small gifts for the participating bands (in place of tickets). In 2016, my band was invited to participate in the first jAM ROOM show held inside a building at a food street in Guangzhou. The building had several small rehearsal rooms, covered with sound-absorbing sponges on both sides of a corridor. The venue at which my band played was one of the rehearsal rooms at the end of the corridor. It was a space of less than 20 square metres, and I could still hear the sound from other rehearsal rooms during the show. Generally, during the show, there is barely any physical distance between the band members and the audience due to the small size of the venue. When a band finishes their set, they just move aside and become the audience for the next band. There is no real difference in the identity of the audience or musicians; everyone is there because they enjoy the same kind of music.

The fourth is **Oh Messy Life ...** This series of shows started in 2019 as a combination and extension of the jAM ROOM and Slam Dunk shows. It is a DIY show with a no-stage set-up which runs the theme of emo/skramz.[5] Figure 1 shows a scene from a typical show. While the shows are not limited to live houses or rehearsal studios, entry is still limited to a certain number of people depending on the chosen venue.

In addition to these four themed shows, QSR has hosted shows for touring bands, documentary screenings and forum sessions. "We want to tell everyone how to participate in the indie music they love; there are many things they can do besides playing in bands" (X. Ji, personal communication, May 2020).

FIGURE 1 At an "Oh messy life ..." show held on August 19, 2019
Source: Wang (2019). Used with permission.

Translocal Network

Releases

As a tribute to Sarah Records,[6] Full Label collaborated with Boring Productions[7] in 2015 on the release of a compilation album called *Our Secret World*. In 2016, QSR co-released a compilation album called *"Emotion, no"* containing the work of eight Asian emo bands with Hong Kong DIY label Sweaty&Cramped.[8] Later, these two labels teamed up with Coral Records[9] from Wuhan to release a second compilation album of this series called *"Emotion too"*. This compilation series was reported in the website Bandcamp.[10] To date, QSR has cooperated with 11 labels from countries such as the US and Japan, and other parts of China such as Shenzhen, Hong Kong, Wuhan, Taiwan and Beijing. The most recent compilation is a charity tape co-released with Nugget Records from Beijing in March 2020. The profits from the sale of these tapes were donated to the Wuhan Small Animal Protection Association to aid pet owners affected by COVID-19. Bands that have released records with QSR come from Fuzhou, Xiamen, Guangzhou, Shanghai, Xi'an, Beijing, Xuzhou, and other cities of China.

Events

QSR's first big event was the China tour of the Taiwanese punk band Touming Magazine[11] along with the Hong Kong math emo[12] band Emptybottles.[13] Since its establishment till May 2020, QSR has hosted and co-organised shows and tours for about 30 groups of musicians and bands from the US, Japan, Taiwan, Hong Kong, Singapore, Australia, New Zealand, France, Germany, Italy and India. QSR also maintains a close relationship with labels from different parts of China, "We want to connect with the underground music scene network in Asia to better help bands in touring or releasing records," Xiao Ji said on establishing connections between local scenes (X. Ji, personal communication, May 2020). With the help of the Internet, QSR can connect with fans, artists, and labels around the world (mainly in East Asia). Thus, the technology has "brought institutions and people in disparate local scenes together in broader systems of cultural production and dissemination" (Kruse, 2010, p. 629).

Difficulties and Strategies

Cultural Censorship

In China, the publication of music and music videos needs to be reviewed by relevant government departments. However, as indie records are not registered, they can bypass the Chinese cultural censorship bodies to some degree. If foreign bands come to China to perform, they must submit the band members' personal information, songs, lyrics, and so on to the authorities for review and registration. As not all bands operated by QRS can pass the censorship process, QSR adopts certain mitigating strategies:

> For some venues that have mandatory requirements for approval, we must submit all the information if we have to. However, we do not have to do it if the show is not hosted in a live house but a rehearsal studio, for example. So, if it is a performance that cannot be registered, we will have to host it in a smaller venue. (X. Ji, personal communication, May 2020)

Funding

Often, releasing records and hosting events may not make ends meet. Funding mainly comes from the selling of records and merchandise, and sometimes it is self-raised by QSR members. Income from events is mostly reinvested in the next event or releases, sometimes even taking part of the income of a band's released work (for example, the income from the selling of an EP of the band I was in was used to host advance shows before they paid us, but we were happy to oblige them). This also explains why "such companies were often, in fact, even more exploitative of their musicians than the major corporations" (Shaw, 1978, as cited in Hesmondhalgh, 1999).

Conclusion

Through a series of events and releases, QSR develops a social network in Guangzhou where local participants establish a unique alternative identity that "identifies their cultural distinctiveness from the mainstream" (Bennett & Peterson, 2004, p. 2) while "the Internet has likely accelerated the process of regional, national, and international sounds and practices interacting with local music" (Kruse, 2010, p. 630). As part of the Asian underground music scene, QSR provides platforms and services for bands who wish to perform in and out of China. Its successful DIY practices and creation of an alternative music scene have proven to young people (whether they are music fans or musicians) that it is possible to find ways for things to work out in this imperfectly free country.

Notes

1 The Guangzhou local DJ group Diggy Boys comprises Pete (a music producer), Xiao Ji (the manager of QSR, and guitarist of a hardcore punk band Die!ChiwawaDie! and indie pop band yourboyfriendsucks), and Fuji Yosuke (a Japanese living in Guangzhou at the time).

2 Daily Craft is an artisanal bread-making workshop that mainly serves the community.

3 Vinylhouse Café is a small record store in Guangzhou that also operates as a coffee shop. There are many repeat customers, so the audience is made up mainly of record store guests and fans.

4 Rozz-Tox was a bar in Loft345. Before being demolished, Rozz-Tox was a popular gathering place for artists and hippies in Guangzhou.

5 Emo is a rock music genre characterised by an emphasis on emotional expression, while skramz is an aggressive subgenre of emo.

6 Sarah Records was a British indie record label that was active in Bristol between 1987 and 1995.

7 Boring Productions is an indie music label from Shenzhen and has co-published two albums with QSR.

8 Sweaty&Cramped is a Hong Kong DIY label closely related to QSR, and often co-organises activities in Guangzhou and Hong Kong.

9 Coral Records is a DIY label operated by Xu Bo, the vocalist of the Wuhan band Chinese Football.

10 Bandcamp is a global music community website where fans can discover music and directly support artists who create and release their music on this platform.

11 Touming Magazine is an indie band from Taiwan.

12 Math emo (midwest emo) is a subgenre of emo.

13 Emptybottles is an emo/math rock band from Hong Kong.

References

Bennett, A., & Peterson, R. A. (Eds.). (2004). *Music scenes: Local, translocal, and virtual.* Vanderbilt UP.

Hesmondhalgh, D. (1999). Indie: The institutional politics and aesthetics of a popular music genre. *Cultural Studies, 13*(1), 34–61.

Kruse, H. (2010). Local identity and independent music scenes, online and off. Popular Music and Society, *33*(5), 625–639.

Lu, X. (2017). *Qi qi yinxiang: Women zui wending de shouru shi yue bao mei yue san kuai de lixi 琪琪音像:我们最稳定的收入是余额宝每月三块的利息* [Qiii Snacks Records: Our most stable income is Yu'ebao's interest of three yuan per month]. StreetVoice. http://dashi.streetvoice.cn/article/琪琪音像我们最稳定的收入是余额宝每月三块的利息/

Motoaki, T. (2011). *Pekin ni okeru sabukarucha no juyo ni kansuru toshi-ron-teki kosatsu 北京におけるサブカルチャーの受容に関する都市論的考察* [Urban theory of acceptance of subculture in Beijing]. Gurobarizeshon to toshi henyo sekai shiso-sha グローバリゼーションと都市変容 世界思想社, 114–140.

Shaw, A. (1978). *Honkers and shouters.* Collier.

Wang, L. (2019). *At an "Oh messy life …" show held on August 19, 2019.* [Photograph].

Appendix

Cat#	Artist (Nationality)	*Title*	Release Date
QSR-001	椰林树影 (CN)	*Untitled Skyporn feat. Man Man Man Man*	2016.03.19
QSR-002	yourboyfriendsucks! (CN)	*Episode 01*	2016.05.06
QSR-003	The White Tulips (CN)	*Shonen SPA*	2016.06.24
QSR-004	Various Artists	*"Emotion, No"*	2016.07.24
QSR-005	椰林树影 (CN) 无高潮 Nein or Gas Mus (CN)	*aeontoiletflushing* *Nowhere is now here*	2016.09.10 2016.09.16
QSR-006	Various Artists The White Tulips (CN)	*QSR×BP 2016~17 SAMPLER* *TARDY*	2017.01.26 2017.02.16
QSR-007	THE 尺口MP (CN)	*爱/Love*	2017.04.21
QSR-008	The White Tulips (CN)	*Fondle (Reissue)*	2017.04.22
QSR-009	Die!ChiwawaDie! (CN) / Struggle Session	*Split*	2017.06.30
QSR-010	Foster Parents The White Tulips (CN)	*Grim* *甜美难忘夜*	2017.06.10 2017.12.08
QSR-011	Wellsaid (HK)	*Setbacks*	2017.12.14
QSR-012	The White Tulips (CN) / Chinese Football (CN)	*双拼 HALF HALF #1*	2017.12.23
QSR-013	Various Artists	*"Emotion too"*	2018.02.14
QSR-014	無高潮 Nein or Gas Mus (CN)	*Nein or Gas Mus*	2018.04.06
QSR-015	动物园钉子户 Zoo Gazer (CN)	*动物园钉子户*	2018.04.01

QSR-016	Curse League (US)	*Laying by the Fire in Good Company*	2018.04.30
QSR-017	VOOID (TW)	*新月 / 矿石*	2018.05.08
QSR-018	桃子假象 Peach Illusion (CN)	*桃子假象*	2018.07.11
QSR-019	Cosmic Child (SG)	*「Blue / Green」*	2018.08.03
QSR-020	Stranded Whale (HK) Cheesemind (CN)	*The Revival* *无糖汽水 / 暗恋公告*	2018.10.01 2019.04.13
QSR-021	Wellsaid (HK)	*Apart*	2019.04.27
QSR-022	Cheesemind (CN)	*海湾公园小夜曲 Bay Park Serenade*	2019.05.16
QSR-023	金巴利道路真理生命联合 (HK)	*金巴利道路真理生命联合*	2019.05.13
QSR-024	パンクロッカー労働組合 (JP)	*BLACK ALBUM*	2019.05.11
QSR-025	Power Milk（CN) / smellyhoover (CN) Cheesemind (CN)	*先返去瞌阵 / 收工喇喂* *真空情书*	2019.06.16 2019.07.26
QSR-026	我是机车少女i'm difficult (TW)	*不是你的春梦not your wet dream*	2019.10.28
QSR-027	Foster Parents Seafoodcake (CN) Various Artists Various Artists	*Idle Archipelago* *Telephone Honey* *爱心录音带 Tapes for Charity—独立流行合辑 An indie pop mixtape* *爱心录音带 Tapes for Charity—电子音乐合辑 An electronic mixtape*	2019.11.29 2020.02.14 2020.03.26 2020.03.26
QSR-028	Cheesemind (CN)	*告别事务所*	2020.03.27
QSR-029	yourboyfriendsucks!(CN)	*第二集 Episode 02*	2020.04.01

※Artists without nationality are foreign bands operating in China

CHAPTER 13

Louder Than Hell: The Rise of Latinx and Native American Metal

Luis Zapata, *Rocklectures.com*

"When the mode of the music changes, the walls of the city shake."
(Allen Ginsberg, paraphrasing Plato)

Rock 'n' roll has been the soundtrack of youth rebellion for almost eight decades. It is one of the most powerful cultural exports of the United States to the world. It may seem cliché to say rock 'n' roll is not just about music, but the moment it gripped a post-war generation of American teenagers, its anthems became words to live by—and future generations would never be the same again.

Kids questioned the establishment and decided they did not need to follow parental rules and expectations. They stopped accepting the status quo, and their outside-the-box thinking contributed to accelerated technological advancement. Talented Latinx and Indigenous musicians who crossed cultural boundaries played a big role in the rise of rock 'n' roll and all that came with it.

When I was a teenager in the 1980s in an extremely violent Peru, rock's metal subgenre provided some of us with shelter, pride, inspiration and empowerment. It was one type of music that was so loud and powerful that it shielded me from the sounds of the violence going on outside in the streets. More than 30 years later, these musicians are still my heroes. However, the tribal essence of Latinx in metal lifestyle has not been properly understood by social scientists because its story has not yet been told (Gaston & Carella, 2018).

Technology: One Step Ahead of Your Parents

If country music arrived on horses and blues chugged in on trains, rock 'n' roll came drag-racing on eight cylinders and roaring on motorcycles. Rock 'n' roll spread via tiny transistor radios, which could be muffled under a pillow to allow clandestine listening to Wolfman Jack's border-radio blasts, Alan "Moondog" Freed's rock 'n' roll dance parties out of Cleveland and New York City, and the jives of Dr Hepcat (real name: Albert Lavada Durst) in Austin, Texas. Before the transistor, radio listening was a family affair; generations congregated around a large piece of furniture and developed musical tastes together.

I would like to think that Marlon Brando gave birth to rock 'n' roll in the 1953 movie "The Wild One". When his character is asked, "Hey Johnny, what are you rebelling against?" he answers, "Whaddya got?". The more passionate, proletariat sector of 1950s youth gave birth to traditional rock culture just as the first hits of Latinx rock 'n' roll appeared. Cuban mambo (the favourite music of zoot-suited pachucos), jump blues (loved by greasers), and African-American rhythms were combined to create the 1958 hit "Tequila," recorded by the Champs.

Latin participation in rock 'n' roll occurred from the beginning with artists Ritchie Valens, Chris Montez and Little Julian Herrera (actually a Jewish Hungarian runaway adopted by a Latino family who had a number 1 hit while impersonating a Latin rock 'n' roll singer), as urban planning dictated home loans based on skin colour; mixing Blacks, Latinx, as well as Jews in the same geographical areas.

In 1958, Link Wray, a Shawnee,[1] had a hit with "Rumble," the only instrumental song that has ever been banned from the radio (Lipsitz, 1986). E Street Band guitarist, Steven van Zandt, said of its raw, angry sound, "Link Wray wrote the anthem for juvenile delinquency." (There was no self-respecting high school cafeteria in America where at least a food fight did not break out when "Rumble" came up on the speakers.) The ferocity in the strumming and use of power chords, distorted signal, and driving drumming in the song would have a substantial impact on guitarists Jimmy Page, Jeff Beck, Pete Townsend, as well as Iggy Pop. This influence would be felt for generations.

In the 1960s, popular music took at least two marked directions in sound and sensibility: one was the folk-oriented *wooden* acoustic music of artists such as Bob Dylan, Richie Havens, Atahualpa Yupanqui, and Victor Jara; the other was the electric-charged sound of the British Invasion, delivered by The Beatles, The Kinks and African-American guitar god Jimi Hendrix, who gained fame after moving to England. Hendrix, who also claimed Cherokee heritage, expanded the language of guitar and immortalised himself with the instrumental anti-war hymn "Machine Gun" and his version of "The Star-Spangled Banner" which he performed at Woodstock in 1969. In both the *Jimi Hendrix Experience and Band of Gypsys* albums, Hendrix incorporated beats reminiscent of traditional Native American drumming.

One of the British invaders' major innovations was the notion that rock 'n' roll no longer needed the roll; it could just rock. The distinction is later expressed in the sound of Led Zeppelin, Humble Pie, The Who, and Black Sabbath. Most rock historians credit Black Sabbath with the birth of heavy metal, characterised by dark lyrics, extremely loud, distorted guitars, and anti-establishment messages. When the band formed in Birmingham, England, the city was still in ruins from World War II. The music of Black Sabbath was the new, angry, industrial sound of the people.

Let There Be Sound

Latinx and Native American musicians were present at the beginning of some very significant eras of loud rock and have contributed to rock's evolution. Generational renewal has kept alive a music to which critics would tend to attribute only shock value, making it a 60-plus-year sound institution. Furthermore, metal has evolved into cultural reformulation by going against canonical establishment, finding echoes in conquered populations around the world. In the 1970s, war-painted New Yorker, Ace Frehley (whose mother was Cherokee), became the quintessential heavy metal guitarist for the band KISS. The band sold millions of albums and tickets around the world, influencing countless loud rockers (Figure 1). Indigenous heritage was even more apparent in Southern hard-rock band Blackfoot, in which all but one original member had Native American blood.

FIGURE 1 KISS Receives its Star on the Hollywood Walk of Fame. From left to right: Ace Frehley, Paul Stanley, Peter Criss, and Gene Simmons.
Source: Shutterstock (Smith, 1999)

Although they sold millions of records and concert tickets, heavy metal acts were heard mainly on college radio for years. Commercial radio actively avoided metal, particularly shying away from bands like WASP, led by the politically outspoken, often controversial Blackfoot, Blackie Lawless. In November of 1983, however, the album *Metal Health* by Quiet Riot, a Los Angeles band comprising Cuban-born bassist Rodolfo Maximiliano Sarzo Lavieille Grande Ruiz Payret y Chaumont (aka Rudy Sarzo) and Mexican-born lead guitarist Carlos Cavazo, displaced The Police's *Synchronicity* album from the number 1 position on the *Billboard* Top 200 album chart. The single "Cum on Feel the Noize" from the album became the first heavy-metal song to reach the top five of the *Billboard* Hot 100. Sarzo went on to perform with Ozzy Osbourne, Whitesnake, Dio, Blue Öyster Cult, and many others.

Following Quiet Riot's success, many metal bands came into the mainstream market, including Twisted Sister, with Nuyorican singer-guitarist Eddie Ojeda. The band scored hits with songs about teenage rebellion, which drew condemnation from then-Senator's wife, Tipper Gore. In a congressional hearing, vocalist Dee Snider testified brilliantly against Gore's censorship efforts.

Notable Latinx metal players also include Cuban Juan Croucier, RATT's bassist; Mexican-American Roberto Agustín Miguel Santiago Samuel Pérez de la Santa Concepción Trujillo Veracruz Bautista (aka Robert Trujillo), bassist for Suicidal Tendencies and Metallica; Bon Jovi drummer Héctor Juan Samuel "Tico" Torres, whose parents emigrated from Cuba; and Slayer's Chilean-born bassist-vocalist Tom Araya and Cuban-born drummer Dave Lombardo.

Most of the top metal bands of the 1980s, including AC/DC, Ozzy Osbourne, Whitesnake, Queen and Iron Maiden, played at Rock in Rio, one of the largest rock festivals in history which debuted in 1985 as a 10-day event for which an entire City of Rock was built just outside of Rio de Janeiro. It attracted 1.5 million attendees, and has since been held in Lisbon, Madrid and Las Vegas. Iron Maiden, Scorpions, Megadeth and Sepultura (founded by Brazilian brothers, Max and Igor Cavalera) all headlined Rock in Rio VIII in fall 2019.

Louder Than Hell

As a kid in Peru, I already loved The Beatles, Santana, Los Teen Tops and others. But I felt I needed music that was wilder, louder, faster and meaner. I hoped that this type of music existed somewhere, as it certainly did not exist on the airwaves of a nationalist military government. Then my mother bought me KISS' *Alive!*—the double live album. I was 10 years old. That was the sound. Older kids hated KISS. You fought for KISS' honour in the schoolyard. They prepared you for what was going to come up later on in life.

One of the most politically outspoken and influential bands in the world Rage Against the Machine, fronted by Mexican-American vocalist Zack de la Rocha, was known for mixing rap and metal and for supporting political efforts such as the Salvadoran political party Frente Farabundo Martí para la Liberación Nacional.

In their most extreme expressions, death metal and black metal embrace more radical subjects and social commentary. Mexican death metal band Brujería, formed in 1989, originally included Dino Cazares, Raymond Herrera, and Jello Biafra; Cazares and Herrera later formed Fear Factory. Brujería's members use nicknames and sing about Satanism, sex and drug trafficking. Tampa, Florida developed a strong death metal scene in the mid-1980s with the emergence of iconic bands such as Cannibal Corpse, Deicide and Morbid Angel. Salvadoran-born drummer Pete Sandoval of Terrorizer and Morbid Angel is known as "the father of blast beat"—a rapid-fire drumming style played with two bass drums, reminiscent of a semi-automatic weapon. It is the signature beat of death metal and black metal bands.

Black metal likely began in the late 1970s in Newcastle, England with Venom, an openly anti-Christian outfit, which was adopted by Scandinavian kids disgusted with the Catholic church's pedophilia scandal. Similar philosophies have taken root in Latin American and Native American metal scenes, giving rise to the Indigenous black metal and Rez metal genres. Heard mostly on Navajo reservations, Rez metal is an angry and dark, yet powerful, expression of longing for cultural respect and survival. (As I write this, I am listening to the late drummer Randy Castillo [Figure 2], whose parents were Chickasaw; he played with Ozzy Osbourne, Lita Ford, Motley Crüe, and other heavy-metal icons.)

FIGURE 2 Randy Castillo
Source: iStock (Gallegos, n.d.)

The most successful Indigenous metal band is called Cemican (Figure 3) from Guadalajara, Mexico ("Indigenous" here refers to the subgenre of metal, not the musicians' ethnicity.). Cemican means "all the life" in Nahuatl, the language of the Aztecs, spoken today by over 2 million people. Using pre-Columbian instruments and Nahuatl names and lyrics, they have played in the world's biggest metal festivals, including France's Hell Fest and Germany's Wacken Open Air.

FIGURE 3 Cemican. From left: Xaman Ek (rituals, dance, pre-Columbian instruments), Mazatecpatl (pre-Columbian instruments), Tecuhtli (guitar/vocals), Tlipoca (drums), Ocelot (bass/backing vocals), and Yei Tochtli (pre-Columbian instruments). Costumes are interpretive.
Source: Courtesy of Cemican (Cemican, n.d.)

Conclusion

In a historical sense, metal and punk remain the most extreme cultural variations of rock. I would even venture to say that just as African-Americans have preserved Gospel through various genres, including rock 'n' roll, Native Americans protect some of their traditions using hard rock. Rudy Sarzo and Carlos Cavazo moved metal music from underground to mainstream, and gave fuel to metal capitals like San Antonio and Los Angeles. Rock 'n' roll has attended its own funeral at least four times that I am aware of, and in all those times, what saved the music and kept the flame alive were the loud rockers. The ones with the warrior mentality. Latinx and Native American musicians contributed to the innovation of the time, and I am happy to help tell their story.

Notes

[1] Shawnee is a semi-nomadic North American tribe that resides in the Ohio Valley.

References

Cemican. (n.d.). *Cemican* [Photograph].

Gallegos, C. (n.d.). *Randy Castillo* [Photograph]. iStock.

Gaston, J. I. L. R., & Carella, G. Risica. (2018). *Espíritu del metal: La conformación de la escena metalera Peruana (1981–1992).* Sonidos Latentes.

Lipsitz, G. (1986). Cruising around the historical bloc: Postmodernism and popular music in East Los Angeles. *Cultural Critique, 5*(Winter 1986–1987), 157–177.

Smith, P. (1999). *Rock group KISS, on Hollywood Blvd where they were honoured with the 2,142nd star on the Hollywood Walk of Fame* [Photograph]. Shutterstock.

CHAPTER 14

In Search of a Sonic Space by Asian Artists: Performance of Indonesian Expanded Cinema with Live Stereophonic Sound in Japan

Madoka Fukuoka, *Graduate School of Human Sciences, Osaka University*

This chapter focuses on attempts by artists to create live performances through the combination and coexistence of traditional cultural elements and sound technology. The object of this study is the collaborative performance of expanded cinema—combining a silent film directed by a celebrated Indonesian film director with live stereophonic sound directed by a Japanese sound artist—that was presented in Tokyo, Japan in July 2019. Indonesian director Garin Nugroho's work of expanded cinema titled *Setan Jawa*, released in 2016, is a silent black-and-white film requiring live sound and music performances in its presentation. The integration of a silent monochrome movie and live music performances is a central element of the work's presentation. Under the direction of Yasuhiro Morinaga, Japanese and Indonesian musicians designed the sound effects and original compositions featuring the voice of KOM_I, a Japanese female singer of popular music whose distinctive vocal performance was perfectly captured and projected by the stereophonic sound system set up for the performance in Tokyo. In addition, dance performances by the lead actors, recitation of poems and mantras, and acting by the singer and the narrator, were presented simultaneously. To stage the performance successfully, the collaboration process between Asian artists was particularly important. The artists explored and experimented on a collaborative creation based on Asian music traditions and Western string ensemble, utilising the new technology of 3-D stereophonic sound requiring 18 speakers.

In this chapter, "popular culture" includes cultural activities conducted in the search and exploration of one's identity, and the performative process towards the existing sense of values. This approach is different from the definition of popular culture based on genre types. "Identity" in this chapter is based on Stuart Hall's definition as "the result of a successful articulation or 'chaining' of the subject into the flow of the discourse" (Hall, 1996, pp. 5–6). With the definition as a basis, this chapter focuses on the process where contemporary Asian artists dive into and explore their own cultural expressions.

The case study described here is viewed as a creative activity of contemporary art. The exhibition of expanded cinema accompanied by live performances attempts to effectively present the cinema's world view through the creation of the space of sound and performances based on the cultural elements of contemporary Japanese and Indonesian musicians, dancers, dramatic artists and singers. The objective of the collaborative project is to create a new space for a live performance through the *negotiation* of various senses of cultural values between the artists. It is also an indication of the Asian artists' sense of value for the international world of contemporary arts, where the traditional dimension of Asian arts has mainly been featured. These characteristics are considered common to the research interests in the study of popular culture where the negotiation of the underlying values has been a focus.

In the following description, I first introduce the work *Setan Jawa*, then examine the concert in 2019 in Tokyo, and finally analyse the importance of the collaborative creations of Asian artists as one of the research topics on popular culture.

Expanded Cinema, *Setan Jawa*

A poor young man decides to make a pact with Setan, a demon spirit, in order to become rich, own a luxurious house, and marry an aristocratic lady. However, it soon turns out that his house continually requires repairs and the young man has to constantly fix it, and in the end, he becomes a pillar in the house after his death. This is the premise of the work entitled *Setan Jawa* by the Indonesian film director Garin Nugroho. The story centres around the theme of *Pesugihan Kandang Buburah*, a kind of ritual or black magic in Javanese mysticism that purportedly brings wealth. The word "*setan*" in Javanese refers to a kind of spiritual being, as anthropologist Clifford Geertz explained in his book titled *The Religion of Java* (1976).

The work is a black-and-white silent film that requires the live performance of sound. The director mentioned two genres as inspiration for the idea of the film; the first source being German expressionist films from the 1920s such as *Metropolis* (1927) and *Nosferatu* (1922). These works were monochrome silent films where sound and music accompaniments were required. In the history of the integration of silent movies and sound, the autonomous dimension of the sound space had been explored. The second source is Javanese shadow puppetry or shadow play known as *wayang kulit*. It is the traditional Javanese art form of storytelling through the use of multiple elements including the projection of shadows, music performance, songs and narrations.

Garin Nugroho used a method of expression called "magic realism", where Javanese dances and traditional masks and objects are used as prominent motifs to realise magical elements. The main protagonists of *Setan Jawa* are:

- **Setio, the main protagonist**. A poor young man, who wants to marry Asih, an aristocratic lady, makes a deal with a demon spirit, Setan. Corrupted by dark magic, Setio loses his humanity and suffers for the pact.
- **Asih, the heroin**. Asih, a young aristocratic lady, marries Setio. When she learns about her husband's pact, she asks Setan for forgiveness; however, Setan requires her body in compensation. Ultimately, Asih must confront Setan.
- **Setan, the wounded soul of a boy from the colonial era**. A demon spirit who has settled in the mountains and becomes attached to Asih.

The film consists of a prologue and seven chapters as follows:

- **Prologue**. Subtitles are projected onto the screen to explain the background of the popularity of mythical practices in the Dutch colonial era.
- **Chapter 1, The Road of Love**. Setio encounters Asih in the streets and falls in love with her.
- **Chapter 2, Mysteries of Body and Love**. Setio proposes marriage to Asih; however, Asih's mother rejects the proposal.
- **Chapter 3, The Mystic Market**. Setio visits the mystic market and makes a pact with Setan.
- **Chapter 4, Indebted to Setan**. He obtains money and a luxurious house, and marries Asih.
- **Chapter 5, Setan's Way: A Broken House**. Setan breaks the house and Setio repairs the damage.
- **Chapter 6, Fate?** Asih learns about her husband's pact, and begs Setan for forgiveness. In return, Setan demands her body as compensation.
- **Chapter 7, Surrender, The Human Way**. Asih must face and overcome Setan.

The first performance was held in Jakarta in 2017 with Javanese *gamelan* music, and the integration of sound and the film was based on Javanese traditional dramaturgy in the performance of shadow play. In the past, live performances have been developed for other kinds of music and sound, such as collaborations of *gamelan* music and symphony orchestras.

Concert Incorporating Live Stereophonic Sound with Cinema in Tokyo, 2019

At the concert held in Tokyo in July 2019, compound ensembles were presented in stereophonic sound. The ensembles consisted of *gamelan* instruments of Central Java, a Western string ensemble, *tarawangsa* (a string instrument of the West Java region), bamboo xylophones and drums of the Banyumas region in southwest Central Java, and the voice and singing of KOM_I, a popular Japanese musical artist.

I have also experienced the stage performance as an audience member. The musicians, narrator, dancers and singer collaborated and performed together to produce a feast for the senses. The stereophonic sound system brought out the vocals and music to set the tone and help produce an air of mysticism. The world of sound created in the performance effectively expressed the atmosphere or circumstances, and the protagonists' emotion in each scene. Various sound effects were used in every scene. The audience could enjoy the experience of being immersed in the 3-D sounds coming from multiple directions.

Yasuhiro Morinaga, as the music director and sound designer, described the world of sound created as being based on the rituals that he had been a part of in some Southeast Asian countries. He recalled the amazing experience of hearing a *troll* sing in the centre of a circle formed by the performers. Morinaga reported that "absorption in the story's world by hearing the stereophonic sound [from] multiple directions" can create the same experience

(Morinaga, 2019, pp. 12–13). He emphasised the effectiveness of the stereophonic sound effects because they were derived from his research and experience of sounds from rituals in Southeast Asia. In an interview session following the performance, Morinaga stated that he emphasised the power of human voices, and by doing so, the performance successfully transcended the difference in language between the Indonesians and Japanese (Y. Morinaga, personal communication, July 2, 2019).

The most striking feature of the concert was the combination of musical sounds, recitations of mantras and narrations, and dancing or acts by performers. From his fieldwork in some parts of Java and other parts of Indonesia, Morinaga referred to the existence of mantras used to summon and send evil spirits back to their world. In the 2019 performance, recitations of mantras were featured effectively. Gunawan Maryanto, an actor and the director of the Central Java-based avant-garde theatre group Garasi, performed the narrations and mantras. Before the Prologue, Maryanto recited the mantra to summon spirits from every direction. In Chapter 1, through "narration 1", he introduced the story as one that could be about anyone who lets desire get the better of them. In Chapter 2, the "mantra of compassion" is recited to appease the spirits. In Chapter 3, "narration 2" reveals that Setio, the main protagonist, has decided to make a pact with a demon spirit, abandoning his soul for the promise of wealth. In Chapter 4, the "mantra of richness" is recited to hail the riches into Setio's home.

Besides these narrations and mantras, three dancers performed in parallel with the film projection on screen. The three dancers represented the actual protagonists in the film: Heru Pruwanto as Setio, Drotea Quin as Asih's mother, and Ari Prasetio as Setan. The narrator Maryanto and the singer KOM_I also played roles that could be viewed as either actor or dancer in different sections of the presentation. Multiple events played out on stage simultaneously including the projection of film, musical performances, dance performances, recitations of mantras and narrations, and singing.

Morinaga described the original nature of Asian performing art forms as the integration of music, song and dance, and tried incorporating these elements into the projection of the film at every opportunity (Morinaga, 2019, p. 12). As mentioned earlier, the performance of live music alongside the projection of silent movies indicates the autonomy of the world of sound to a certain degree. In addition, the live performance in 2019 pointed to the autonomous nature of the various kinds of live performances including music, sound, narration, voice and dance.

As one of the international cultural exchange activities between Japan and Indonesia, the collaboration between musicians and artists of both countries was emphasised. Morinaga stated that the collaborative performance is not merely an anthology of various kinds of music in Indonesia or Japan, but a necessity that expands these elements of traditional music to the future while remaining rooted in the concepts of indigenous land and history. To realise this purpose, he placed great emphasis on the process of creation, taking cognisance of all the performers' discussions of each tradition or musical element of the region. He also stressed the importance of conducting fieldwork in various regions in Indonesia (Morinaga, 2019).

Based on these ideas, the artists from various regions worked together to successfully realise the goal of creating an original space of stereophonic sound consisting of Asian traditional music, Western music, popular music, voices, narrations and singing.

Conclusion

In the programme book of the performance in Tokyo, the director Garin Nugroho describes the use of 3-D stereophonic sound technology as follows:

> It would be the opportunity [to pay] homage [to] the history and imagination of dramatic arts such as silent films and shadow play. In the celebration of Asian arts where mysticism and digital technology coexist, I will present [the] film *Setan Jawa*. (Morinaga, 2019, p. 10)

By adopting mystical realism through the incorporation of Javanese dances and various traditional masks and objects, the film featured traditional Javanese cultural elements as the source of innovative expression of contemporary arts. In addition, the 2019 performance featured the collaborative efforts of Japanese and Indonesian artists. Based on their own cultural experiences, these Asian artists created an innovative space of sound and performance, delivering it to the audience using cutting-edge digital technologies. These contemporary artists worked on the collaborative production based on their own artistic experiences encompassing different Asian music traditions, Western music traditions and popular music. In addition, the performance utilised the new technology of stereophonic sound that required the use of 18 speakers to showcase the vocals and create an air of mysticism. By doing so, they realised a performance space that could be created only by Asian artists living in the contemporary era. The performance highlighted the importance of the collaboration process between the Indonesian and Japanese artists with varied artistic experiences. This indicates one of the ways for Asian artists to enter the contemporary art scene where the main collaborations had been executed between Asian and Western artists.

The main research interests in the study of popular culture have been the negotiation of various kinds of senses of value. The process of searching for identities through cultural activities has also been the main focus of the study on popular culture. The case study in this chapter indicates some challenges in the contemporary art world faced by Asian artists in considering the coexistence of tradition and innovation in Asian contemporary art forms. It is the Asian artists' own demonstration of existing stereotypes in the contemporary art world where the traditional dimension of Asian art forms had been featured.

To consider today's Southeast Asian popular culture, it is necessary to examine various types of scenes of cultural creation, including new trends in the contemporary art scene. This chapter examined Asian artists' collaborative performance creation in the contemporary art scene. The consideration suggests the significance of including scenes of art creation in the contemporary art world in the research interests of current studies on popular culture.

References

Geertz, C. (1976). *The religion of Java*. The University of Chicago Press. (First published in 1960)

Hall, S. (1996). Who needs "identity"? In S. Hall & P. Du Gay (Eds.), *Questions of cultural identity* (pp. 1–18). Sage Publications.

Morinaga, Y. (2019, July). Indonesia and Japan: In search of resonating sounds. *Setan Jawa: A silent film with a live 3D sound concert* [Programme book of 3D sound concert of *Setan Jawa* in Tokyo]. Japan Foundation Asia Centre.

CHAPTER 15

Echoes of Times: A Study of Choral Arrangements of Taiwan Pop Songs

Mali Liu, ***IC Broadcasting Co, Chinese Culture University***

A well-known song is often the epitome of an era, representing the voice of the people, reflecting the pulse of society. During Taiwan's martial law, music was used to shape the consciousness of the masses by praising the political party, the state and the leaders, in conjunction with government decree and propaganda. After the lifting of martial law in 1987, Taiwan moved towards democracy and freedom, and more diverse songs appeared in the pop music scene. Mass culture was no longer manipulated by the ruling party but was initiated by the opposition and civic groups instead.

Cultural criticisms since the second half of the 20th century, especially in the humanities and social sciences, have often misappropriated the dialectical theme of the Adorno-Benjamin debate which centres around the issue of artistic autonomy. Theodor Adorno (1903–1969) was a German philosopher, sociologist, psychologist, musicologist, and composer known for his critical theory of society, while Walter Benjamin (1892–1940) was a German Jewish philosopher, cultural critic and essayist. Adorno believed that "culture industry" should replace "mass culture". The masses are not the measure but the ideology of the culture industry, even though the culture industry itself cannot scarcely exist without adapting to the masses (Adorno, 1991). However, a song can emerge in response to the needs of the times. It is not only an expression of the sentiments of the composer, but also of politics, influenced by those in power. Sometimes it purifies the heart and represents the voices of the people, striking at the pulse of society.

This chapter is based on three different music types, analysing patriotic songs after the Retrocession of Taiwan in 1945, campus folk songs after 1970, and social movement songs after the lifting of martial law in Taiwan in 1987. A representative work from each music type is used as an example to explain how it became a hit and then a classic. The examination can sort out the significance of the times of these classics, and explore the artistic values they demonstrate after being adapted for choral singing.

The Martial Law Era

During the martial law period from 1949 to 1987, songs were mainly in Mandarin. "800 Heroes Song" is the most representative of all the patriotic songs after the retrocession or return of Taiwan to China from the Japanese. The song is also known by the title "China Will Not Perish" and was later changed to "China Shall Be Strong". With lyrics written by Tao-sheng Gui and music composed by Zhi-qiu Xia, the song was completed circa 1937 to commemorate the heroic efforts of the National Revolutionary Army in defending Sihang Warehouse in the final stage of the Battle of Shanghai. It was written to praise the heroic acts of the so-called 800 soldiers of the 524 Regiment of the 88th Division, and to prop up morale in the fight against the Japanese. This song uses the dotted rhythm powerfully. In the movie 800 Heroes released in 1976, it was used as the theme song to evoke strong emotional resonance. "China Shall Be Strong" is one of 20 songs selected by the Department of Education of the Taipei City Government deemed to inspire patriotism (Guo, 2011).

Zhi-qiu Xia is a professor at the Central Conservatory of Music in Beijing. He composed both the solo and the choral editions of the song. In the latter, the homophonic and contrapuntal techniques are used. The piano part supports the harmonies, enriching the aural experience and artistry. In the early days of the Retrocession, the anti-Japanese sentiments were transformed into that of anti-Russian and anti-communist, leading to even greater resonance. The translation of the lyrics are as follows:

> China shall be strong, China shall be strong,
> Look at our national hero Colonel Jin-yuan Xie.
> China shall be strong, China shall be strong,
> Watch the 800 warriors fighting alone to defend the eastern battlefield.
> Everywhere is artillery, everywhere is jackals.
> They would rather die than retreat, would rather die than surrender.
> Our nation's flag flies proudly amidst the sea of chaos, flies proudly, flies proudly, flies proudly.
> 800 heroes with one heart, unstoppable to the thousands-strong enemy.
> Our actions are strong and powerful.
> My compatriots, my compatriots, get on the battlefield, and follow the example of the 800 heroes.
> China shall be strong! (4×) Shall be strong! (4×)

"Descendants of the Dragon" is a nostalgic campus folk song that was popular during the martial law period. In December 1978, the United States (US) government announced the severance of diplomatic relations with Taiwan and the establishment of diplomatic relations with the government of the People's Republic of China. De-jian Hou, a student of National Chengchi University at the time, wrote the lyrics, composed the music overnight, and published the score and lyrics in the newspapers the next day.

This song uses the strophic form, with only five notes. The melody is of conjunct motion, with eight phrases in each stanza. The lyrics are concise, clear and powerful. Performed by the ever-popular singer Jian-fu Li, the song had constant media coverage and was widely promoted with the support of the government. Coupled with the popularity of campus folk songs, the song quickly became extremely well known. The song was later performed by Hong Kong singers Ming-man Cheung and Michael Ching-Kit Kwan, and spread throughout Mainland China.[1]

"Descendants of the Dragon" was like the national anthem in the pop music world, and later became the theme song of the 1981 film *The Land of the Brave* directed by Li Hsing. However, when De-jian Hou defected to China in 1983, the song was banned in Taiwan until 1989. Because of its significance, the Chinese composer Ce Ren, once a professor at Capital Normal University, arranged the song for a mixed choir and piano version, using the homophonic and contrapuntal technique to amplify the structure and harmony. The first edition of the score is a manuscript of numbered musical notations, which was later published in Ce Ren's collection of "Choral Music".

In the Far East there is a river,
　its name is the Yangtze River.
In the Far East there is a river,
　its name is the Yellow River.
Although I've never seen the beauty of the Yangtze,
　in my dreams I miraculously travel the Yangtze's waters.
Although I've never heard the strength of the Yellow River,
　the rushing and surging waters are in my dreams.
In the Ancient East there is a dragon,
　her name is China.
In the Ancient East there is a people,
　they are all the descendants of the dragon.
I grew up under the claws of the dragon,
　after I grew up I became a descendant of the dragon.

Black eyes, black hair, yellow skin,
    forever and ever a descendant of the dragon.
One hundred years ago on a tranquil night,
    in the deep of the night before enormous changes.
Gun and cannon fire destroyed the tranquil night,
    surrounded on all sides by the appeasers' swords.
How many years have gone by with the gunshots still
    ringing out,
    how many years followed by how many years.
Mighty dragon, mighty dragon open your eyes,
    forever and ever open your eyes.

Post-Martial Law Period

"She is Our Darling" is one of the most significant songs from this period. In 1993, musician Ming-chang Chen was commissioned by the Garden of Hope Foundation to write a song for the "Save Child Prostitutes" campaign. Chen's works generally express a strong sense of localism and concern for society. After the 1999 earthquake (known as the 921 Earthquake) in Taiwan, "She is Our Darling" became a song that expressed solidarity with victims of the severely devastated area. In 2004, it was the theme song of a peace rally called "228 Hand-in-Hand Rally" which attracted millions of participants. Because the melody is easy to follow, and the lyrics are amiable and touching, the song often appears in the election campaigns of the Democratic Progressive Party (DPP) or public benefit activities.[2]

In 2016, Yu-shan Tsai rearranged this song for a mixed chorus and a women's chorus, applying the homophonic style and adding a discant melody line in high voice to make the music more expressive. Tsai obtained a Master of Piano Performance at the Peabody Institute of Music in the US. After she started collaborating with the renowned choir Formosa Singers, Tsai worked on the choral arrangements of various Taiwanese songs. The repertoire includes more than 100 songs of various origins, such as Mandarin, Hoklo, Hakka, and the aboriginal language, making up for the dearth of native works in Taiwan's choral world. The fresh and versatile style not only preserves the original spirit of the song, but also makes choral music more interesting. The lyrics are as follows:

> A flower growing on the land, cherished by mom and dad,
> If the wind blows, you need to cover with the quilt,
> Don't let darkness befall her,
> Unbloomed flowers need care from you and me.
> Give her a piece of growing land,
> Holding hands, heart to heart,
> Let's stand together, she is our darling.

"Island's Sunrise" is a more recent song, written for a student-driven protest movement called Sunflower Student Movement. On March 18, 2014, students occupied the Legislative Yuan, the supreme legislative organisation of China, to protest through nonviolent resistance the unequal Cross-Strait Service Trade Agreement signed between Taiwan and China. The movement has awakened the Taiwanese consciousness and brought more attention to important political, economic, and livelihood issues. People began to realise the corruption of Taiwan's political environment. (You, 2018).

"Island's Sunrise" is a Taiwanese song written by the rock 'n' roll band Fire Extinguisher. It profoundly expresses people's desire for a democratic society and their firm belief in fighting against government corruption. The original edition was a rock song performed with great energy. Two young musicians, Po-Neng You and Pai-rui Ye, scored a mixed a cappella choral arrangement with syncopation to retain the rhythm of the original song. The lyrics are as follows:

Colours grow, colours creep,
My tinted flesh outline your feet.
Your vast limbs, tightly we knit,
Your face is cast with my breath, my heat.
The hunters start to seize,
We're lost at sea, adrift like leaves.
Have our hollers reached your heels?
We hope our whispers slightly touched your crown.
Darkness breaks (At the crack of dawn),
The horizon lined with a hopeful crowd.
A voice echoes, beckons,
Wave by the wings below the sun.
Darkness breaks (At the crack of dawn),
Flags raised high, wall breaks down.
Link my spirit to your heart,
Together we stand proud.
Set sail, don't fear, sky crystal and clear,
The heavy fog may slow me down.
Hold that fire high above the wild,
Fight for the glorious day to come.
Darkness breaks (At the crack of dawn),
Darkness breaks (At the crack of dawn),
With pounding hearts, we are marking this (the) start.
Darkness breaks (At the crack of dawn),
Express your dream, grow with our song.
Teardrops fall in river,
They spread and sparkle along.
Darkness breaks apart (At the crack of dawn),
Express your dream grow with our song.
Dear, that day will come,
With this brilliant and fearless throng.

Conclusion

A song which has various arrangements and adaptations is proof of the song's popularity and influence, as it draws new composers, music publishers and singers to reinterpret it for a new audience. Therefore, a song can become a common memory of an era. Apart from resonating with the people and carrying nostalgic emotions, song adaptations allow the spirit of the song to be passed in different ways, allowing future generations to better understand the zeitgeist of the past through choral performances. Songs for the general public usually have simple arrangements that avoid the need for excessive technical singing skills, preserve the integrity of the original melody, and focus on the homophonic style so as to encourage it being sung by the public.

Before the lifting of martial law in Taiwan, songs were written in response to national policies and government propaganda, with an emphasis on discipline. The majority of songs were marches that focused on patriotism and praised the leaders for their virtues. "800 Heroes Song" and "Descendants of the Dragon" are very typical examples. However, with the changing times and social environment, the shift in national policies, and the emergence of outstanding composers in Taiwan, a wide selection of quality choral works have since been composed. Choirs have a wide variety of songs to choose from, and both the solo and choral versions of "800 Heroes Song" and "Descendants of the Dragon" have long been forgotten.

After the lifting of Taiwan's martial law, cross-strait tensions eased and the economy developed rapidly. Songs were still in line with national policies, but the style became more flexible. There was less focus on political decrees and more on humanistic concerns. Lyrics in Hoklo expressed stronger grassroots sentiments, and were more touching and resonating. "She is Our Darling" is the most representative example. At that time, the DPP was in power and this song was constantly sung. "Island's Sunrise", on the other hand, was written during the Kuomintang regime (since the end of World War II in 1945 to the end of the Taiwanese martial law period in 1987) and appeared as a result of social activism. As the political situation was much more liberal than in the 1970s, "Island's Sunrise" resonated well with the masses.

While contemplating the present and recalling the past, no matter what period or under which regime, songs exist to serve the public; they resonate with both the old and the young, and are inspiring, edifying, entertaining and appreciated by all. Choral arrangement is a continuation of the spirit of the original song through singing.

Notes

[1] More information on the "Descendants of the Dragon" (in Chinese) can be found on Wikipedia: https://bit.ly/3apk0Yi

[2] More information on "She is Our Darling" (in Chinese) can be found on Wikipedia: https://bit.ly/3poiMRp

References

Adorno, T. W. (Ed.). (1991). *The culture industry: Selected essays on mass culture*. Routledge.

Ko, C. H. (2011). *Country, market and music: The evolution of Taiwan patriotic songs during martial law, 1949-1987* [Master's thesis, National Taiwan Normal University].

Ren, C. (1978). Long de chuanren 龍的傳人 [Descendants of the Dragon] [Vocal score].

Tsai, Y. S. (2016). Yi shi zan de baobei 伊是咱的寶貝 [She is Our Darling] [Vocal score]. Formosa Singers.

You, P. N., & Ye, P. R. (2018). Daoyu tianguang 島嶼天光 [Island's Sunrise] [Vocal score]. Chorphillia.

Xia, Z. Q., & Gui, T. S. (1937). Ge babai zhuangshi 歌八百壯士 [Praise to 800 Heroes] [Vocal score].

CHAPTER 16

Gender Troubles in Japanese Popular Music Culture?: The Case of Female Idols from "Gay Town"

Mana Kamioka, *Keio University*

This chapter explores the problems and issues of the Japanese female idol industry through a case study of the gay idol group Nichome no Sakigake Coming Out (二丁目の魁カミングアウト Coming Out of the Second Street). They are an idol group from Shinjuku Ni-Chome (Shinjuki block no. 2/the Second Street), a well-known gay district in Tokyo; and all its members identify as gay men. They have affirmed that they would never give up being idols despite their sexual orientation, advocating that "Gays can be idols". This affirmation may sound confusing since sexual orientation is not a hindrance to becoming an idol in Japan; so what does this statement mean? Through this chapter, I clarify the meaning of this motto in the context of the Japanese female idol culture. In Japan, female and male idols operate separately in the music industry, with some female idols being considered gay icons in the Japanese gay community. In other words, "idol" here refers particularly to the female idol. Since its formation, the group Nichome no Sakigake Coming Out has been performing on the same stage in the role of female idols without having to cross-dress. Therefore, they are not just a dance cover group that covers girl groups' songs, but they perform as actual idols, striving to find their footing in the female idol culture. Through this case study, I discuss gender issues in Japanese popular music culture and reveal that there is a possibility of transcending gender norms in Japanese idol culture.

Idol Culture Problems

Nichome no Sakigake Coming Out call themselves not just "idols" but "gay idols", a unique and genderless label. By declaring themselves "gay idols", their sexual orientation differentiates them from other idols. Mikitty Honmono (ミキティー本物), the group's producer and one of its members, has said in several interviews and articles that their "gay idols" label is a response to and resistance against the conventional idol culture. He has said that gay idols are an unprecedented challenge to the norms of the culture, which means the band can proudly try to establish a "gay idol" standard (musicite, 2017; Yagi, 2019). This resistance is due to controversial issues that exist in the idol industry. I discuss three main issues within the idol culture as addressed by Nichome no Sakigake Coming Out in the following paragraphs.

CDs for Conversation, Not Music

First, there is the problem of selling exaggerated quantities of CDs as the idol industry still shows a tendency to focus on CD purchases. It is quite common for idol fans to purchase multiple copies of the same CD or DVD; that is, a fan supports their favourite idol by buying 10, 20, or even 100 copies of their CDs or DVDs. This is a distinctive system in idol culture, and is widely known in Japan as the "AKB48 method" because the trend started with the iconic girl group AKB48. Fans of the girl group regularly buy their CDs for a ticket to a meet-and-greet event or to vote in a poll that determines the members' popularity. Currently, buying more than one copy is a normal and expected behaviour of idol fans. Such purchases come with special bonus gifts: a handshake with the idol for the purchase of one CD; a photograph for the purchase of two copies; a group shot for three; an autograph for four; a 30-second video for five, and so on. While studies of idol culture have examined the benefits of such systems, we can understand this as a problematic phenomenon of turning CDs into currency, in which fans acquire CDs as a kind of currency rather than a music medium. The meet-and-greet events are a commodification of the intimate relationship between fans and idols. Uno (2013) pointed out that "AKB48 does not sell their music anymore" (p. 131). Indeed, the experience of spending time with one's favourite idol, which cannot be reproduced, is valuable to a fan. Thus, idol songs are prone to become an afterthought to time dedicated to fan interaction.

However, Nichome no Sakigake Coming Out has rejected this custom. Mikitty has repeatedly said, "I don't want to sell 10,000 CDs, I want 10,000 people to listen to it" (musicite, 2017) and criticised "systems that [enable] fans … to spend a lot of money" (Mikitty, 2019). The group does not have a meet-and-greet system based on the buying of CDs or other items, but instead sells meet-and-greet tickets themselves. A group photograph or a few shots of the fan with any three members costs 500 or 1000 yen. A 500-yen ticket is for a "salty" (塩対応 *shio taio*) photograph, in which members pose expressionlessly and do not converse with fans, while a 1000-yen ticket is for a "godly" (神対応 *kami taio*) photograph where members welcome fans warmly and enthusiastically. Salty and godly versions of photographs are also technical terms derived from AKB48's idol culture. They are used in jest, but the group also realises that intimacy with fans is a crucial entertainment element of their work.

Identity in Music

Second, Nichome no Sakigake Coming Out protests that music should be high on the list of priorities in idol culture. As I have pointed out, perks like handshake events have ironically been holding more weight than the music itself in recent years. Nichome no Sakigake Coming Out has longed not only for the performativity of female idols, but also their music. Placing music at the centre of their work may be their own push for a musical renaissance. One of the typical aspects of idol performance is that the idols do not write their own lyrics and music. Idols often perform songs and choreography created by other musicians or dancers, and their schedules are controlled by management offices called *jimusho* (事務所). Those who do not understand the circumstances around idols may well think that idols lack creativity in their work. However, Mikitty writes and choreographs all of Nichome no Sakigake Coming Out's songs. Their songs are based entirely on their own values, but most of the lyrics are not actually about the experiences, struggles, worries, or romance of LGBTQ people. Mikitty has said, "There is no mention of homosexuality in the lyrics, but I want to explain with simple words that anybody worries about the same things, regardless of their sexuality, and [that] we are quite same" (Yagi, 2019). Instead of focusing on sexual orientation or gender identity, the group emphasises that their songs are enjoyable for everybody.

At the same time, their music aims to transcend sexual orientation and gender identity. For example, in their song titled "My Dream is to be Someone's Bride" (ボクの夢はお嫁さん *Boku no Yume wa Oyome-san*), Mikitty chose the word *boku* (ボク), a first-person pronoun mainly used by boys, as the subject of the song. While the members usually refer to themselves using *watashi* (私)—a first-person pronoun generally used by women at casual or neutral occasions—almost all of their songs are sung using the first-person pronoun *boku*. In the Japanese language, there are a variety of gendered first-person pronouns. Some Japanese songs effectively utilise these terms for a kind of cross-gender performance (CGP). However, it is unclear whether "My Dream is to be Someone's Bride" is indeed a CGP. The song uses a tricky title but does not sing directly about marriage or dreams. The lyrics talk about how those who have been treated as grown-ups since the age of 20 cannot be grown-ups in the way that they have imagined when they were younger. They sing their worries about the future and the dream of meeting someone. "Meeting the one" makes one think of marriage, but the institution of matrimony is not a reality for the band. Here, they sing about a relationship between people that is not just based on patriarchal family norms. The group also performs another song that makes listeners imagine a wedding ceremony. When singing "In Sickness and In Health" (病める時も 健やかなる時も *Yameru Toki Mo Sukoyakanaru Toki Mo*), they dance with the pinky-swear gesture and are clad in white outfits that are a combination of a wedding dress and a tuxedo. On the day they performed the song for the first time, Mikitty tweeted to fans: "The choreography with the little finger means that we can't promise anything now, but there are many things we can pledge to each of you" (Mikitty, 2018). The song is also not based on the current imagination of matrimony. The lives of gay people, sexual minorities and those who choose not to marry may be filled with anxiety about the traditional family structure that continues to be the standard. Understanding this, they sing about a situation not at all based on heterosexual norms. The idol industry is unconsciously based on heteronormativity, and questioning this is their third act of resistance.

About Sexual Orientation and Gender Identity

Third, the gender identity of Nichome no Sakigake Coming Out's members is not specifically disclosed. Members have said that they almost gave up on their dream of becoming an idol because they are *men*. They perform as female idols, not male idols, but that is not a factor in determining their gender identity. However, it is true that they have entered the field of female idols as *male*. Ironically, the heterosexual norms made this challenge to enter the field of female idols possible because people consider that they never fall in love with female idols.

In the idol industry, idols are frequently forced to act like boyfriends/girlfriends to their fans. AKB48, for example, has a rule that forbids the members from having any kind of romantic relationship. This has created a tradition that idols should not date. While the rule is not actually contractual, it is widely practised within the industry. It goes without saying that this rule is based on heterosexual norms. On the other hand, the members of

Nichome no Sakigake Coming Out are considered neither women nor men; their outfits while performing are neither too feminine nor masculine. While mainstream idols are often characterised by their femininity or masculinity, Nichome no Sakigake Coming Out does not emphasise either. Furthermore, due to their sexual orientation, fans or managers of female idols do not have to worry about or become jealous of the members becoming close to the girls. This is presumably Mikitty's strategy as he strictly forbids bisexual men from applying for auditions. The situation has raised a few questions: Why do fans not approve of their favourite female idols having boyfriends? Is it okay if female idols have girlfriends? Are all female idols female? What does the gender of idols depend on? Issues of gender identity or sexual orientation might not be a problem but are ignored in this field. Nichome no Sakigake Coming Out naturally raises questions about heteronormativity and gender identity. Intentionally or not, their attempt to create a new music genre called *gay idols* casts doubts on the gender and heterosexuality norms in the idol industry.

Conclusion

This chapter discussed issues of the Japanese female idol industry through the case of the gay idols, Nichome no Sakigake Coming Out. Their affirmation that "Gays can be idols" is a critique of gender regulation that is pervasive in the industry and also brings into question the gender regulation of female idols. To challenge the norm, the group offers a new label: "gay idols". Through their performance, audience, fans, other idols and everyone involved in the idol industry are encouraged to question the gender norms and heterosexuality inherent in their musicking. They are idols, not artists, which means to them more than anything else. In short, the gay idols provoke the masses to think and imagine the possibility of transcending the gender norms in Japanese idol culture.

References

Mikitty, H. [@*Mikitty_sakigake*]. (2018, April 20). *病める時も 健やかなる時も』初披露でした。小指の振り付けは、誓うことは今は出来なくても、一人一人と約束できることはたくさんあるよっていう振付です。二丁目の魁カミングアウトとしては19曲目！大切に大切に歌い続けます。ちゃんと届いたのー！?！?* [We perform Yameru Toki Mo Sukoyakanaru Toki Mo for the first time. The choreography with the little finger means that we can't promise anything now, but there are many things we can pledge to each of you. This is the 19th song of Nichome no Sakigake Coming Out! I will keep and song it forever. Did you get it!?!?"]. Twitter. https://twitter.com/Mikitty_sakigake/status/987001135931129856

Mikitty, H. [@*Mikitty_sakigake*]. (2019, March 20). *最近メールで色んなところから、アーティストのリスクなし、負担ゼロで〇〇が出来ます！作れます！とかいう提案が届くんだけど、メールを最後まで読んでいくと結局はファンが大量にお金を使わないといけないシステムなんだよね。ファンが負担になる事はアーティストにとって大きなリスクなのに* [I've received some messages or suggestions like you can do XX with no risk for money! Lately, but reading it all, I realised that fans have to spend a lot of money. Even though it's high-risk for us to put a burden on fans]. Twitter.
https://twitter.com/Mikitty_sakigake/status/1108286879953125376

musicite. (2017, June 28). Ni cho-me no Sakigake Coming Out interview. https://www.musicite.net/gk/sp/post_216.php

Uno, T. (2013). *Nihon bunka no ronten* [Issues of Japanese Culture]. Chikuma Syobou.

Yagi, S. (2019, May 15). Interview: Ni cho-me no Sakigake Coming Out. *Timeout*. https://www.timeout.jp/tokyo/ja/music/interview-2tyoumenosakigakecomingout

CHAPTER 17

Popular Music and Fandom in the Smartphone Era

Masae Yoshimitsu, *University of Nagasaki*

This chapter examines the relationship between popular music, entertainment industries and fan communities after the spread and proliferation of smartphones in East Asia. One of the key concepts of popular music during the smartphone era is the participation and empathy of fans in the music's production and distribution. With popular music content being optimised for smartphones, this chapter presents a case analysis of an idol singing competition television (TV) show.

First, in preparation for the case analysis, this chapter examines representative media research to analyse the behaviour of fans. Second, a case study is conducted from the perspective of previous research. The main focus of the analysis is an idol singing competition TV show called *Idol*, created by a South Korean entertainment conglomerate and licensed in China and Japan. Finally, the similarities and differences between the South Korean, Chinese, and Japanese programmes and fan behaviour are discussed.

The research method combines content analysis of broadcast programmes and comment analysis, known as online ethnography in media research (Miller & Slater, 2000). Appropriate reference to official programme announcements and media coverage will ensure the objectivity of this consideration.

This chapter starts by examining the issue of affective economics. Then, using case studies from different East Asian countries, the chapter looks into how the involvement of empathetic and emotional audience raises concerns about the fairness and justice of televised idol singing competitions and the dangers they can introduce to producers.

Value of Active Audiences and Fans' Empathy

The *Idol* singing competition, a televised reality show, has been successful thanks to the element of interaction with viewers. It has created a huge celebrity market and prompted the reorganisation of the global media entertainment and popular music industries. Jenkins (2006) analysed the success of *Idol* from an "affective economics" perspective. Jenkins defined "affective economics" as "creating a deeper and more emotional connection between consumers and products" (p. 61). This theory finds potential value in active audiences and fans. Jenkins (2006) further explained this concept with the example of the famous Idol singing competition TV show. The prototype for this was the British TV show *Pop Idol* broadcast in 2001. Adopted globally, competition-based reality shows have become some of the most successful entertainment formats. The success of *Idol* is due to high viewer interaction, where viewers vote on the phone via text messages or on official websites. With the introduction of the voting system via smartphone or the Internet, viewers enjoy the right to decide who will survive in the show, increasing empathy for competing performers.

Information Disclosure for Justice and Fairness of Competition

Jenkins (2006) proposed that, "the media industry is trying to generate content that will attract loyals, slow down zappers, and turn casuals into fans" (p. 74). It has been pointed out that talk or gossip about shows generally has a great influence on converting zappers (channel-surfing viewers) and casuals to loyal fans. According to Jenkins (2006), "gossip is finally a way of talking about yourself through critiquing the actions and values of others" and that "reality television provides consumers with a steady stream of ethical dramas" (p. 84). Boyd (2014) also discussed the impact of gossip about reality TV celebrities in social media on young people who have "attention as a currency" (p. 147). According to Boyd, teens are learning the "value of attention, cost of gossip, power of drama" from "media-led templates such as reality TV" (p. 147). Reality TV viewers confirm morality and sociality by sharing gossip about the programme. By talking about performers' behaviour, viewers indirectly discuss the norms of their own lives. Apart from performers' behaviour, fans also use their internalised ethical standards to constantly monitor the programme's voting mechanism and competition rules. When fans find bias or unfairness in the competition, they can hold a protest or a boycott campaign.

According to Jenkins (2006), in the case of the popular singing competition show *American Idol*, "one of the primary drivers of traffic to network Web sites" was the loyal fans' "search for the hidden truth" (p. 95). The truth sought by loyal fans includes the contestants' ability to be idols, the standards of the contest, and the process of voting. If they found that commercial interests interfered with fair voting, they would request for disclosure of information such as voting details and for rectification in order to protect contestants.

Fraade-Blanar and Glazer (2017) described fan backlash as follows: "About the protest movement by fans, the 'us vs. them' mentality, fighting for a cause is exciting and romantic and it's even more true when one side does indeed have the moral high ground" (p. 246). Further, Fraade-Blanar and Glazer (2017) said that "sometimes transparency creates trust, but sometimes transparency shatters that thin veneer of authenticity" (p. 276), depending on whether the disclosed information threatens the "identity" or "status" of the show within the fan community. From this point of view, when disclosing information, it is necessary to carefully consider whether it will threaten the reality and authenticity of the programme and the loyal fans' belief in justice.

Value of East Asian Audiences and Excessive Loyalty

The reality music competition TV show *Produce 101* will be analysed as an East Asian case study. *Produce 101* was created by the South Korean entertainment conglomerate CJ E&M. The show aired from January 22, 2016 to April 1, 2016. The purpose of the programme was to create a new idol group by viewer voting via smartphone or the Internet, choosing 11 members from a pool of 101 trainees from many entertainment companies. This TV show became a hot topic on social media among young people in Asia. Subsequently, Chinese and Japanese media and entertainment companies worked together to produce and broadcast licensed versions.

According to Yu (2018), the success of the TV show was due to the show's declaration that viewers were the "national producers" and that the members of the debut group would be decided by a "100% referendum" (p.61). Han (2017) proposed that the show introduced an "active audience participation and immersion"

(p. 57) by incorporating a system of "growth using gamification strategies" (p. 57). Viewers voted in the programme's official and related website, but voting was only available to South Korean residents. Basic voting was free, but there was a charge for deciding on the group members at the final stage. Fans even raised funds and promoted their favourite participants at subway stations and bus stations. In addition, fans worked on increasing the number of views on music and video distribution sites (Liu, 2017). Since Season 2, fans have advertised not only in South Korea but also in Times Square in New York (Herman, 2017). The idol group formed from this TV programme will acquire a fan base that has proven their willingness to invest in and advertise the group. However, according to Han (2017), all of the reality music competition shows on the Mnet television channel have been luring viewership using so-called "devil editing" (p. 57) or biased editing for dramatic purposes. Fans have protested over-editing, the practice of presenting events out of sequence and broadcasting bias.

In the fourth season of *Produce X 101* (where the show focused on the top 10 or "X" contestants), loyal fans pointed out the questionable ranking operations of the programme and filed a lawsuit by forming a *Produce X 101* truth investigation committee (Yim, 2020). The show aired from May 3, 2019 to July 19, 2019. While the goal of the programme's producers was to "protect the planning company [or talent agency] and trainees", the producers were eventually detained and the employees of the talent agency were placed under house arrest (Yoo, 2019). The idol group that debuted from the programme was disbanded and the television series ended.

This South Korean case study illustrates a very deep emotional connection between the consumer and the product. Fans' empathy for idols increases in proportion to their investment. As consumption increases, emotional connections deepen and the market grows. However, over-commercialism made the programme unrealistic, triggering fans' sense of justice and becoming a significant social problem.

Excessive Investment Battle

Chinese and Japanese media and entertainment companies produced and broadcast licensed versions of the Korean programme. *Produce 101 CHINA* was co-produced by 7-D Vision and Tencent Penguin Pictures under license from Mnet owner, CJ E&M. The show, which aimed to create a Chinese girl group, aired from April 21, 2018 to June 23, 2018. On the social media platform Weibo, the show was more talked about than the soccer World Cup, which was held at the same time. The Chinese version had many more paid voting options than the South Korean version, resulting in a fan investment battle (Hangzhou Women's Clothing Network, 2018). Many of the fans who participated in the money game were called the "Super Girl Generation" and were young girls in 2005 when the *Super Girl Voice* talent show was broadcast. As this generation grew up and gained money and power, the fans voted as if the performers they were supporting were their own children. *Produce 101 CHINA* aimed to create idols that modern Chinese women could identify with. According to the news and media website *The Guardian*, competing performers who deviated from Chinese beauty standards—being white and thin—have also become popular (Kuo, 2018). While the female director of the programme sought to create a female image that would not be an object of consumption, the enhancement of the pay-to-vote system enabled the over-exploitation of female fans (Shao, 2019).

According to Liang and Shen (2016), crowdfunding by Chinese fan groups attracted the attention of investors and caused a surge in the manufacturing of Chinese idols in the creative industry. Liang and Shen (2016) further said that the women participated in these fan groups because they felt they were able to satisfy the imagined identities of their ideal self through idols. In the Chinese version of the show, the femininity and abilities of competing performers were discussed, but the fairness of large numbers of paid votes was not. However, the Chinese authorities have deemed such excessive investment games inappropriate and banned the word "idol" from being used in the show for fear of idol worship. Nevertheless, the sequel to *Produce 101 CHINA* is being produced and will be broadcast with a different title.

Dream for a Global Idol Group

Produce 101 JAPAN was broadcast in Japan from September 26, 2019 to December 11, 2019. The mission of this programme was to produce a boy band for the global music market. Yoshimoto Kogyo, a Japanese entertainment conglomerate, produced the programme with the cooperation of CJ E&M in South Korea. SoftBank affiliates broadcast the programme and provided some accompanying content. Only the first and last episodes were broadcast on the Tokyo Broadcasting System channel, while the full series was streamed online. The first part of *Produce 101 JAPAN* was filmed in a South Korean training camp. However, when the Japanese version was being broadcast, the Mnet vote manipulation investigation became a social issue. *Produce 101 JAPAN* issued an official statement, saying that they were not affiliated with the South Korean production team and used a separate voting system where votes were analysed by a group of third-party lawyers (Oricon News, 2019).

The difference between the Japanese version and those in other countries is that voting is completely free right up to the end. Fans who had watched the Korean version of *Produce 101* were pleased that they could support their favourite competitors on the show like how the Korean fans did. Japanese fans were eager to vote in support of only one idol, rather than creating an ideal idol group. While the global idol group debuting from *Produce 101 JAPAN* needed performers who had experience with global K-Pop idol groups, fans thought such an experience was unnecessary. Fans then proceeded to protest, resulting in performers dropping out of the programme. While the global idols needed to attract the support of overseas fans, Japanese fans were concerned that large-scale voting from overseas could skew the results from votes by Japanese fans. Thus, fans demanded the restriction of voting from outside Japan. As a result, the programme proceeded in a direction that made it difficult to include an international member and to promote a global fan base. The members of the boy band JO1 formed on the show consisted of only Japanese who had little experience in the performing arts. Despite the coronavirus outbreak, the group's debut single was successfully released on March 4, 2020 and became an instant hit.

Conclusion

This chapter examined the relationship between fan behaviour and reality TV entertainment, particularly the music competition TV show *Produce 101*. *Produce 101* is an entertainment programme tailored to digital-savvy East Asian youths who are encouraged to vote for the winning idols via smartphones or the Internet. Under the leadership of a media entertainment conglomerate, the programme includes a range of cross-border collaboration projects that have opened up a new youth entertainment market. However, the behaviour of fanatical youths and their sense of loyalty and justice for their idols can sometimes lead to setbacks for the show. While media and the entertainment industry need to pay more attention to the need for transparency and disclosure, it is not always a good idea to give in to fan demands. Finally, this chapter suggests that there is a need to consider ways to interactively share music that makes everyone happy.

Acknowledgements

This work was supported by JSPS KAKENHI Grant Number JP20K12405.

References

Boyd, D. (2014). *It's complicated: the social lives of networked teens*. Yale University Press.

Fraade-Blanar, Z., & Glazer, A. M. (2017). *Super fandom: How our obsessions are changing what we buy and who we are*. Profile Books Ltd.

Han, E. (2017). *Analysis of game-factor with viewer-participating-TV contents: Focus on viewing experience of idol survival program, department of content convergence* [Master's thesis, Ewha Womans University].

Hangzhou Women's Clothing Network. (2018, June 1). "Produce 101" fans' epic battle. https://xw.qq.com/cmsid/20180601A1L81M00

Herman, T. (2017, November 12). K-Pop audition shows produce big results, but cause concerns over industry's future. *Billboard*. https://www.billboard.com/articles/columns/k-town/8031250/k-pop-audition-shows-produce-big-results-south-korea-music-industry

Jenkins, H. (2006). *Convergence culture: Where old and new media collide*. New York University Press.

Kuo, L., & Wang, X. (2018, June 9). China's Beyonce: Meet Wang Ju, the pop idol breaking down beauty barriers. *The Guardian*. https://www.theguardian.com/world/2018/jun/09/chinas-beyonce-meet-wang-ju-the-pop-idol-breaking-down-beauty-barriers

Liang, Y., & Shen, W. (2016). Fan economy in the Chinese media and entertainment industry: How feedback from super fans can propel creative industries' revenue. *Global Media and China, 1*(4).

Liu, W. (2017). *Research on Training Program Transmedia: Storytelling Strategy Focused on the case of <Idolm@ster> and <Produce 101 Season 2>* [Master's thesis, Konkuk University].

Miller, D., & Slater, D. (2000). *The Internet: An ethnographic approach*. Berg.

Oricon News. (2019, November 15). PRODUCE 101 Japanese version 'No fraud' Official statement of suspicion in Korea. https://www.oricon.co.jp/news/2148810/full

Shao, M. (2018, May 24). "Creator 101" Producer Qiu Yue: What kind of idols do young people like. *Three Sounds*. http://baijiahao.baidu.com/s?id=1601610443889871525&wfr=spider&for=pc

Yim, H. (2020, January 22). X1 fans take to street to call for another shot. *The Korea Herald*. http://www.koreaherald.co.jp/view.php?ud=20200122000849

Yoo, S. (2019, December 30). "Produce 101" disgraced for the first time in 4 years ... is it good or bad for the K-pop market? *Chuo Nippo*. https://news.joins.com/article/23669217

Yu, L. (2018). *A narrative analysis of <Produce 101> Season 2, based on the competition and training* [Master's thesis, Kyung Hee University].

CHAPTER 18

Popularising Heritage and the Electronic Keyboard in Malaysia and Indonesia

Mayco A Santaella, *Sunway University*

During the 1980s, access to instruments, new recording technology, and dissemination platforms in marginal regions of Malaysia and Indonesia resulted in the development of new regional genres produced and consumed *in situ*. Using local music idioms and sung mostly in the local language, these genres became both ethnic and regional signifiers of alternative modernities (Gaonkar, 2001) until the present day. Occasionally referred to as *pop daerah* (regional pop) in Indonesia, these genres developed from local celebratory contexts and expanded the boundaries of the music and dance heritage of each locale. Such is the case of the new *dero* genre in Central Sulawesi, Indonesia and the *sangbai* in Sabah, Malaysia. This chapter discusses the two genres as the popularisation of heritage based on local music and dance idioms that continue to serve ethnic-specific functions. The analysis pays particular attention to the use of the electronic keyboard for both the development of new repertoire and the production of local performance contexts. At the micro level, *dero* and *sangbai* exemplify traditional music features, local modes of production, and regional performance contexts. At the macro level, the genres epitomise examples of aesthetics, approaches, and concomitant logics of praxis that culturally bind the "Sulu Zone" (Warren, 2007) region in the 21st century.

From *Ende* to *Dero*: Popularising Heritage Among the Pamona in Indonesia

The Pamona are the largest ethnic group of Kabupaten Poso (Poso Regency), with small settlements in neighbouring regencies. The community is linked to the historical Luwu Kingdom (now a regency in South Sulawesi). The Pamona are mostly Christian due to the presence of missionaries since the late 19th century. The Dutch missionary Albert Kruyt had a house in Poso and wrote some of the earliest accounts of the area. Some of the first photographs and accounts of *ende* were done by Albert Grubauer, a German ethnologist who spent time in Central Sulawesi during the early 20th century.

Ende is a communal structured movement system accompanied by a gong as well as one or two double-headed drums. The participants move in circular motion and, at times, hold the hand or elbow of the person next to them. This results in a shared motion and rhythm by all participants which may be more than 100 people. The movement motifs differ between the various communities, and sometimes within a single ceremony. The patterned footwork is repeated in cycles and may include gentle steps or stronger stamping motions. *Ende* movement motifs among the Pamona include the *ende ntonggola* (two steps to the right and one to the left, slightly backwards), the *ende ntoroli* (two steps to the right and one to the left) and the *ende ada* (similar to the *ende ntoroli* but without the hand-holding). Similar communal round movement systems are found among other communities in the region such as the Kaili and the Kulawi in Central Sulawesi and the Toraja in South Sulawesi (Santaella, 2019).

The popularisation of the *ende* tradition among the Pamona resulted in a new genre known as *dero*. The new *dero* became a popular form among young Pamona community members and was eventually consumed throughout Central Sulawesi as well as beyond the province. Among the Pamona, the popularisation of *ende* took different forms. The most evident was the development of new regional songs, at times characterised as *pop daerah* (regional pop), which could serve as musical accompaniment to the *dero* movements. The electronic keyboard functions as the main accompaniment to these songs, with the capacity to provide a melody, chord accompaniment, and the characteristic rhythm. The preset rhythmic pattern is usually between 70 and 80 beats per minute (BPM) in order to accompany *dero* movements. During live performances, the keyboard serves as the main instrument that accompanies both hired singers as well as audience members that may sing a song or two. Following the success of *dero* in the province, other developments took place in new dance choreographies within the *kreasi baru* (new creation) genre. Performed at numerous festivals in the district, regency, and province, the movements maintained cyclical features and included characteristic wrist patterns following the *dero* beat. The choreographies used newly composed pieces with gong and drum accompaniment and, at times, included other traditional instruments of the Pamona. Lastly, the popularisation of *dero* was heard on other local genres such as *karambangan*, which consists of solo guitar plucking accompanied by verses. In this case, the characteristic *dero* rhythm adapts to the smooth and gentle *karambangan* beat usually performed between 50 and 60 BPM.

The popularisation of *dero* was part of a national expansion of new pop *daerah* songs, which developed significantly in eastern Indonesia during the 1980s and 1990s. Probably the most famous song from eastern Indonesia was the 1993 song "Poco Poco" composed in Maluku by Arie Sapulette and popularised by Yopie Latul who sang the song with an upbeat electronic music accompaniment at the time. Similar to "Poco Poco", *dero* songs were composed and produced in the region and played during local ceremonies such as weddings. The use of the keyboard as well as electronic music beats made it easier for local studios to release albums disseminated in cassette, VCD and eventually MP3 formats. *Dero* productions reached all regencies of Central Sulawesi as well as other provinces, specially the Toraja region of South Sulawesi. The popularisation of *dero* also produced a demand for keyboard players to perform at governmental events, ceremonies, and other celebrations. Live keyboard accompaniment allowed for singing (with transposition to any key), tempo variations, and song requests. Since the late 20th century, this has been the practice for the Pamona specifically and Central Sulawesi at large until the present day.

From *Tagunggu'* and *Gabbang* to *Sangbai*: Popularising Heritage Among the Bajau in Malaysia

The Bajau is the second largest ethnic group of Sabah in Malaysia, with different communities mainly divided into east coast Bajau facing the Sulu Sea and the west coast Bajau who have settled inland mostly around Kota Belud. Among the east coast Bajau, there are communities that have lived along the coast for a number of generations, and others that continue carrying out sea-dwelling economic activities and have settled in nearby islands or in new floating villages along the coast. Regardless of dialect differences, the Bajau are *sama'* speakers, a language that binds Bajau communities in east Malaysia, the southern Philippines, and (with increased differentiations) in eastern Indonesia. Bajau communities in east Sabah and the southern Philippines also share the presence of the *gabbang* and the *tagunggu'* ensemble which accompanies the *igal* structured movement system.

The *gabbang* is a bamboo or wooden xylophone that accompanies extemporaneous verses. The *gabbang* player executes both a melody and a rhythmic accompaniment on the xylophone and usually other individuals improvise verses based on established melodies. The *tagunggu'* ensemble commonly consists of a *kulintangan* (seven to nine gong kettles laid in a row), a pair of agung (deep rim hanging gongs), and a *tambul* (double-headed cylindrical drum modeled after the western snare drum). The *kulintangan* player is accompanied by a *solembat* player who reproduces the rhythmic pattern of the *tambul* on the higher gong kettle of the *kulintangan*. The *tagunggu'* ensemble accompanies the *igal* movements characteristic of the Bajau. The *igal* movements are carried out within specific rituals (such as the *magpaii-baha'u* and *magpaigal-jin* cleansing rituals) but more commonly during *pagkawin* wedding ceremonies. During weddings, the participants may execute *igal* movements demonstrating agility and dexterity in honour of the newlyweds, and other participants may give money to the dancer in order to show appreciation for the capacity and movements of the dancer. The celebrations culminate in the *maglami-lami* part of the evening where everyone can participate in social dancing. While traditionally *maglami-lami* used to be accompanied by the *tagunggu'* ensemble (at times by the *gabbang*), the popularised genre known as *sangbai* is now commonly used during a *maglami-lami* social dancing event.

The *sangbai* genre consists of *angaleleng* or singers who deliver both through-composed and extemporaneous verses accompanied by an electronic keyboard. The genre was popularised during the 1980s and slowly began to replace the *tagunggu'* ensemble during wedding ceremonies and *maglami-lami*. The electronic keyboard reproduces rhythmic and melodic patterns of the *gabbang* and the *tagunggu'* ensemble using preset instruments such as the marimba and the drum set. "Dalling Dalling" (My Darling) is an example of a famous piece that was composed in the southern Philippines, incorporated into the *gabbang* repertoire, and then performed as *sangbai* (Ellorin, 2015). Aside from being accessible, loud, and allowing live singing, the popularity of *sangbai* is also due to its ability to accompany *igal* movements. Rather than accompanying specific forms of *igal* (as with the *tagunggu'* repertoire), the *sangbai* allows a relative liberty to improvise using an array of existing movement motifs, often developing new ones *in situ*.

Popularised Heritage at the Margins

The development of local music industries since the 1970s was supported by the use of cassettes. During this time, the genre known as *pop daerah* developed in Indonesia and included the prominent *pop Sunda* (West Java), *pop Batak* (North Sumatra), and *pop Minang* (West Sumatra). The songs had popular music features characterised by the use of western instruments, chords, and scales. But unlike national pop tunes, they were sung in the regional language, appealing to local audiences and, consequently, developing local music industries. Within these local industries, the use of keyboards became both efficient and vital during the production process. Keyboards were able to produce melodies, chords, and rhythmic accompaniment. Simultaneously, as reported by van Zanten (2014) in his analysis of *pop Sunda*, this approach standardised the pitch and scales of new popular songs. However, not all regional popular music was considered *pop daerah*. There are modern compositions and music renditions using traditional instruments in West Java that would not be considered *pop Sunda* (Subagio, 1989). Similarly, while dangdut did influence the development of some *pop daerah* songs, there are also regional renditions of the genre outside of Java such as *dangdut Minang* and *dangdut Batak*. At the margins of *pop daerah*, there are popularised renditions based on traditional music and dance that have become a genre of their own such as *dero* in Central Sulawesi and *sangbai* in Sabah.

The *dero* and *sangbai* experience is not isolated from the development of both national and local music industries. However, they are not considered regional pop, rather, popular renditions of the local heritage. This is partly due to standardised approaches to *pop daerah* with the use of western instruments, chord progressions, and a characteristic rhythmic structure with standardised tempos. In this sense, *pop daerah* often resulted in regional renditions of national pop music sung in local languages. Alternatively, both *dero* and *sangbai* use melodies, rhythmic structures, and tempos based on the local traditions. Additionally, both genres allow the execution of innovative renditions of movements based on traditional dance. Lastly, *dero* and *sangbai* are validated as modern approaches to the production of ethnic-specific celebratory contexts, developing new possibilities as they replace the performance of traditional music and dance (to which not all agree).

In order to support the execution of music idioms, dance, and a context based on local traditions, the electronic keyboard plays a fundamental role. For *dero*, the use of the electronic keyboard allows the setting of a recurring rhythm (nowadays similar to techno music) and the delivery of melodies based on both local and international tunes. The tempo variations accompany the execution of specific motifs by participants as they carry out continuous circular movements. Lastly, live accompaniment allows interaction between the musician (and singer, if there is one) with the audience and those doing *dero*, providing a modern variant of the traditional *ende* that allows for the interaction of younger community members. For *sangbai*, the use of the keyboard or *pakiring* provides a recurring rhythmic accompaniment and melodic motifs based on the *tagunggu'* and *gabbang* traditions. The recurring rhythmic patterns allow the execution of *igal* movements by numerous participants, who enjoy relative freedom to both reproduce movement motifs based on traditional *igal* as well as develop new ones. The keyboard also allows interaction accompanying the *angaleleng* or singers who, using extemporaneous verses, describe the movements, dancers, event and other features of what becomes a modern variant of the *maglami-lami* social dancing experience.

Conclusion

Since the 1980s, the electronic keyboard has played a key role in the development of new genres such as *dero* and *sangbai* in eastern Indonesia, the southern Philippines and east Malaysia. The analysis of both production and performance contexts provides an insight into the selection of instruments, rhythms and melodies that support local aesthetics. The popularisation of heritage through *dero* and *sangbai* in Central Sulawesi and the Sulu Zone respectively are examples of distinct approaches to the development of modern genres and spaces based on local celebratory contexts. Located at the margins of the nation states of Indonesia, Malaysia, and the Philippines, the genres serve as ethnic and regional signifiers of alternative modernities. Both *dero* and *sangbai* challenge national and Anglophone conceptualisations of what is considered "pop" or "popular music", and encourage academics to look into alternative experiences of popular performance genres, particularly those developed by local musicians, within a local music industry that caters to a local audience at the margin of nation states.

References

Ellorin, B. B. (2015) *Trans-cultural commodities: The Sama-Bajau music industries and identities of Maritime Southeast Asia* [Doctoral dissertation, University of Hawai'i at Mānoa].

Gaonkar, D. P. (2001). *Alternative modernities.* Duke University Press.

Santaella, M. A. (2019). "Doing Rano" among the Kaili of Central Sulawesi: A choreomusicological analysis of the body as cultural locus of the sound-movement continuum. *Asian Music, 50*(2), 33–57.

Subagio, G. (Ed.) (1989). *Apa itu lagu pop daerah* [What is regional pop]. Citra Aditya Bakti.

van Zanten, W. (2014). Musical aspects of popular music in West Java. In B. Barendregt (Ed.), *Sonic modernities in the Malay world: A history of popular music, social distinction and novel lifestyles (1930s–2000s)* (pp. 321–352). Brill.

Warren, J. F. (2007). *The Sulu Zone, 1768–1898: The dynamics of external trade, slavery, and ethnicity in the transformation of a Southeast Asian maritime state* (2nd ed.). National University of Singapore Press.

CHAPTER 19

Representing Masculinity Through the Wind: Historiography of China Wind and the Chinese Nation

Na Li, *Zhejiang Yi Gao Cultural and Creative Co, Ltd*

At the turn of the 21st century, Jay Chou developed a unique musical style under the Mandopop category known as *Zhongguo feng*, with the literal meaning of "China Wind". The meaning can also be widely interpreted as "Chinese Style", since the Chinese character *feng* (wind) is used to imply *fengge* (style). China Wind refers to a hybrid of Western popular styles and Chinese traditional or folk musical elements. This musical form has experienced great success in the broader Chinese market since it first debuted. Chou's success with China Wind has encouraged many other Taiwanese Mandopop composers and singers—for example, Leehom Wang, David Tao, and Kenji Wu—to adapt similar styles in their music, incorporating their understanding of the Chinese Style based on their cultural backgrounds.

The focus of this chapter is on the Taiwan-based China Wind style, especially that of Jay Chou, since the style was first created and defined by Taiwanese musicians and strongly associated with the works of its founder Chou. By exploring the construction of "hardness" and "softness" in this form through the production of recordings and music videos, this chapter first examines bifurcated versions of masculinity presented through male characters and performers considering "gender identity as performative" (Goffman,1979; Butler, 1990; Auslander, 2004). In addition, I also explore how the notion of "Chineseness" and the symbolised Chinese culture have been gendered. More importantly, I illustrate how, in reception, Chinese sociocultural values and the power of the nation have interacted with gender dynamics. Furthermore, through audiences' decoding of "national power", this chapter discusses the understanding of national identity and the self-identification of Chinese audiences with different cultural backgrounds in this generation. Most of the interviewees or participants of this research are university students and citizens of Mainland China, and overseas Chinese students studying in Birmingham, the United Kingdom (UK). All interviews were conducted between 2016 and 2018.

Masculinity Versions in China Wind Music

Many of the interviewees' main and first impressions of China Wind music are characterised by a sense of "chivalrous tenderness". As Interviewee A (a big fan of Jay Chou's who is in his late 20s) states, "Actually, I think *xiagu rouqing* (chivalrous tenderness) is the main theme of China Wind music, especially in Jay Chou's China Wind works".

Halberstam (1998) suggested that masculinity is constructed based on its tight link with maleness but various alternative versions of masculinities have emerged at the same time. Although the alternative versions of masculinities analysed in Halberstam's book are linked with queer or female masculinity, which is not exactly what China Wind music involves, the understanding of masculinity and especially the construction of different modes of masculinity are still useful in the case of China Wind, for example, in relation to the *wen* and *wu* male gender types presented by the male characters and performers of this style. Louie and Edwards

(1994) pointed out that *wen* and *wu* originally and specifically "refer to Zhou Wen Wang and Zhou Wu Wang"—two ancient kings of the Zhou period, whose personality traits and governing techniques resulted in two models of ruling: "Wen Wang used culture to rule and Wu Wang relied on military power" (p. 140). According to Gao (2007), the *wen-wu* concept was developed influentially in the Tang Dynasty, where these two terms had often been used for distinguishing officials based on their different talents (pp. 201–206): *wen* (scholar-officials) and *wu* (military-officials).

Therefore, *wen-wu* is a conceptual pair that is applied to construct and shape Chinese masculinity. *Wen* is often used to imply "cultured behaviour, refinement, mastery of scholarly works", while *wu* indicates qualities of "martial prowess, strength, mastery of physical arts" (Louie & Edwards, 1994; Louie, 2002; Brownell & Wasserstrom, 2002, p. 28).

In China Wind music, the masculine image of this style is mainly delivered to the audience using a visual medium (music videos) through a male martial arts hero using his swords. The presentation of his swords through visual elements constructs the hardness or strength of the male hero, showing the link between male, power and masculinity, and indicating the hero as the *wu* (武, martial abilities/physical strength) masculinity.

However, unlike the hard image presented through his physical strength, the hero is gentler and more tender towards women. The audience then perceives the soft expressions of the male role to be as distinctive as his swords; due to this sense of gentleness and softness, the hero here exhibits some features of *wen* (文, civil, sophisticated) masculinity.

However, the *wu* and *wen* masculinities are not only produced and perceived through a micro perspective, such as the two modes of male gender types, but are also linked with state nationalism

(Louie, 2014). For audiences, the cultural influences from China Wind music or the concept of the Chinese style also represent the national voice and the status of Chinese national power.

The Hardness of the Nation and *Wu* Masculinity

Many of the China Wind songs stress a particular type of Chinese culture—Chinese martial arts or Chinese *gongfu*. In screen-based products such as films and television series, Chinese *gongfu* generally symbolises the power and strength of the national spirit. Promoting themes of heroism or swordsmanship that tap into the Chinese national spirit, mainstream values and patriotic traditions is an important way for China Wind musicians to show the hardness or strength of the nation in order to connect the broadest Chinese audience. In portraying these particular themes, China Wind music videos frequently involve a hero and a villain, and the narrative usually focuses upon how the Chinese hero fights the (foreign) villain in order to save people and his country. This can be seen, for example, in the narrative of "Huo Yuan Jia" and "Nunchucks", two China Wind songs by Jay Chou.

The male protagonist in these kinds of music videos are set to a very powerful and aggressive masculine image. The hero persona and martial arts theme designed by China Wind male musicians illustrate the hard masculinity or power of China Wind music, while the production of patriotism and nationalism in this musical form shows the importance of presenting the hardness or strength of the nation—the *wu* masculinity. In other words, it is a straightforward way to display the physical strength of the nation, representing *wu* masculinity, and to link this sense of hardness with China Wind music.

The Soft Power of the Nation and *Wen* Masculinity

In addition to the presentation of hardness and *wu* masculinity, many overseas Chinese students interpret China Wind or the concept of the Chinese style as being representative of the soft power (*ruanshili*) of the nation. For them, the Chinese musical and cultural characteristics as reflected by China Wind or the idea of the Chinese style are used to show and highlight the attraction of national cultures to enhance the global status of China. Interviewee B (a PhD student studying in the UK) provides the representative statement of this opinion:

> I think the production of Chinese style and Chinese characteristics [in music] is aimed at showing our soft power to the world. We have shown our military and especially economic strength in the global stage in recent years. However, the stronger the hard power we have illustrated, the weaker the soft power has been indicated. Without the strong presentation of the soft power, our nation's comprehensive strength cannot be enhanced. Therefore, it is hard to get a higher status [for China] through international relationships. (Interviewee B, personal communication)

In contrast to the concept of hard power, the soft power, according to Joseph Nye (2003), is "the ability to get what you want by attracting and persuading others to adopt your goals". Soft power is then frequently used to refer to non-coercive elements or approaches: the "cultures, political values and foreign policies" (Nye, 2011, p. 84). In 2014, Xi Jingping, the current paramount leader of China, announced that "we should increase China's soft power, give a good Chinese narrative, and better communicate China's messages to the world" (Shambaugh, 2015). Therefore, revealing the strength of the nation through a sophisticated approach and showing the value of China's long-lasting histories and cultural heritage are considered a useful means to demonstrate the soft power of the nation. Thus, the shared sophisticated approach, the delivery of sociocultural values and the sense of softness indicate the inner relationship between soft power and soft masculinity—the *wen* masculinity.

Although the *wen-wu* concept is used both by the authorities and the masses as a tool to display the national power and its global status (Louie & Edwards, 1994), the meaning of soft power as interpreted by audiences is not identical to the context as explained by Nye or promoted by the authorities. For audiences, building the concept of a Chinese style through music, such as illustrating the folk or traditional musical elements and culture through music, is a useful means to show the soft power of the nation. However, not all cultural productions lead to soft power. China Wind artists and the style are also not officially promoted by the state or affiliated institutions as representations of the soft power of China on the international stage.

The concept of soft power is mainly used as a tool by Chinese audiences to measure national capabilities. Through the reception of China Wind music, it shows that audiences' understandings of national power are influenced by their (imagined) international reception of the Chinese nation or the Chinese identity. Through interviewees' interpretations of the connection between gender dynamics and national power, it becomes clear that searching for the meaning of China Wind or the idea of a Chinese style is not just a question of music historiography, but rather of the historiography of the nation. It indicates audiences' expectations or willingness of writing the history of the Chinese nation.

Conclusion: The "National Identity" of China Wind

The passion for and support of the China Wind style in the nation are due to symbolised sources in the music that match people's identification of national identity. The music style also satisfies their patriotic sentiments, as noted by Interviewees B and C:

> We like China Wind because we have strong national dignity. With the trend of globalisation and China's quick socio-economic growth in 2000s, we need to have something that can represent our Chinese identity from the cultural aspect. China Wind has become such a popular music type because it achieves the goal; it speaks for us [Chinese]. (Interviewee B, personal communication)

> We like China Wind music not only because we are familiar with the Chinese tunes or instruments but also it matches our patriotic heart. (Interviewee C, personal communication)

The majority of the interviewees, especially university students, attribute China Wind's popularity to the fact that "China Wind represents the value of Chinese cultures and it speaks for us [the Chinese]". The interviewees perceive and define China Wind as "our music". They believe that China Wind represents an image of national identification of the Chinese people despite the fact that this style was originally created by Taiwan-based musicians.

As Bhabha (1994) stated, "the question of identification is always the production of an image of identity and the transformation of the subject in assuming the image" (p. 45). Chinese popular music, from its beginning in the 1920s Shanghainese Pop, has served as a mirror of social reality for specific social conditions. However, China Wind, on the contrary, does not completely represent social reality due to its symbolic Chinese cultural elements. When China Wind music first appeared in public in 2000, tension between Mainland China and Taiwan was exacerbated after the Democratic Progressive Party (DPP) in Taiwan won the presidency with the election of Chen Shuibian. The Chinese mainland authorities insisted on the "One China" principle, while Taiwan's DPP claimed its position as an independent authority. Consequently, audiences on the mainland and in Taiwan, as a result of their different educational and political systems, started fighting for their own understanding of national identification through the Internet and social media. This manifested more recently in the Vicky Zhao and Zhou Ziyu incidents. The main point of contention between audiences from the mainland and Taiwan, aside from their different understanding of democracy, is the difference in self-identity, particularly of being Chinese and Taiwanese. Taiwanese audiences may stress the difference between these two communities, whereas mainland audiences insist on their sameness. However, more recently, statements and emotions on this topic have become more forceful between the mainland and Taiwanese audiences, as can be seen in the Chinese social media Weibo posts and comments.

China's rich historical and cultural heritage as evidenced in China Wind music provides audiences with a sense of "us" or "national pride" within different interpretations. Audiences' various understandings of China Wind music and the "Chinese nation" reflect pertinent and widespread historiographical debates happening outside of academia in this generation. Audiences from different Chinese communities may have their own dialogues with the music based on their shared cultural memories or unique social experiences, as suggested by Wang (2011). China Wind music or the concept of Chinese style allows musicians to produce and promote their music without the restriction of place, space or political systems, and also provides the text for Chinese audiences in different regions to rethink and re-explore their identities within different sociocultural contexts.

References

Auslander, P. (2004). I wanna be your man: Suzi Quatro's musical androgyny. *Popular Music, 23*(1), 1–16. https://doi.org/10.1017/s0261143004000030

Bhabha, H. K. (1994). *The Location of Culture.* Routledge.

Brownell, S., & Wasserstrom, J. N. (2002). *Chinese femininities/Chinese masculinities: A reader.* University of California Press.

Butler, J. (1990). *Gender trouble: Feminism and the subversion of identity.* Routledge.

Gao, M. S. (2007). *Zhongguo zhonggu zhengzhi de tansuo* [Exploration of Chinese politics]. Taiwan Five South Book Publishing Company Limited.

Goffman, E. (1979). *Gender advertisements.* Harvard University Press.

Halberstam, J. (1998). *Female masculinity.* Duke University Press.

Louie, K. (2002). *Theorising Chinese masculinity: Society and gender in China.* Cambridge University Press.

Louie, K. (2014). Chinese masculinity studies in the twenty-first century: Westernizing, easternizing and globalizing wen and wu. *NORMA, 9*(1), 18–29. https://doi.org/10.1080/18902138.2014.892283

Louie, K., & Edwards, L. (1994). Chinese masculinities: Theorizing wen and wu. *East Asian History, 8*, 135–148.

Nye, J. S. (2003, January 10). Propaganda isn't the way: Soft power. *International Herald Tribune.* http://www.belfercenter.org/publication/propaganda-isnt-way-soft-power

Nye, J. S. (2011). *The future of power.* Public Affairs.

Shambaugh, D. (2015, June 16). China's soft-power push: The search for respect. *Foreign Affairs.* https://www.foreignaffairs.com/articles/china/2015-06-16/china-soft-power-pus

Wang, Y. W. (2011). The transition in national identity and popular music in Taiwan: Chou-style in Mandopop. *Cultural Hybridity: Remix and Dialogic Culture.*

CHAPTER 20

Is "HINOMARU" a Patriotic Song?: From the Point of View of Reception

Nene Taira, *Kansai University*

In 2018, the song "Hinomaru" by Japanese rock band RADWIMPS became a topic of controversy on the Internet due to allegations of nationalism present in the song. In 2016, the band had released "Zenzenzense", the theme song of a successful animated film *Your Name.* (*君の名は。*), and it became a huge hit reaching number one on the *Billboard* Japan Hot 100. In 2019, they released their 11th album *Weathering with You,* which was used as the soundtrack for another Japanese animated film *Weathering with You.* This album also garnered a lot of attention. These theme songs were performed at NHK Kohaku Uta Gassen, the annual New Year's Eve television special viewed by a wide audience across generations. Today, RADWIMPS is one of the representative J-pop artists.

RADWIMPS released the song "HINOMARU" on June 6, 2018. Among the central themes of the song is one's strong attachment to the nation. The title refers to the national flag of Japan that depicts a red disc symbolising the sun in the centre of a white background. The lyrics of the song include phrases from the old form of the Japanese language, such as *okuni no mitama* (the spirit of the country) and *saa iza yukan* (come on, let's go). The slow tempo and distinctive sounds of the opening drums and bells create a majestic atmosphere. This song was recorded as a coupling track for the single "Catharsist". The title track "Catharsist" was used by the Japanese television network Fuji Network System as the theme song for the 2018 FIFA World Cup tournament. However, "HINOMARU", the track on the B-side, caused a stir on the Internet, with many praising and also denigrating the song. Ishido (2018) reported:

> The lyrics have become a hot topic of conversation online, with a variety of opinions for and against the song. Some fans praised it, saying, "I want it to be a national anthem". A fan transcribed the lyrics into a notebook and tweeted, "For the first time ever, I wanted to write them and I was obsessed with writing them". There are many critical comments on the Internet, such as "I'm horrified", "Here comes something amazing again", and "A song that looks like it was created by someone who isn't even a right-winger writing lyrics innocently". (Ishido, 2018)

In fact, there were many differing opinions on the song on the Internet. Some lauded the song as a prayer for Japan's 2011 earthquake and tsunami recovery, and thought of it as a cheering song. Some criticised the song as being akin to a war song, while others called it a patriotic song. Some researchers were wary about the song being called patriotic, as patriotism in Japan is often associated with an exclusive ideology. Exclusive ideology appears in hate speech against Koreans living in Japan, which has become a social problem in recent years. Patriotism and the rights of the Japanese people are often claimed as the reason for excluding people with foreign roots. Therefore, people were concerned that those who praised the song might be xenophobic or chauvinistic.

However, there are several factors that are not clarified in the preceding problem proposals. First, the articles reporting on the controversy have not disclosed why people's opinions are divided. Second, the analysis which assumes "HINOMARU" as being a patriotic song does not consider the opinion of those who do not interpret the song as being patriotic. The concept that people take away from the song is not necessarily patriotism with an exclusive ideology. For some, the song may remind them of their love for the everyday aspect of living in the country. The question we have to ask here is how people received "HINOMARU". The first point that requires clarification is thus what is the song received *as*. The second point that requires clarification is the reason why the attitudes of people who listened to the song are different.

Method

Tweet Content Analysis and Interview Survey

In this study, content of tweets was analysed and interviews were conducted. The tweets subject to content analysis were collected using the "Advanced Search" feature on Twitter. This feature allows users to narrow down search results by combining words or dates (Twitter Help Center, n.d.). The tweets were searched and collected with two narrowing criteria:

- **Tweets as examples of various receptive attitudes:** Tweets containing all the keywords "hinomaru song" and written in Japanese between June 5 and June 10, 2018 were collected on December 28, 2019.
- **Tweets showing differences in attitudes towards reception of patriotic songs:** Tweets containing all the keywords "hinomaru patriotic" and written in Japanese between June 7 and June 10, 2018 were collected from December 26 to December 27, 2019.

Interviews were conducted from November 12 to December 4, 2019 at various locations in Osaka, Japan. The subjects of the interview survey were students and members of society living in Japan selected by snowball sampling. Snowball sampling is a method of increasing the number of samples by asking one survey participant to introduce the next survey participant.

Results and Discussion

Four Types of Reception

People's reception of "HINOMARU" can be divided into four major types (Figure 1). The types of reception are based on two axes, "Approximation to its reception as a patriotic song" and "Perspective that shaped the attitudes of the people who received the song".

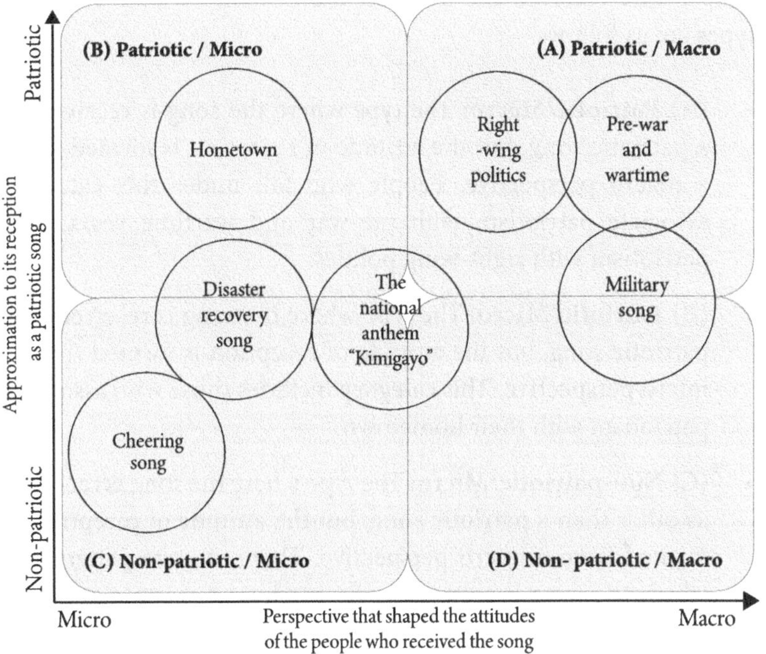

FIGURE 1 Four types of reception to "HINOMARU"

The first axis represents an approximation to the reception of the song as a patriotic song. The interpretation of the song as patriotic is found in the preceding arguments and analyses, and is one of the mainstream receptions. The song was not only received as a patriotic song, but also associated with other songs such as the national anthem "Kimigayo", rock songs, disaster recovery songs and cheering songs.

The second axis represents the perspectives that shaped the attitudes of those who received the song. The perspectives can be divided into micro and macro; micro is an emotional and intuitive perspective, while macro is a logical and objective one.

The reception of the song was categorised into four major types, with the approximation to its reception as a patriotic song on the vertical axis and the perspective that shaped the attitudes of the people who received the song on the horizontal axis. The four types are as follows:

- **(A) Patriotic/Macro:** The type where the song is received as a patriotic song, but the attitude of reception is formed from a macro perspective. People who fall under this category associate patriotism with pre-war and wartime years, and patriotism with right-wing politics.
- **(B) Patriotic/Micro:** The type where the song is received as a patriotic song, but the attitude of reception is formed from a micro perspective. This category includes those who associate patriotism with their hometown.
- **(C) Non-patriotic/Micro:** The type where the song is received as other than a patriotic song, but the attitude of reception is formed from a micro perspective. There are two patterns in which the song is seen as partly patriotic but contains other interpretations. The first pattern is that the song is similar to the Japanese national anthem "Kimigayo", while the second is where it is received as a disaster recovery song. In another pattern where the song is not interpreted as patriotic but in a completely different way, the song is received as a cheering song instead.
- **(D) Non-patriotic/Macro:** The type where the song is received as anything other than a patriotic song, but the attitude of reception is formed from a macro perspective. An example of a classification of this type is the reception of

the song as a military song. However, there were tweets that overlapped with tweets associating patriotism with the pre-war and wartime periods, or type (A). According to Tsujita, the categorisation of music produced during the wartime years is vague. Furthermore, the use of patriotic and military songs is not clearly separate (Tsujita, 2011). As a result, it is difficult to make a clear distinction between type (A) and the reception of a song as a military song as there will be some overlap between the two.

Conclusion

To summarise, "HINOMARU" is not only seen as a patriotic song but has also been interpreted in a variety of ways using different perspectives. The survey found that interpretations and receptions can be divided into four main types.

The future direction for this study is to try to unravel why attitudes towards the reception of the song are divided. What is the difference between those who regard it as a patriotic song and those who consider it as something else? What is the difference between people with an emotional, intuitive, micro perspective and those with a rational, logical, macro perspective? The underlying social factors need to be identified.

Finally, I will address the theory of a divided society, which has received much attention in recent years, as a hypothesis of the social factors dividing the reception of the song. This divide can be succinctly summarised by Shiobara (2019), who defined Japan's divided society as "conflicts of interest and inequalities between different categories of people, and interaction and contact between those people has decreased and mutual hostility has grown and a situation where the imagination of the other person is declining" (p. 110).

Moreover, the relationship between social stratification and the distribution of knowledge is a factor that diminishes the imagination of the opponent. According to Shiobara (2017), "[i]magination is an effort to understand others and society through the use of knowledge" (p. 21). All the same, the intellectual effort to use that imagination will be limited "by the different modes of knowledge and the way it is distributed across different social classes" (Shiobara, 2017, p. 21). In other words, the Japanese society will remain divided because knowledge belonging to each social class is different, making the achievement of understanding difficult despite imagination.

Can the hypothesis that people are divided because of different knowledge have something to do with people's reception of songs? This can be an issue to be studied in the future, which may include considerations of the meaning of the word "knowledge".

References

Ishido, S. (2018, June 8). RADWIMPS' new song "HINOMARU" caused a sensation, "in the name of God of the land of the rising sun". *Huffpost.* https://www.huffingtonpost.jp/2018/06/08/radwimps_a_23454012/

Shiobara, Y. (2017). *The Sociology of division and dialogue: Imagination for living in a global society.* Keio University Press.

Shiobara, Y. (2019). Exclusionism and multiculturalism in divided societies: Cases of Japan and Australia. *Quadarnte, 21*, 107–120. http://repository.tufs.ac.jp/bitstream/10108/93321/1/ifa021011.pdf

Tsujita, M. (2011). *The complete collection of war songs: The age of nationalism and ideology read in lyrics.* Shakaihyoronsha.

Twitter Help Center. (n.d.). How to use advanced search. *Twitter.* https://help.twitter.com/ja/using-twitter/twitter-advanced-search

CHAPTER 21

Music Heals: An Analysis of BTS' Fan Song "Magic Shop"

Nur Lina Anuar, *UCSI University*

In the late spring of 2013, a seven-member hip-hop boy band from a homogenous country of South Korea debuted in a heavily saturated world of commercial K-pop. Like many new idol groups from small companies, the group BTS (방탄소년단 bangtansonyeondan) struggled to find fame. However, they continued working on reinventing themselves and began finding their footing in the punishing Korean music industry two years later, by presenting theoretic storylines in their music videos with alternative R&B sounds that suited a more commercial market. The year 2017 saw them break into the Western music world in the United States and they quickly became a global sensation, even making it to *Time Magazine*'s Top 100 Most Influential People of 2019. This chapter examines the music and lyrics of the group's fan song, "Magic Shop", from the *Love Yourself* album series and how their fans, who go by the acronym ARMY, have used this song to help them get through their most challenging days.

K-pop Fandom Culture

Fans are an integral part of a music artist's career. They are the ones who would take a keen interest in the artist and contribute to the artist's popularity. In return, the artist can show, in various ways, their appreciation to their fans for their enthusiasm and support. This can be in the form of fan events like meet-and-greets or conventions. The culture of fan conventions or meetings began as early as the 1940s. These are events where fans of particular TV shows, movies or even comic books participate in activities hosted by an organiser. In South Korea, fandom culture is well known in the music and anime industry (Jeon, 2015). Fandom culture began in the 1970s and has since steadily grown in popularity. The culture exploded in the 2000s when fan clubs began emerging more frequently, reflecting the popularity of the first-generation idol groups at their peak. It was also a time when the Internet became much more developed and accessible in South Korea. Artists found various ways like fan meetings and events to connect and interact with their fans, and show their appreciation for the support they receive.

BTS was formed by a then-small company, Big Hit Entertainment, and in the early days of the group in 2013, they met with fans in venues that had fewer attendees than a wedding reception. There would be less than 40 people at an unofficial fan meeting, which took place at a storefront after hours at the end of the day. The BTS members also had to wear jerseys with their names printed on the back for fans and people to recognise and remember their names (beansss, 2019). Fast forward to seven years later, their fan meetings now draw huge crowds; there were some 69,000 attendees at the BTS 5th Muster: Magic Shop[1] event in June 2019, and 150,000 attendees in total at the Japan Official Fan Meeting Vol. 5: Magic Shop across one weekend each in November and December 2019.

BTS has written songs dedicated to their fans, with lyrics pronouncing "Thank you for being by our side for the last three years" (from a track titled "I Know", released during the band's 3rd anniversary) and "Thanks for believing in someone like me, dealing with all these tears and wounds" (from their first official fan song titled "2! 3!"). Based on that context, this chapter analyses the music and lyrics of BTS' second official fan song "Magic Shop" found in two of the three *Love Yourself* album series *Tear* and *Answer* (Jeon, 2018a, 2018b).

Research Question

The process of music writing can go through countless revisions with the help of collaborators, and BTS is known to write their own music and lyrics with the help of a song-writing team under Big Hit Entertainment. Through their songs, BTS tells stories of personal struggles and challenges, and share real stories of current agendas and trends in music. As shared by the band's producer Pdogg, that approach is how BTS amasses fans along their journey as music artists, and these fans grow with them every step of the way (Min, 2017).

Language has features of pitch, rhythm and tempo which are communicative emotions in speech. These features provide the basis for humans to have an innate musical sense, thus being able to feel the emotions through music without understanding the lyrics (Patel, 2008; Slevc & Okada, 2015). With many hands involved in the composition of songs, it is fascinating how fans claim to feel connected to a song when it is written by so many people. Fans commonly share that they find solace and healing in BTS' songs due to the relatable factor that these songs have. So, how is it that the songs resonate so deeply with fans who claim that BTS has emotionally changed their lives for the better?

Methodology

It was with their *Love Yourself* album series that saw their fanbase grow tremendously outside of South Korea. BTS albums have strong themes of youth, love and empowerment. These thematic concepts have been one of the factors for the success of their trilogy series. In the *Love Yourself* trilogy, the group sings about the excitement of love ("Trivia 承: Love"), the pains of betrayal ("Fake Love") and the enlightenment of self-love ("Epiphany"). In a narrative form, these songs—which contain social commentaries on how judgmental a society is—has made their music relatable universally, and thus, able to reach out to a wider audience. This is mixed with other styles like Latin, jazz and rock, creating new experimental sounds and music styles. Lyrically, BTS writes mainly in Korean, with English words used sporadically.

I ran a quick questionnaire participated by mainly Malaysian and Singaporeans, and 77.7% of the 198 respondents selected "Magic Shop" as one of their BTS "feel good" songs (the other being "Anpanman"). Both these songs are found in the *Love Yourself: Tear* and *Love Yourself: Answer* albums of the trilogy series. While the slower ballads lend themselves to emotional healing (statements such as "feel better", "heals my soul", "gives me hope" are mentioned by respondents), their up-tempo songs help lift spirits and motivate listeners to carry on and power through difficult times (respondents used words like "pump up" and "psyched up").

Analysis

"Magic Shop" was primarily written by Jungkook, the youngest member of BTS, who wrote it with their fans in mind (KBS World, 2018). The song lists three other BTS members who contributed to the writing of the lyrics, along with local and international collaborators. Jungkook mentioned in a press conference that the song is a message telling fans that when things get tough, one is welcomed to visit the "magic shop" (Doyoubangtan, 2018). At the magic shop, visitors who come with concerns, worries or fears are welcomed by the shop owners who offer advice by sharing their own stories and experiences. In this case, the shop owners are BTS and the visitors are the fans. The storyline of this song bears a slight resemblance to the book *The Miracles of the Namiya General Store* by Keigo Higashino, published in 2012.[2]

"Magic Shop" is written in a major key with four diatonic chords used throughout the entire song. The simplicity of the harmonic progression reflects one of the main characteristics of the pop style. The verse-chorus form is also a typical pop-style song structure, whereby the verse is rapped and the chorus sung. "Magic Shop" starts with a fade-in swoop, giving an auditory image of one being sucked into a realm and standing at or in front of the magic shop. The opening melody is speech-like, with the soft baritone of member V whispering, "I know that you're hesitating because, even if you speak your true heart, it all comes back as scars". This is followed by the next phrase, which is melodically similar to the first, but with the more affirmative tenor voice of Jungkook singing, "I won't say obvious things like 'cheer up', but I'll rather share with you my story". Even without understanding the translation or meaning of the words, the tone colour and articulation of the selected member singing the melody gives listeners an auditory image of a possible meaning of the text that is being sung.

At a tempo of 75 beats per minute, "Magic Shop" is on the slower spectrum of a human heartbeat which is between 60 and 100 beats per minute. This would give listeners a sense of unhurried calmness, although the sample beats used are groovy enough to reciprocate the rhythmic rap verses. In the rap verses, BTS tells the story of their relationship with ARMY. The first rap verse shares how BTS believes that the support they receive from fans can help the group overcome doubts from naysayers. Group member and leader, RM, raps that BTS and ARMY will fall back on each other for support no matter how big the fandom grows. The second rap verse opens with member J-Hope singing a repetitive melodic phrase referencing the stages of a flower's life cycle similar to moments in one's life (Figure 1). Ironically, while the lyrics compare flowers at various stages of their bloom to the emotional ups and downs in life, the melody is repeated in the four phrases of this second verse. Then, member Suga raps about how BTS members always compare themselves to others, resulting in them being consumed by their own greed. The lyrics can be interpreted as BTS not wanting their fans to be hurt by the words of haters.

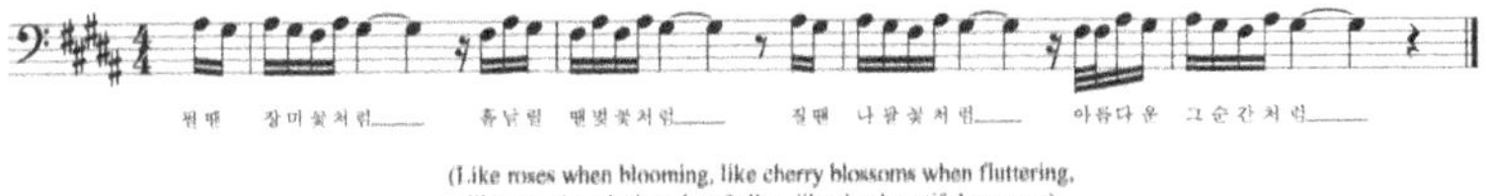

FIGURE 1 Transcription of Second Rap Verse of "Magic Shop"
Source: Tan (2021)

The pre-chorus has a soothing melody, with its first phrase "On a day I hate being myself, on a day I want to disappear forever" being sung in whispery tones by member Jin. The phrase is sung from the perspective of a fan, which then shifts back to BTS in the next melodic phrase telling the fan to create an imaginary door. This is followed by the melodic phrase "Once you open the door and enter, this place will wait for you" sung in a more assertive style by member Jimin. The final phrase of the pre-chorus goes "It's okay to believe Magic Shop will comfort you". The ending of this phrase in the pre-chorus is the highest point or climax of the entire song, which is uncommon in pop songs. Normally, the climax of a song is identified by a modulation to a different key or is at the end of a last chorus with a dramatic slowdown in tempo leading to a pause. This brings prominence to the importance of BTS' lyrics in their songs, highlighting that storytelling is the essence of their music.

The chorus has a laidback feel with repetitive pitches in the melody. The lyrics, which correspond to a stagnancy similar to a person relaxing, read "Drinking a cup of hot tea, looking up to the galaxy" and are followed by a stepwise ascending melodic line with the words "You'll be alright, oh here it is Magic Shop". This presumably gives the assurance that everything is alright because the Magic Shop is a safe place. Musically, the diatonic melody and harmonies further support the familiarity factor to the auditory senses, giving listeners a sense of calmness. In the bridge, BTS shares how they too have fears of life's uncertainties. However, they sing that the answers to those fears and uncertainties are all within ourselves.

In the song, BTS refers to themselves as the "Magic Shop" and their fans the "galaxy". Both these words have significance for both BTS and the fans, and they occur at the highest point in the entire song (Figure 2). The word "galaxy" is mentioned six times throughout the song, in both Korean and English. The word has more prominence in the bridge, particularly when the group comes together to sing in the final phrase: "You'll find the galaxy inside you". It gives a two-way emphasis that: (a) the galaxy implies that self-belief is within one's self, and (b) their fans, the ARMY, are the most important people to them.

FIGURE 2 Emphasis on the Phrase "Magic Shop" and Word "Galaxy"
Source: Tan (2021)

Respondents from the questionnaire shared that the melody and singing voices of BTS were the elements that made them feel happy and content. A respondent shared that the lyrics resonate strongly with her and she understood that the main message was to not give up and that "even if today was a bad day, there is still a chance that tomorrow will be a good day". Other respondents also shared that

"Magic Shop" is their go-to song to lift their spirits. In general, the message mirrors a common saying that "there is light at the end of every tunnel" and that the light is actually one's own self.

Conclusion

From the beginning, BTS has always maintained that the narrative style of their songs is a way for the younger generation to connect with their music (IZE Korea, 2019). The song "Magic Shop" does just that. It tells the story of a tired soul finding comfort in an imaginary realm called the Magic Shop. BTS reciprocates this idea by finding their own comfort and healing in their fans, ARMY (Kim, 2019). It is especially heart-warming when both artist and fans sing together, "So show me, I'll show you". BTS' music, as enhanced with relatable stories in their lyrics, has brought healing to a generation of listeners and help them understand themselves and each other. Music critics from *Rolling Stone* and *Billboard* have reviewed BTS music positively, praising the storytelling technique in the lyrics and the new creative beats, sounds and styles in their songs (Herman, 2018; Leight, 2018). It is clear that BTS does not only endear itself to existing fans, but also to new listeners as they continue their music career.

The sheer popularity of BTS remains a fascination to people who are unfamiliar with the group or K-pop in general. Is it really the music which has contributed to the hype surrounding them today? Or could it just be pure interest in the group that has gotten people to take notice and unconsciously become fans? Nevertheless, the impact of BTS on the global music industry is largely credited to how their music resonates with fans across all ages, genders and also borders.

Since BTS is into the second cycle of their seven-year contract, there is much to look forward to and listen out for as they continue to work on their ever-evolving craft. It would be interesting to see where else their music can go now, since they have covered the themes of adolescence and young adults, self-doubt and self-love. One thing is for sure, to quote South Korean president Moon Jae-in: "Their melody and lyrics transcend regional borders, language, culture, and institutions" (Peters, 2018). This suggests that future scholarly research on BTS should delve deeper into the storytelling technique in their lyrics and how they craft their music to share with their listeners and fans.

Notes

[1] Muster is a combination of a concert and a fan meeting held annually by BTS for their fans, ARMY. For such events, BTS "musters" or assembles the army which, in this case, refers to the fans.

[2] *The Miracles of the Namiya General Store* is a novel about a store owner Namiya who accepts letters from people seeking advice. The story has multiple characters who are unrelated but interwoven through time and space.

References

beansss. (2019, October 30). In light of BTS's "Speak Yourself" finale, netizens recall the boys' first unofficial fan meeting with only 32 fans present. *Allkpop*. https://www.allkpop.com/article/2019/10/in-light-of-btss-speak-yourself-finale-netizens-recall-the-boys-first-unofficial-fan-meeting-with-only-32-fans-present

BTS pledges to "tell the story of our generation with our lyrics". (2019). *IZE Korea*. https://www.ize.co.kr/articleView.html?no=2019040102057238751

Doyoubangtan, A. (2018, May 24). Press conference for Love Yourself: Tear. *BTS Translation*. https://doyoubangtan.wordpress.com/2018/05/24/press-conference-for-love-yourself-tear

Herman, T. (2018, August 25). BTS reflect on life & love on uplifting "Love Yourself: Answer". *Billboard*. https://www.billboard.com/articles/columns/pop/8472127/bts-love-yourself-answer-album-review

Jeon, S. (2015). *Yeon-yeindeul paendeom-e daehan midieoui 연예인들 팬덤에 대한 미디어의 영향력* [The impact of media reporting on the celebrity to fandom] [Master's thesis, Inha University].

Jeon, J. K. (2018a). Magic Shop [Recorded by BTS]. On *Love Yourself: Answer* [CD]. Big Hit Entertainment.

Jeon, J. K. (2018b). Magic Shop [Recorded by BTS]. On *Love Yourself: Tear* [CD]. Big Hit Entertainment.

KBS World (2018, May 25). *BTS "Beautiful" (美친) Press Conference Part 2 [SUB : ENG]* [Video]. YouTube. https://youtu.be/60ltyOWDzfc

Kim, Y. (2019). Review 13. In *BTS: the Review: A comprehensive look at the music of BTS* (pp. 227–228). RH Korea.

Leight, E. (2018, May 18). Review: BTS' "Love yourself: Tear" is K-pop with genre-hopping panache. *Rolling Stone*. https://www.rollingstone.com/music/music-album-reviews/review-bts-love-yourself-tear-is-k-pop-with-genre-hopping-panache-630441/

Patel, A. D. (2008). *Music, language, and the brain*. Oxford University Press.

Peters, M. (2018, May 28). South Korean President Moon Jae-in congratulates BTS on first No. 1 album. *Billboard.* https://www.billboard.com/articles/columns/k-town/8458071/south-korean-president-moon-jae-bts-first-no-1-album-billboard-200-chart-kpop

Min, K. (2017, May 26). Pdogg discusses BTS's secret recipe: Producer talks about how they met and how they put song together. *Koreajoongangdaily.joins.com.* https://koreajoongangdaily.joins.com/2017/05/26/etc/Pdogg-discusses-BTSs-secret-recipe-Producer-talks-about-how-they-met-and-how-they-put-song-together/3033870.html

Slevc, L. R., & Okada, B. M. (2015). Processing structure in language and music: a case for shared reliance on cognitive control. *Psychonomic Bulletin & Review, 22*, 637–652

Tan, P. S. (2021). Transcription of Second Rap Verse of "Magic Shop". [Transcription].

Tan, P. S. (2021). Emphasis on the Phrase "Magic Shop" and Word "Galaxy". [Transcription].

CHAPTER 22

"Malaysia Truly Asia": A Nation-Branding Campaign Song Firmly Rooted in Multi-Ethnic Origins

Shazlin Amir Hamzah, ***Institute of Ethnic Studies (KITA), Universiti Kebangsaan Malaysia***

The song "Malaysia Truly Asia" was composed in 2000 specifically for the Visit Malaysia campaign by the Ministry of Tourism, Arts and Culture. Written by the legendary musical maestro and National Laureate Dato' Ahmad Nawab, the song made its debut during the Citrawarna Malaysia (Colours of Malaysia) festival held in conjunction with the tourism campaign. The song was specifically interspersed with musical elements of the three biggest ethnic communities of Malaysia—the Malay, Chinese, and Indian. Its music arrangement was a combination of the *kompang* (single-headed frame drum), Kelantan *Wayang Kulit* (shadow puppetry) music, *serunai* (quadruple reed wind instrument), *tabla* (a pair of double-headed drums), accordion and *seruling* (flute). Essentially, popular patriotic music plays a significant role in depicting a country as a tourist destination in a national tourism campaign. In addition, popular patriotic music specifically has the ability to represent and conjure emotions of affinity for the country. For Malaysians, these songs connect them to the predominant ideology of an "authority-defined" national identity—one that links the Malay ethno-national politics with a British colonial past (Shamsul, 1996).

Songs are malleable as they can be created to tell stories, and these stories help create a collective imagination of a group. This function is similar to how, as Anderson (1983) stressed, print-capitalism forms narratives for individuals in a society to think about and relate themselves to others in ways that provide them with a sense of belonging, solidarity and national identity. In Malaysia, music is a cultural marker and local musicians are often expected to play a significant role in the process of nation-building or branding (Chopyak, 1987). In 1946, Radio Malaya was set up as a government-owned broadcaster which propagated "authority-defined" (Shamsul, 1996) communication and messages through music. A little while later, television was introduced in the country and Radio Television Malaysia (RTM) was established in 1963. RTM began broadcasting locally composed and arranged music that promoted the national culture (Chopyak, 1987).

A nation-branding project results in the diffusion of a country's good reputation. It is largely a way of creating symbols for a particular society to associate and identify themselves with an "imagined community" (Anderson, 1983). Similarly, a product's brand image is created and disseminated through advertising. The vast difference between the brand image of a product and a country is that the reputation created by the image of the former is mainly for commercial purposes. For countries, the brand image has a profound impact on the way the country is perceived (Shazlin, 2019). Music, songs and jingles are essential components in every advertising and branding campaign. More interestingly, music for nation-branding campaigns is often one that reflects a shared history and culture as it contains a collective myth and symbols that hold the identity of the people together (Dinnie, 2009). Using information from an interview conducted with Ahmad Nawab, the composer of the song "Malaysia Truly Asia", I discuss the origins of this popular tune as a nation-branding tool in Malaysia. This song has been a part of a destination-branding campaign targeted at a global market since it was first composed, and has evaded the often-contested meanings of a nation for the postcolonial state that is Malaysia (Shamsul & Sity, 2012).

Branding the Malaysian Nation

According to Jordan (2013), nation branding is the self-conscious effort taken by governments to produce a particular image of the nation state. This effort involves the invention and reinvention of a political or social reputation. When the Federation of Malaya achieved its independence from the British in 1957, the dawn of modern nation-building began for the postcolonial state. It must be emphasised that for postcolonial countries, the "state" is separate from the "nation". The conceptual definition of the "state" is an entity that has a rule of law, a territory and citizenship, while "nation" is an imagined community. The state existed and was left as a legacy by the colonials who used it to fulfil their colonial needs. The main governance structure of the country, once it achieves independence, remains as that of the colonial state (Shamsul & Sity 2012). Essentially, what existed at the time of independence was a country that was primarily dominated by the Malays (Chopyak, 1987; Shazlin, 2016). This was the beginning of the nation-branding project for the country, where the government earnestly placed efforts at inventing symbols and mobilising them to educate people about their nation and its national identity.

In Malaysia, achieving independence required unity among the various ethnic groups. Prior to independence, what existed was not a unified sense of Malayan nationalism but three streams of nationalism tied to ethnicity—the Malays, Chinese, and Indians (Chopyak 1987; Salleh 2005; Shazlin 2016). Music, particularly through mass media and education, was given an important role in the process of unification by the Malaysian government. Popular patriotic songs were commissioned by the government specifically to serve the purpose of nation-building and have remained powerful from constant repetition on the radio. Due to malleable characteristics of songs, popular patriotic songs have the ability to become the border markers in the state.

This chapter is based on facts drawn from an interview with composer Ahmad Nawab, covering his life experience as a musician in Malaysia from the 1950s until today. In a span of six decades, he has composed over 2,000 songs and almost 70 singers from all over the region have recorded his songs (Augustin & Lochhead, 2015). His views are a manifestation of the imagined national ideals of an everyday individual, rooted in a belief of a shared collective and historical identity in a multi-ethnic region.

Dato' Seri Ahmad Nawab: Composing "Malaysia Truly Asia"

Ahmad Nawab was born in Penang in 1933 to Nawab Khan who, having originated from Pakistan, had travelled as a musician in an opera group known as Wayang Parsi for performances around the archipelago. Nawab's childhood in Penang was amidst a colourful melting pot of people from various ethnic origins from Minangkabau, Sumatra to Malabari, India and all the way to Teochew and Hainan in China. During the 1950s, Penang was a bustling multi-ethnic cosmopolitan point of commerce in the region where modern and popular culture flourished. Penang became the centre for local syncretic performances such as *wayang parsi*, *bangsawan* opera theatre, *boria* and *dabus* (Syed Othman, 2008; Mohd Haqkam, 2010). Night clubs and hotels offering spaces for singing and entertainment mushroomed like never before to service the influx of people on the island.

Nawab moved to Kuala Lumpur at the age of 20 and became a saxophonist for the Bukit Bintang Cabaret in BB Park, a popular carnival park in Kuala Lumpur. By 1960, he joined RTM and was the first Malay to play the baritone saxophone with Orkestra RTM. By the 1970s, he had already helped hone the skills of various singers such as Salamiah Hassan, Uji Rashid, Sharifah Aini, siblings Khadijah and Latiff Ibrahim, Jamal Abdillah, Datuk Shake (Hafidah, 2000), and eventually Ramlah Ram in the 1980s. In 1988, Ram became the first Malay artist to be awarded with the Double Platinum Disc Award for raking in over 450,000 copies in CD sales of the album *Kau Kunci Cintaku (Dalam Hati Mu)* [My Love is Sealed in Your Heart] composed by Nawab (Ramlahramgroup, n.d.). Throughout his career, Nawab has composed over 2,000 songs sung by local and international artists. He has been involved in producing over 150 albums, recorded in Indonesia, the Philippines, Singapore, Thailand, Taiwan, and Hong Kong.

In November of 1999, Nawab was approached by the Ministry of Tourism, Arts and Culture Malaysia to compose a song for the country's tourism campaign titled "Malaysia Truly Asia". The task was to compose a song that fit the lyrics provided to him and to incorporate musical elements from various cultural groups. Considering the colossal responsibility placed on his shoulders, Nawab contacted Khadijah Ibrahim, who he believed to be the most suitable singer to record the song, for a demo tape to be presented to the ministry. Impressed by the song presented by Nawab, the committee at the ministry's Malaysia Tourism Promotion Board immediately requested for it to be produced and recorded. The song lyrics were intentionally written and sung in English for the global campaign, and were eventually translated into 17 languages. The song was performed by an orchestra of 50 musicians and recorded in Kuala Lumpur. Nawab himself flew to each of the 17 countries to coach their finest singers on how to sing the song in their respective languages including Cantonese, Mandarin, Japanese, Italian, Dutch, Hindi, Tamil, Russian as well as French.

A Campaign that Exemplifies Malaysia's Culture of "Embeddisation"

Hanafi (2018), in an article written about the branding of Malaysia, stressed the importance of intangible cultural heritage—particularly dance, music and martial arts, as well as food heritage—in branding the country and uniting different ethnic groups. There has been a considerable amount of research done on "Malaysia Truly Asia" as a branding campaign, with varying analyses and conclusions as to the effectiveness of the said effort. "Malaysia Truly Asia" has been promoted and featured through several short videos, the first featuring Khadijah Ibrahim's singing voice and released in 2010. In 2014, Yuna's singing voice was featured in a video promotion entitled "The Essence of Asia". It can be said that efforts were earnestly being made to brand Malaysia as inclusive and "truly Asia" for its rich cultural heritage. The video with Yuna's singing features the *Datun Julud* dance (by the Orang Ulu people of Sarawak), *Zapin Sindang* dance (by the Malays of Sarawak), *Alu-alu* dance (by the Melanau people of Sarawak) and the *Rejan Be'uh* dance (by the Bidayuh people of Sarawak). This video begins with traditional and ethnic musical instruments such as the *seruling* (flute), *pipa* (Chinese classical instrument), Malay gamelan and Indian *tabla* (a pair of twin hand drums) (Hanafi, 2018). Strains of the Chinese *erhu* (two-stringed bowed musical instrument) and the Indian *tabla* mingled with the *dikir barat* (a musical performance done in groups) reflect the country's multi-ethnic setting. In addition, the *gong* (percussion instrument in the form of a big circular metal disc that is hit with a mallet), *tangyu* (Chinese violin fiddle musical instrument), *bungkau* (traditional instrument of the Dusun people of Sabah), bamboo flute, Indian *sitar* (plucked string instrument used in Hindi classical music) and *kompang* (single-headed frame drum) were also included. ("VM2020 Official Song Boasts Traditional Instruments and Beats", n.d.).

Nation branding can also be wrongly equated with efforts of destination branding, which is the kind of branding which makes use of commercial techniques such as corporate identity, public relations, advertising and graphic design (Anholt, 2008). Instead of promoting and marketing a country to attract visitors, nation branding aims to make people see the country in a different light. Anholt (2008) emphasised how the long-running "Malaysia Truly Asia" campaign is wrongly cited as a successful case of nation branding. According to him, the campaign is a destination branding campaign carried out with the intention of increasing visitors to the country. Nation branding, stressed Anholt further, is different because there is no single product or promotional goal. He insisted that in order to make people see the country in a different perspective, commercial promotional techniques are likely to be inadequate if not entirely inappropriate for the task.

Morais (2013) in her research described "Malaysia Truly Asia" as a campaign that places Malaysia as a country which represents all of Asia. Analysing the images used in the campaign's print and television advertisements, she noted how Malaysia is only represented by female ambassadors with uniformly light skin and almost interchangeable faces. The campaign is specifically targeted to male leisure travellers and any audience would be led to conclude that the erasure of bloodlines is truly Malaysian and thereby truly Asian. By erasing bloodlines, Morais pointed to the fact that the success of the campaign was seen to rest on convincing readers and viewers that in the melting pot that is Malaysia, racial boundaries have been smitten so successfully that the result is near homogeneity. In this sense, there is no room for anyone's skin colour to be other than light. She added further how this would work against the expectations of the would-be visitor of what he or she will find in Malaysia.

Morais (2013) also observed the difficulty in representing Malaysia as "truly Asia" because of the varying ideas of what the nation really is. This is due to the fact that the truly Asian demography of Malaysia is threatened by the reality of a country that hungers and is in a hurry for development modelled after industrialised countries in the West. Salleh (2005), who also studied the campaign, shared this view and contended that tourism can and has been used to create and assert a national identity. It is believed that through tourism policies and promotional activities, the authorities can create the desired Malaysian identity and present it to the world and the country itself. Over the years, the focus of promotional activities has been more on multi-ethnic and multi-cultural Malaysia. This new openness is said to be the reaction of *Bangsa Malaysia*, the concept of a Malaysian Nation mooted by Tun Mahathir in the early 1990s. The concept refers to citizens who identify themselves with the country, speak the Malaysian language and accept the Malaysian Constitution. The idea of the Malaysian nation is still being negotiated, and the process of becoming a nation may not be an easy one. This is because it involves both the authorities and the people of various ethnic groups in the difficult search for a commonly accepted parameter or basic constituents. Negotiation between ethnic groups requires a degree of openness and tolerance (Salleh, 2005). This ties in with Jordan's (2014) argument on the tension and contradiction between nation branding and national identity.

Nonetheless, after delving deeper into how "Malaysia Truly Asia" was originally composed, it is revealed that the song is more than just another tourism advertising jingle. The choice of Ahmad Nawab to compose the song with pre-written lyrics was a top-down ("authority-defined") decision made by the Malaysia Tourism Promotion Board. However, studying the thoughts of the composer discloses more about the everyday reality of Malaysian identity, as opposed to something that is propagated arbitrarily by the government through a tourism campaign. Nawab came from a very colourful background, having been raised in a melting pot of multi-ethnic Penang. By the 1930s, Penang had already become a cultural hub as a result of the confluence of various cultural influences from which music also flourished. Nawab was exposed to diverse traditions of musical performances and Penang's amusement parks, such as the Fun and Frolic Park, Wembley Park (which he was a part of) and the New World. These amusement parks had different stages and halls, so that an entrance ticket brought customers into a large area where subsidiary performances were being offered on different stages. These include *bangsawan*, films, *ronggeng* parties, joy rides cars, and dance halls, supplemented by food and gambling (Augustin & Lochhead, 2015). In a nutshell, the inclusion of various ethnic and cultural elements into "Malaysia Truly Asia", a song which belongs to a modern pop genre, is a manifestation of a shared cultural heritage that exists in the psyche of the songwriter and is exhibited through the eventual mass acceptance of his song as a reflection of a collective phenomenon.

To comprehend this, it is imperative to understand the evolution of societal formation within the Malay Archipelago (Southeast Asia today), where Malaysia is located. It needs to be emphasised that there had surely been a slow evolution of socio-political transformation of the region from the pre-colonial period all the way to the colonial era and post-European rule. This Malay world exhibits wide-ranging ethnic, linguistic and cultural variations. It is the result of the region being an heir to Hindu, Buddhist, and Islamic traditions as well as to three European colonial government systems and administrations—British, Dutch, and French. This has a big influence on the socio-political transformation of the region (Shamsul, 2009). Shamsul emphasised that the evolution of politics and governance in the Malay world is the result of a complex multi-linear "embeddisation" process. This means each new culture or civilisation that arrives is layered on top of the previous one, reinventing and reconstructing it to suit the needs of the day. The precolonial era of the Malay world was characterised by a plurality of cultures that signified a free-flowing natural process not only articulated through migration but also cultural borrowings and adaptations. Colonial rule introduced knowledge, social constructs, vocabulary, idioms, and institutions hitherto unknown to the indigenous peoples of the precolonial era. Malaysia as a nation developed throughout the different phases of governance from the precolonial and colonial periods to the postcolonial period. Malaysia's contemporary identity today is a result of the impact of layers of "embeddisation" originating from its precolonial civilisation and cultures within the archipelago.

Conclusion

Regardless of the frequency of any nation branding campaign, the symbols invented and mobilised for the purpose of representing Malaysia as a modern nation are never detached from a long and complex history of cultural borrowing and embeddedness of elements shared within the archipelagic *nusantara*. Influences that include Hindu, Buddhist and Islamic variants have all graced and made a lasting impact on the evolution of governance, each with its own nation-of-intent in this country. The intangible cultural heritage within a country and its performing arts and music will always have an important position in the country's tourism sector and branding efforts. Despite the fact that the nation of Malaysia is still very much a work-in-progress, what can be observed is that the collective heritage will remain a representation of Malaysia irrespective of whether the country is viewed as "truly Asia".

I have examined several other popular patriotic songs of Malaysia such as the national anthem "Negaraku", "Tanah Pusaka", "Bahtera Merdeka" and "Pahlawan Tanah Air" and concluded that these songs promote the idea of a collective and shared national identity by repetitive dissemination through mass media (Shazlin 2016, 2018, 2019). The survival of ethnic elements for a community rests on attitudes, sentiments, and perceptions that are embedded in the myths, symbols, and values of a society. Even when changes are bound to occur over time, the importance and relevance of collective myths and symbols as part of branding Malaysia will continue to live on and transcend time.

References

Anholt, S. (2008). 'Nation branding' in Asia. *Place Branding and Public Diplomacy, 4*(4), 265–269. https://doi.org/10.1057/pb.2008.22

Augustin, P., & Lochhead, J. (2015). *Just for the love of it: Popular music in Penang 1930s–1960s.* Strategic Information and Research Development Centre (SIRD).

Chopyak, J. D. (1987). The role of music in mass media, public education and the formation of a Malaysian national culture. *Ethnomusicology, 31*(3), 431. https://doi.org/10.2307/851665

Dinnie, K. (2009). *Nation branding: Concepts, issues, practice.* Elsevier.

Hafidah, S. (2000, July 1). Ahmad Nawab's midas touch. *New Straits Times.*

Hanafi, H. (2018). View of branding Malaysia and re-positioning cultural heritage in tourism development. *Journal of Southeast Asian Studies,* (Special Issue 2018 (Rebranding Southeast Asia)), 74–91. https://doi.org/https://doi.org/10.22452/jati.sp2018no1.6

Jordan, P. (2013). Nation branding: A tool for nationalism?. *Journal of Baltic Studies*, 1–21. https://doi.org/10.1080/01629778.2013.860609

Mohd Haqkam, H. (2010). *Datuk Dr. Ahmad Nawab bin Nawab Khan (Datuk Ahmad Nawab): Tokoh Seniman Negara ke-7.* Jabatan Kebudayaan dan Kesenian Negara, Kementerian Penerangan Komunikasi dan Kebudayaan.

Morais, D. (2013). "Malaysia: Truly Asia": Double consiousness in Malaysia's tourism advertising, or the double jeopardy of being Malaysian. *Project Muse. Imagined Identities: Identity Formation in the Age of Globalism*, (May), 191–210.

Ramlahramgroup. (n.d.). *Laman Rasmi Ramlah Ram* [Ramlah Ram's official website]. http://ramlahram.com/

Salleh, Y. (2005). Negotiating identity in Malaysia: Multi-cultural society, Islam, theatre and tourism. *Asian Journal of Social Science, 33*(3), 473–485. https://doi.org/10.1163/156853105775013625

Shamsul, A. B. (1996). Nations-of-intent in Malaysia. In S. Tonnesson & H. Antlov (Eds.), *Asian Forms of the Nation* (pp. 323–347). Taylor & Francis Group.

Shamsul A. B. (2009). *Culture and governance in Malaysia's survival as a nation*. Institut Kajian Etnik (KITA).

Shamsul, A. B., & Sity, D. (2012). Nation, ethnicity, and contending discourse in the Malaysian state. In R. Boyd & T. W. Ngo (Eds.), *State making in Asia* (pp. 134–143). Routledge. https://doi.org/10.4324/9780203338988

Shazlin, A. H. (2016). Branding the Malaysian nation: Tracing the role of popular songs in the construction of an imagined community. *Southeast Asian Social Science Review, 1*, 152–173.

Shazlin, A. H. (2016). *Penjenamaan bangsa: Lagu-lagu patriotik popular dan pembentukan jenama Malaysia.* Universiti Kebangsaan Malaysia.

Shazlin, A. H. (2018). Negaraku: The national anthem binding Malaysians in integration. In *UKM Ethnic Studies Paper Series No. 59*. Institut Kajian Etnik (KITA).

Shazlin, A. H. (2019). A Malaysian nation brand: The dissemination of it by radio Malaya via the song Tanah Pusaka. *Jurnal Komunikasi: Malaysian Journal of Communication, 35*(1), 90–102. https://doi.org/10.17576/JKMJC-2019-3501-07

Syed Othman, S. M. Z. (2008). *Seniman Negara Ke-7: Datuk (Dr.) Ahmad Nawab*. Jabatan Kebudayaan dan Kesenian Negara (KEKKWA).

VM2020 Official Song Boasts Traditional Instruments and Beats. (n.d.). *The Star*.

CHAPTER 23

Trans-Pacific Trajectories of "China Nights": From a Japanese Wartime Song to Memories of the Far East in the United States

Shin Aoki, *Tokyo Woman's Christian University*

"China Nights" (also known as "China Night") is the English title of the Japanese wartime song "Shina no Yoru" originally released in 1938. However, even in 2020, multiple versions of this song can be found on YouTube in the Japanese, English, and Chinese languages. Among the titles of the uploaded videos are "Shina no Yoru" in Japanese characters and in English alphabet, "China Nights" in English, as well as several versions of the title in Chinese. Of these, a majority of the comments on the videos with English titles are in English (most likely made by Americans), and despite it being a Japanese song, there are comparatively fewer comments in Japanese. There are also some comments in Chinese, Korean, Thai, and Portuguese.[1] In this chapter, by briefly tracing the trajectories of "Shina no Yoru"/"China Nights" in the last 80 odd years, I discuss the trans-Pacific journey of a wartime pop song from the World War II (WWII) period through the Cold War era to the present.

A Japanese Wartime Song Transforming into a Favourite Among GIs

Released by record label Nippon Columbia in 1938, "Shina no Yoru" was a popular Japanese song during the Asia–Pacific War (1931–1945) and contained stereotypical images of China in its lyrics and sound. The record by Hamako Watanabe (a Japanese female pop singer who had musical training in a conservatoire in Japan) and the 1940 Toho film titled *Shina no Yoru* featuring the song, became hits in Japan which soon spread to East Asia and Southeast Asia under Japanese imperialism (Aoki, 2017).[2]

After WWII, the song started acquiring new listeners—the American servicemen in occupied Japan. As early as December 1946, *Pacific Stars and Stripes* (the newspaper for the US military personnel in the Far East) reported on the popularity of "Shina no Yoru" for GIs and the subsequent reissue of the record by Nippon Columbia. After catching the ears of American officers and soldiers in the early part of the occupation, the song's popularity lasted through the late 1940s and peaked during the course of the Korean War, which made it well known to Americans serving in Japan, Korea, and other parts of the Far East where the US military had marked its presence. Inspired by this popularity, in addition to reissuing Watanabe's original 1938 recording in 1946, Nippon Columbia released a new recording of "Shina no Yoru"/"China Nights" by the Chinese singer Hu Mei Fang (known as Ko Bihou among the Japanese) in 1953, and marketed souvenir albums to American servicemen in the 1950s, listing "Shina no Yoru" as the first song on the A-side. Many US military personnel stationed in or visiting Japan bought these records and the music boxes of "Shina no Yoru", and enjoyed listening to the song in bars that catered to them. Furthermore, they had fun singing small parts of its original Japanese lyrics, or the GIs' own English parody of the phrase "Shina no Yoru" as "She ain't got no yo-yo" (Aoki, 2017). The song seems to have been frequently heard and sung by GIs in the Far East, at least until the 1960s, considering that a number of veterans stationed in Okinawa through the 1960s have made comments on YouTube referring to the tune's popularity.

"China Nights" Crossing the Pacific

After crossing the Pacific with returning servicemen, "China Nights" started receiving acceptance in American pop music as a popular Oriental song evoking the imagery and memories of the Far East. The song retained these meanings in America through the 1950s and 1960s, as evinced by the fact that at least 35 singles and albums that included "China Nights" were released in the US during this period, and only two releases (an album and one single from it) were found in the 1970s.[3] Moreover, research on "Shina no Yoru"/"China Nights" through an online newspaper archive confirms that most of the contemporary articles referring to the song in the US mainland were written in the 1950s and 1960s.[4]

In the US, from the end of WWII to the early 1960s, there was a steady stream of written works, stage productions, and films that forged and celebrated *mutual understanding* between America and non-communist Asia, which attempted to promote US–Asian integration amid tensions of the Cold War. The Asian population represented in these cultural productions appeared as characters who were different from white middle-class Americans but had a shared humanity that could cross racial and cultural divides. Cultural historian Christina Klein termed this mode of representation as "Cold War Orientalism" (Klein, 2003). From this perspective, it is significant that "China Nights" is a western-styled three-minute pop song imitating stereotypical Oriental sounds such as the gong and the erhu. A *Billboard* reviewer commented that "China Nights" was "an attractive, fragile Japanese pop song" with "a smooth oriental–occidental backing" (Billboard, 1952), and it was easy for American listeners to learn part of its melody and

Japanese lyrics and sing along. Through this musical experience, "China Nights" turned into a material through which Americans could begin to understand and relate to Japan or the Orient.

As a cultural product in the context of Cold War Orientalism, the recording and performance of "China Nights" in the United States (US) from the 1950s to the 1960s can be characterised from three aspects. First, "China Nights" became one of the standard tunes of the music genre of the period known as Exotica. Exotica music, filled with sounds of the imagined East and the Tropics, was consumed by white middle-class men in the living rooms of their suburban homes or in lounges of resorts (Hayward, 1999). As a popular tune comfortably evoking the Orient to the ears of the American middle class, "China Nights" was included in instrumental albums with the theme of the East or the non-Western world.

Second, the reception of "China Nights" in the US held unique meanings for Hawaii. The role of Hawaii as the geopolitical nexus between the US and Asia was strengthened after WWII, when American military personnel and civilians who visited Hawaii grew in number. Thus, the islands became the *gateway* between the US mainland and Asia (Klein, 2003). In Hawaii during the 1950s, "China Nights" was presumably the song that symbolised and marked the return trip from the Far East to the gateway, in view of the fact that American military bands were playing "China Nights" as a send-off song for departing servicemen at the port of Yokohama (Phelan, 1953) and later as a welcome song for returning servicemen from the Far East at the port of Honolulu (J. Wright, personal communication, August 2, 2017). In addition, it is noteworthy that there were Hawaiian newspaper articles testifying to the song's popularity among Japanese immigrants in the late 1940s. Unlike other parts of the US, the Hawaiian Islands—where a significant Japanese population have lived since the late 19th century—already had a history of familiarity with "Shina no

Yoru" as a Japanese wartime song. Due to the multilayered history of "Shina no Yoru"/"China Nights" in Hawaii, the song continued to be performed there well into the 1970s, far longer than in the US mainland.

Third, the most striking feature in the context of Cold War Orientalism is the gendered and racialised differentiation of the singers of "China Nights" in the US. As per my research, there were no recordings of "China Nights" by African American or white female American singers in the 1950s and 1960s, even though my interviews with Korean War veterans in 2004 revealed that the song used to be sung and has been remembered by African American ex-servicemen.[5]

Singers who made recordings of vocal versions of the song (in Japanese or English) were approximately divided between nine Oriental singers (including one group) and six white male American singers. Among the Orientals, six were Asian-born women (three solo singers and one group) and men (two singers) who went to the US, and three were Hawaiian-born women. Of these, a group of three Korean women who called themselves The Kim Sisters included "China Nights" in their repertoire when they entertained the US troops in Korea, and the song was selected as the opening number for their first appearance on *The Dinah Shore Chevy Show* in 1960 (Rickets, 1956; Seid, 2016). The Japanese singer Romi Yamada, who had also sung "China Nights" on a TV show in 1962, remembers that the song was frequently requested during her stay in the US in the early 1960s even though she did not make a recording of "China Nights" (Yamada, 2010). Considering these accounts and the higher proportion of Asian female singers, "China Nights" in the 1950s and 1960s was a song that the mainstream American media and audience expected to be performed by female singers with Oriental backgrounds. Singing "China Nights" charmingly without defying this orientalising gaze was an important first step to being favourably accepted in Cold War America. Focusing on the white male singers, four of the six were country musicians, and three had served in the Far East during the 1950s. Among them, Dick Curless had already played "China Nights" while stationed in Korea in 1954, and after returning to the US, recorded the song three times in his career (Rickets, 1954; Curless, 1965). Although I cannot make any meaningful interpretations of these country versions of "China Nights" with the limited information available, it is notable that there was a marked tendency in the backgrounds of the singers, that is, young Asian women who went to the US hoping for cultural and economic success, and young white men who had served in the Far East during and immediately after the Korean War. The lingering popularity of "China Nights" in America until the 1960s was a cultural by-product of the US expansion into Asia during the early stages of the Cold War. The fact that the only "China Nights" single in the 1970s—the third recording by Dick Curless—appeared in 1973 when the American troops withdrew from Vietnam, suggests that the song epitomised the American fantasy of a mutual understanding with Asia in the middle of the 20th century.

"China Nights" Renewal

The reception of "China Nights" in America has, of course, had other contexts besides the ones previously discussed. One example of the cultural transformation that occurred in a more local sense is that a "Shina no Yoru" record brought back by a Hopi (a Native American tribe) GI serving in Japan was changed to a tribal song and dance in their community, known as the *Hopi Ghost Dance* (Masuyama, 1993; Dawahoya & Hopi singers, 2004). In recent years, reception of the song in a more intimate context has also appeared in the ongoing new media, YouTube. "China Nights" videos have been uploaded to YouTube since the beginning of its service in 2004, and comments on these videos indicate that the song triggers memories of several generations of Americans who have emotional ties with the time they spent in the Far East. Some emotions evoked by "China Nights" on YouTube are related to their parents (including Japanese mothers married to American servicemen) who had often played the record in their childhood days. As seen in the case of other old pop songs, various versions of "China Nights" uploaded to YouTube have renewed and kept alive the memories of individuals who once encountered the song in the past.

Conclusion

"China Nights" became a hit among US servicemen in post-war Japan and established its status as a song that evoked memories and imagery of the Far East in American popular music from the 1950s to the early 1970s. Furthermore, it seems to have been the most famous Japanese popular song in the US until the massive hit "Sukiyaki", sung by Kyu Sakamoto, was released in 1963. However, "Sukiyaki" did not immediately erase the popularity of "China Nights". Record releases of "China Nights" and articles referring to the tune decreased in the early 1970s when the US lost the war in Vietnam, and the idea of a mutual understanding with Asia was revealed to be an American Cold War fantasy. "China Nights" concurrently lost its status as a popular Asian song in the US. Nevertheless, in the early 21st century, several generations of Americans still have memories of the song that are reawakened as they encounter "China Nights" once again on YouTube.

Notes

[1] Unlike the videos with English titles, there are many Japanese comments to the YouTube videos that have titles in Japanese characters. In this chapter, all the findings of "Shina no Yoru"/"China Nights" on YouTube are based on research conducted on January 10 and January 13, 2020.

[2] It should also be noted that "Shina no Yoru" as disseminated in East Asia and Southeast Asia during the Japanese colonial invasion conjures up different trans-Asian post-war histories and memories.

[3] All the findings on the record releases of "Shina no Yoru"/"China Nights" in this chapter are based on research I have been conducting on Discogs.com (https://www.discogs.com/), an online audio recording database, and Newspapers.com (https://www.newspapers.com/), an online newspaper archive, while collecting and identifying the records themselves.

[4] This finding is based on research conducted through Newspapers.com (https://www.newspapers.com/) on March 4 and March 5, 2019.

[5] Larry Allen, an African American singer and pianist who entertained US military personnel in the Far East during the 1950s, created records including "Shina No Yoru"/"China Nights"; however, the recordings were made in Japan and presumably not for public sale. In addition, Eve Boswell and Joyce Frazer—white female singers in the British Commonwealth—recorded this song as "Moon Above Malaya" in the early 1950s.

References

Aoki, S. (2007). Singing exoticism: A historical anthropology of the G.I. songs "China Night" and "Japanese Rumba". *The Journal of American History, 103*(4), 943–955.

Billboard. (1952, July 5). International record reviews. *Billboard*, 41.

Curless, D. (1965). *Tombstone every mile* [Album]. Tower.

Dawahoya, B., & Hopi singers. (2004). *Hopi social dance songs* [Album]. Canyon Records.

Hayward, P. (Ed.) (1999). *Widening the horizon: Exoticism in post-war popular music*. John Libbey & Company Pty Ltd.

Klein, C. (2003). *Cold war orientalism: Asia in the middlebrow imagination, 1945–1961*. University of California Press.

Masuyama, E. (1993). "Shina no Yoru" kara "Buffalo Dance Song" he: Beikoku Hopi Indian heno Denpan to sono Kayo-seiritsu-katei nitsuite. *Nippon Kayo Kenkyu, 33*, 69–76.

Phelan, L. (1953, April 28). Sayonara port. *Pacific Stars and Stripes*, 8–9.

Rickets, A. D. (1954, July 3). Far east footlites. *Pacific Stars and Stripes, 21*.

Rickets, A. (1956, June 13). On the town. *Pacific Stars and Stripes, 5*.

Seid, D. (2016). Forgotten femmes, forgotten war: The Kim Sisters' disappearance from American screen and scene. *Center for Gaming Research Occasional Paper Series, 38*, 1–10.

Yamada, R. (2010). *Gakufu wo Daite* [Embracing Music Scores]. Kadokawa-gakugei-shuppan.

CHAPTER 24

The "Modern" in Sundanese Music Broadcast over the Radio in the 1930s and 1940s

Shota Fukuoka, *National Museum of Ethnology*

From the late 1980s to the early 1990s, *pop Sunda* (Sundanese pop music), sung in the Sundanese language, was prevalent in West Java, Indonesia. Many music cassette tapes of *pop Sunda* were released and sold in music shops in major cities of West Java. This trend seems to be linked to the world music boom of the time. For example, in Japan, two CD releases featuring a *pop Sunda* singer Detty Kurnia in collaboration with Japanese and Southeast Asian musicians were out in the first half of the 1990s. Her group performed at WOMAD, an international festival of world music and dance, held in Yokohama. The *pop Sunda* repertoire mainly came from three different periods: the late 1930s and the early 1940s when a category of songs entitled *kawih* was developed with the start of full-scale radio broadcasting in West Java; the 1950s and 1960s when songs called *lagu daerah*, an iconic repertoire of the regions, proliferated throughout Indonesia; and the late 1970s and 1980s when the genre entitled *degung kawih* became popular in West Java. In this chapter, I focus on the development of *kawih* in the late 1930s and the early 1940s.

In contrast to classical and folk music, people have generally viewed popular music as unique to modern society. Most popular music in the non-Western world including Southeast Asia was created by incorporating Western popular music styles. The process was often conceived as the "modernisation" of music. As a result, until the late 20th century, Indonesian popular music tended to be conceptualised as modern. Today, music genres unique to West Java that employ the native language and instruments, usually fall in the traditional rather than modern or popular category. The *kawih* repertoire is also recognised as being traditional. However, in West Java in the 1930s and the early 1940s, *kawih* was a symbol of modern attempts in Sundanese music. In this chapter, I discuss what people found to be modern in Sundanese music in the early days of radio broadcasting.

The Beginning of "Modern" Sundanese Music

In a book published in 1942, the Sundanese artist MA Salmun, who frequently contributed articles on traditional Sundanese art to magazines, wrote:

> The word *raehan* (arrangement) became popular only after the advent of radio studios. Moreover, what is called classic and modern to me is divided according to the year when radio broadcasting started. In other words, I categorise the period until 1934 as classic and after 1935 as modern. (Salmun, 1942, p. 211)

NIROM and VORL[1] were the two major radio stations transmitting the "Eastern Broadcast" services for indigenous residents in West Java at the time. They began broadcasting in 1934 and 1935, respectively. The word "*raehan*" is a clue to the difference between the classical and modern eras described by Salmun; the word means creating a new song based on existing patterns. Numerous new songs were created and broadcast over the radio. This new repertoire marked the new era of Sundanese music.

The magazines for radio listeners, *Soeara Nirom* (Voice of NIROM) and *Pedoman Radio* (Radio Guide), provide some information on the pieces of Sundanese music that were broadcast on radio at that time. Based on this data, I examine the characteristics of the repertoire.

Development of *Kawih*

RA Darja, a staff member of the Radio of the Republic of Indonesia at its Bandung branch, often analysed Sundanese music in *Pedoman Radio*. He wrote that a new trend in Sundanese music was born with the advent of radio in West Java. According to him, the repertoire sung by female singers, or gamelan tunes, came to be played in a rhythmically dense style, and the lyrics were conceived to suit the title of the tune; new tunes came to be composed based on the existing *patokans* (Darja, 1949).

A temporal unit called *matra*, a concept similar to measure in Western music, provides the basis of the form of gamelan tunes. The pattern of gongs consists of four *matras* delivering the basic unit of the tune. In principle, players accompany the tune based on the last notes of the second and fourth *matras*. These tones constitute the framework of the tune, the pattern of which is called a *patokan*.

In *gamelan* tunes, the concept of a "piece" has two levels: the *patokan*, which defines the structural framework of the tune, and the *lagu* (the melody). For example, a tune called *Es Lilin* (popsicle) has a *patokan* called Senggot. Players can accompany many other tunes with Senggot if they have the same *patokan* tones. In other words, a basic playing pattern of the *patokan* can be applied to various tunes. The *gamelan* tunes have come to form a repertoire shared in several music genres. Darja pointed out that several genres, including "additional tunes" of *tembang* (a genre of Sundanese classical songs), have the same style and structure as *gamelan* tunes (Darja, 1950).

The "*gamelan* tune" is equivalent to *kawih* in Sundanese. It originally referred to the song sung by a female singer, *sinden*, in the gamelan. Although each *kawih* has a roughly fixed melody based on *patokan* tones, a *sinden* sings it with an elaborately improvised embellishment that an amateur can rarely imitate. Relatively freely, she can choose whichever lyrics that fit the specific verse form of the piece.

Kawih existed in the pre-radio era. However, the newly created repertoire has a certain degree of novelty. In radio magazines, we often find the name "*kawih*" with the word "extra" (or *ekstra*). The term might have been derived from the repertoire sung as an interlude to a play performed by itinerant theatres such as *bangsawan*, an important media of popular music before radio existed. A song sung between acts in *bangsawan* performances was called an "extra turn" (Tan, 1993). This suggests that a new repertoire of *kawih* was developed in response to popular music being distributed by itinerant theatres and other media.

The rhythmic density of the new repertoire can be attributed to the influence of *kroncong*, a popular music genre flourishing at the time. The lyrics were relatively free from a particular verse form and had a consistent meaning based on a theme or story suggested in the title (Darja, 1949, 1950). Artists created a variety of lyrics related to nationalism, lessons for children, romantic stories, specific news and the like. Both the melody and the lyrics became essential factors for defining a song and helping it succeed.

Kawih and *Tembang*

Male aristocrats used to sing classical songs called *tembang*. Their main repertoire, *mamaos*, was a song free of rhythm that did not follow a fixed metre. However, if we look at the repertoire of *tembang* broadcast on the radio, we can find that there were also songs described as extra. That means that the genre began incorporating *kawih* as part of the broadcast repertoire. Most of the singers who sang those songs were female.

Sinden, the female singers in *gamelan*, tended to be viewed as being socially inferior, as was the case with other entertainers. From the perspective of Sundanese aristocrats, it would be unthinkable that such a singer and repertoire would enter the world of *tembang*. However, radio broadcasting was a new platform for music that made this phenomenon possible, provided it received the support of the audience.

Today, *kawih* has become established as a repertoire of *tembang* called *panambih* or additional songs. A typical performance of *tembang* begins with a few *mamaos* and ends with one or a few *panambih*. Sukanda, who studied the history of *tembang*, wrote that the *panambih* repertoire was created in the 1930s (Sukanda, 1983). He criticised the *sinden* who had not adequately learnt *tembang* but sang *panambih* and released records. He stated that ordinary people (*masyarakat awam*) did not know right from wrong (Sukanda, 1983).

Williams (2001) pointed out that in the early period of *tembang*, most of the singers were male, but from the mid-20th century onwards, an increasing number of women became *tembang* singers. Nowadays, almost all such singers are female. Lindsay (1997) mentioned that in Central Java, radio was a tool that democratised music in that it brought court music outside of the palace. In West Java, radio was also a factor that brought new value to existing genres. It helped bring music to a larger audience and gave musicians, particularly female singers, opportunities to participate in a broader range of music. Several music genres shared the repertoire of kawih and promoted interaction between the genres.

The "Modern" in Sundanese Music

Ethnomusicologist Bruno Nettl noted the following four points as effects of the recording industry on the non-Western world: (a) A small number of performers have come to dominate the listening of a large public; (b) Music has decreased in terms of traditional functions and has become more associated with recreation; (c) Variety in musical style has tended to give way to unification; and (d) Records have forced time limits on music, resulting in an emphasis on shorter forms and composed genres (Nettl, 1985, p. 63). In West Java, a similar tendency can be seen to some extent.

In radio broadcasts in the 1930s and 1940s, the success of star singers, especially female singers, attracted a broad Sundanese audience. Female singers became famous not only in the genres which they were initially engaged in, but also in the genres which male aristocrats had dominated. Yampolsky (2014) pointed out that compared to gramophone recordings which required more cost and labour, radio was more flexible in terms of exploring new talent. A few musicians' dominance over the listening of a large public also meant that many Sundanese people came to listen to the same programmes on a regular basis. The notion of "Sundanese music" going beyond differences in music genres might have contributed to the consciousness of Sundanese culture going beyond social class distinctions.

People began listening to music on the radio as a daily pastime. Such recreational listening provided a venue that was relatively free of the context and value that had previously governed Sundanese music genres. However, occasions for music performance from the pre-radio era did not simply disappear. As the occasions diversified, the values underlying each musical context could come into conflict with each other. This is particularly evident in the case of *tembang* and other music genres enjoyed by the aristocracy. Amid the diversification of occasions for music performances and the conflicting values that came with such diversification, listening to music through mass media became increasingly prevalent.

In West Java, the unification of the diversity of musical styles appeared as the expansion of a shared repertoire, a new *kawih*, through increased exchanges among genres. This process occurred alongside the growing significance of the composed pieces. To attract the listeners' attention, musicians composed one new *kawih* after another, featuring lyrics conceived according to the theme indicated by the title, and with a relatively simple-to-remember melody. As the use of the term *extra* suggested, *kawih* introduced into Sundanese music some of the characteristics of the popular music of the time.

Based on the information described in radio listeners' magazines, Yampolsky (2014) suggested that the incorporation of European and American popular music of the 1920s and 1930s qualified the music as modern at that time. He excluded *tembang* from the modern genre since it had not integrated popular music. However, as Salmun and Darja stated, devising a new *kawih* repertoire marked a new, modern era in Sundanese music. Radio provided the venue for that development.

Conclusion

There was some criticism of "modern" Sundanese music. Salmun wrote in a 1949 article:

> From 1935 to 1945, it was the fashion to arrange (*mengubah*) Sundanese songs. There were various reasons for this. First, the performers were forced to make new songs whenever they played for a broadcast so that the audience would not get bored ... Second, there were some (not many) composers trying to mass-produce music for financial reasons. The song broadcast for that reason is, of course, not a realisation of a heartbeat, but a kind of commodity that was manufactured. It is no different from any other fashionable product. When a fad passes, the song disappears, and it does not live like a classical piece of

> music that symbolises a heartbeat. If the changes in music since 1935 are considered progress, I do not understand the meaning of progress. (Salmun, 1949, p. 105)

In 1942, Salmun positively recognised that Sundanese music had entered a new era with the creation of new songs following the advent of radio. However, in the 1949 article, he criticised the newly composed repertoire tailored to commercial mass production. In 1950, the first music school to teach Javanese music was established in Solo, Indonesia. Subsequently, similar schools were built to teach regional music in several parts of the country. Amid these developments, a debate took place with regard to what Indonesian music should be like. The music of each ethnic group that makes up Indonesia gradually changed its character from "modern" to "traditional" due to such discourses, organisations, and institutions. As a result, Sundanese music is regarded as traditional music as opposed to modern music. However, in West Java, new genres such as *degung kawih* have emerged from traditional music, and were popularised by the record industry in the 1970s and 1980s. It reminds us that traditional music also has the potential to produce a new repertoire in line with sociocultural changes, and to contribute to popular music.

Notes

[1] NIROM stands for Nederlandsch-Indische Radio-omroepmaatschappij (Dutch East Indies Radio Broadcasting Corporation) and VORL stands for Vereeniging van Oostersche Radio Luisteraars (Association of Eastern Radio Listeners).

References

Darja, R. A. (1949). Lagu2 Sunda didepan Tjorong Radio. *Pedoman Radio, 34*(1949.2.20), 8.

Darja, R. A. (1950). Tembang dan gamelan. *Pedoman Radio, 21*(1950.10.22), 6–7.

Lindsay, J. (1997). Making waves: Private radio and local identities in Indonesia. *Indonesia, 64*, 105–123.

Nettl, B. (1985). *The Western impact on world music: Change, adaptation, and survival.* Schirmer Books.

Salmun, M. A. (1942). *Padalangan.* Balai Pustaka.

Salmun, M. A. (1949). *Seni Sunda. Indonesia: Madjalah kebudayaan, 1*, 100–107.

Sukanda, E. (1983). *Tembang Sunda Cianjuran.* Proyek Pengembangan Institut Kesenian Indonesia.

Tan, S. B. (1993). *Bangsawan: A social and stylistic history of popular Malay opera.* Oxford University Press.

Williams, S. (2001). *The sound of the ancestral ship: Highland music of West Java.* Oxford University Press.

Yampolsky, P. (2014). Music on Dutch East Indies Radio in 1938: Representations of unity, disunity, and the modern. In B. Barendregt (Ed.), *Sonic modernities in the Malay world: A history of popular music, social distinction and novel lifestyles, 1930s–2000s* (pp.47–112). Brill.

CHAPTER 25

The Aesthetics and DIY Ethics of DJs as Asian Music Collectors

Taeyoon Kim & Haemin Ryu, *Sungkonghoe University*

In this chapter, we examine the change in the status of disc jockeys (DJs) as creators of a music subculture following the shift in the production and consumption of music as a result of advancements in recording technology. Across the genres and subcultures in the music industry, DJs have been treated more peripherally than live-performing musicians. As the importance of recorded music increased during the revival of discs and post-production arts in club culture, the role of DJs expanded from merely playing music recordings at parties to presenting new music creations. In the recent music scene in Seoul, South Korea, DJ-based performances and parties have emerged, and the music industry in the post-digital era has begun emphasising the importance of content beyond recorded music. Amidst discrepancies in cultural ethics and creative responses to the rapid changes in music production and consumption, some DJs are finding Asia to increasingly be the capital of a new music subculture. At this point, vinyl-centric turntablism and the building of playlists featuring Asian music are part of a major methodology reflecting the way in which DJs "approve" of Asia. In this chapter, we delve into the following questions: How did DJ parties become commonplace in the indie music scene? What is the "cultural hipness" in Asian music that brings together hipsters, music listeners, and people in the art scene? Finally, what is the difference between the Western and Seoul perspectives of Asian music?

Of Books and Retro Records

In 2015, a book entitled *Go Go! Korean Rock Travel Journal* published in Seoul included short reviews of 1970s South Korean rock records, and essays on 1990s indie music venues and record shops. In his early days in South Korea, the book author Yohei Hasegawa joined indie rock bands as a guitarist, while becoming an increasingly avid record collector. As a Japanese born in the 1970s, he visited Korea in the 1990s with the sole purpose of purchasing popular music records he could not find in other countries. In the book, Hasegawa recalls the shock he experienced after listening to the Korean rock band Sanulrim, a pioneer in the Korean rock music scene at the time. Its sound did not follow that of typical popular Western rock music due to the band's lack of exposure to Western music, as imports controls were imposed by authoritarian leaders in 1970s South Korea. Hasegawa joined some bands in South Korea, and became fascinated with Asian music (Hasegawa, 2015). Although he no longer plays in bands nowadays, Hasegawa now produces mixtapes that trace the so-called Japanese city pop genre from the 1980s.

Towards a More Hip Space-Time

Yang (2010) indicated that during the late 1990s to 2000s, Asian-American hip-hoppers could be separated into two generations. The first generation could be recognised as DJs, similar to turntablists in the South Bronx hip-hop scene in New York, while non-Asian-American hip-hoppers could be recognised as emcees and so on. In the case of the second generation, Asian-American hip-hoppers positioned themselves strategically as part of both old-school American hip-hop and ethnic-cultural diversity.

During the 2000s, the indie music scene in Seoul saw a retro movement which looked at the past for inspiration. One of DJ Soulscape's (hereafter "Soulscape") two full-length CDs titled *The Sound of Seoul* (2008) captured and remixed the records of many Korean bands that appeared in the United States military camp town shows in Seoul during the 1960s and 1970s. Although Soulscape had already been a successful hip-hop turntablist, these two records and his other collection, *More Sound of Seoul* (2009), drew the attention of hip-hop listeners and hipsters. If Soulscape found inspiration in music that was popular before the democratisation of Korea, Hasegawa delved deeper into the so-called city pop genre—influenced by the urban atmosphere of the Japanese economic growth period in the 1980s—which spread to Korea through DJing and mass media. Hasegawa (2015) and Soulscape agreed that they both focused on the aesthetics brought by the discord between the Westernisation and localisation of East Asian popular music (pp. 292–315). The conspicuous role of the DJ in the indie music scene was an attempt to reject the Western-centric gaze, and a series of DJ parties called Asian Music Party (AMP) planned by DJ Yesyes (hereafter "Yesyes") allowed both forms—DJ party and Asian music—to co-exist. The first AMP was held in 2015, and altogether, seven events took place up to 2019. At the first AMP, Soulscape, Hasegawa and Soi48 (a duo comprising Keiichi Utsuki and Shinsuke Takagi) appeared, and thereafter various DJs from Asia performed (Figure 1).

FIGURE 1 The 5th Asian Music Party
Source: Author's own (Kim, 2020)

Before the first AMP, Yesyes' idea of incorporating Asian music in DJ parties can be traced back to several earlier occasions. The first was the opening party of an international interdisciplinary arts festival called Festival Bo:m, planned by Yesyes in 2014. In this festival, Yesyes emphasised the use of Asian music in a DJ party for the first time. In a discourse on post-production in 1990s contemporary art, curator and art critic Nicolas Bourriaud (2002) used the term "culture of use" to argue that artworks should never be separated into production and consumption. Instead, artworks should be treated as a consecutive process by means of recycling or reinterpretation. Within that context, rave party DJs were pointed out to have created new music by "copying and pasting together loops of sound, placing recorded products in relation with each other" (Bourriaud, 2002, p. 18). Yesyes' approach in copying and pasting and intersecting different Asian music is similar to that of an "Asian music curator" or "rock curator" (Reynolds, 2014, pp. 142–170). To Reynolds, however, the remixing and curating of music is only a secondary genre combining and appropriating music influences, not a creative one.

The second was the realisation by Yesyes and his friends that rock music was not something they wanted to pursue. This realisation came after having watched a live performance of Canadian indie rock band Arcade Fire on YouTube in the early 2010s (Hong & Shim, 2019). Finally, when Yesyes joined a private networking party in Yahiro, Japan, he witnessed the interest in Asian music by Asian people. It was at that moment that he was able to quell his misguided belief that Asian people do not listen to Asian music (Yesyes, personal communication, September 7, 2017).

In investigating club culture, Thornton (1995) explained that subcultural capital (or cultural and social knowledge of members of a particular subculture) forms a cultural hipness or an "alternative hierarchy" in which "the axes of age, gender, sexuality, and race are all employed … to keep the determinations of class, income and occupation at bay" (pp. 154–164). In the use of Asian music in DJ parties, the aforementioned axes encourage the intersection and harmony of music from different Asian regions, regardless of the differences in the socio-economic developments within each region.

Bringing Together and Diving Into Networks

AMP created a big impact on the Seoul music scene, leading to a boom in derivative DJ parties. With Yesyes inviting many Asian DJs to Seoul in the late 2010s, some DJs have begun incorporating Asian music into their sets. One of them, DJ Mimi (hereafter "Mimi"), has introduced records she collected from other Asian regions in a series of DJ parties called Mimi Pops.

Yesyes, as the owner of the record label Helicopter Records, focuses on importing records and mixtapes released by Asian DJs in their respective regions. As Yesyes himself selects the records and mixtapes to be imported, many music listeners regard him as a music tastemaker. For example, the series of mixtapes known as *A Night in Taipei* (2017) were originally mixed CDs released in Japan by Yuichi Kishino, Yachi Hideki, and Sakata Ritsuko from their collection of Taiwanese music (Kishino & Hideki, 2017). Yesyes re-released these works, changing the medium from CD to cassette tape through his own label. The other mixtape, titled *Live at Kabukichō* (2018), involved Yesyes re-releasing the music collected by Soi48 from Thailand, Cambodia, and Japan from several eras. All these releases are digitally available for download. Inspired by Yesyes, Mimi continued producing mixed CDs, appearing on DJ stages in Malaysia, Indonesia, and Thailand, and even appearing on radio broadcasts. She released her first full-length mixed CD titled *Asian City Night* (2020), which also inspired the name of her record label A.C.N Records. The album cover showcases the kind of aesthetics she pursues: an illustration of a girl in the Japanese manga style and a tracklist of songs in the city pop style, bringing to mind the Japanese popular culture of the late 20th century (Figure 2).

FIGURE 2 A Night in Taipei (*top left*), Live at Kabukichō (*bottom left*), and Asian City Night (*right*)
Source: Author's own (Kim, 2020)

Shin (2018), citing journalist Simon Reynolds, referred to Japanese subcultural performativity as an "empire of retro of the hipster international". Shin also mentioned "post-hipster hipsterdom" (p. 396) in reference to the attitude of hipsters in Seoul who do not follow trends from Japan. For example, while Mimi was inspired by Japanese city pop, she also seeks eclectic Asian music trends from all over. She hosts the only Asian music podcast series called *Groove in Seoul* with her colleague So-yeon on Totally Weird Radio, a music broadcasting station from the London record label Acid Jazz. In the podcast, she introduces Asian music as being "worthy of a representative channel of Asia" (Mimi, personal communication, September 9, 2019). She usually visits various places in Asia to collect records and establish inter-Asian networks. In 2019, she performed at Wonderfruit, a large music festival held in Thailand, by invitation of Zudrangma Records in Bangkok. Nowadays, she actively engages in her work which includes planning Mimi Pops, establishing and running her own record label, and producing her second mixed CD.

The Ethics of Asian Music DJs

While exploring how Asian music DJs emerged in the Seoul indie music scene, certain observations can be made. First, although both Asian music and DJ parties fit well with contemporary art, both forms are not artworks but rather subcultural goods. Second, despite producing subcultural goods, the DJs do not compose music or play an instrument; instead, they use recorded, thus digital, music. This creates a dilemma between the culture of use and the notion of authenticity of popular music.

Indeed, hipsters, music listeners and the general public agree with the idea that Asian music comprises interesting work. Since mid-2020, the Korean government's Education Broadcasting System (EBS) has been providing a free podcast series called *Music A*, which curates popular music from each Asian country with various guests (Education Broadcasting System, 2020). As Negus (2019) pointed out, "the recording [on CD, as download, as stream] is displaced" (p.19) in the post-record music industries. From this perspective, although EBS is not a huge commercial music venture, its aim is not to create subcultures but to gain public interest in Asian music.

Above all, the records by Yesyes and Mimi are produced with the aim of being sold. They are produced in limited quantities through do-it-yourself (DIY) methods[1] and can only be purchased through subscription or by attending the artists' parties or indie venues. The process of producing such records includes manufacturing and packaging them, providing online links, and promoting the records via various channels, not unlike traditional recording industries. These activities are fairly difficult even for live performers. While it cannot be said that Yesyes and Mimi produce artworks, they indeed create a common contemporary art aesthetics through recycling and reinterpretation.

In 2018, GQ Korea published an article on 10 notable DJs and their mixtapes (Wooyeong, 2018). Only a few of these DJs incorporate Asian music in their sets, but this does not diminish the influence of the music as it has since been a staple for many other DJs in Seoul's Asian party scene. Such DJs have also produced records which can be found in other Asian regions.

Conclusion

The term "cultural hipness" was originally meant to denote an alternative hierarchy in the social strata (Thornton, 1995). With the rise of the DJ, the term has been altered to encompass both the retro movement and inter-Asian connections it inspires. Cultural hipness is slightly different from contemporary art and the idea of authenticity of popular music. While DJs are inspired by past music and recycle or reinterpret it for a new audience, they use traditional DIY methods to produce records. The inter-Asian connections DJs establish in the music scene transcend the differences in race, ethnicity and national minorities. The question of how DJs encounter and negotiate the different music activities in various Asian regions will be an interesting subject to explore.

Notes

[1] A do-it-yourself (DIY) culture includes the immediacy of "direct action" and "lifestyle politics", etc. In terms of production, DIY is related to independent production of materials such as fanzines and music. See more details in McKay (1998).

References

Bourriaud, N. (2002). *Postproduction: Culture as screenplay.* Lukas & Sternberg.

Education Broadcasting System. (2020, April 21). *Thailand#1* [Audio podcast]. Music A. http://www.podbbang.com/ch/1775706

Mimi, DJ. (2020). *Asian city night* [CD]. ACN Records.

Mimi, DJ., & So-Yeon. (2019, December 4). *Groove in Seoul* [Audio podcast]. Totally Weird Radio. https://totallywiredradio.com/groove-in-seoul/

Soulscape, DJ. (2008). *The sound of Seoul* [CD]. Studio360.

Soulscape, DJ. (2009). *More sound of Seoul* [CD]. Studio360.

Shin, H. (2018). Urban commoning for *Jarip* (self-standing) and survival: Subcultural activism in "Seoul Inferno". *Inter-Asia Cultural Studies, 19*(3), 386–403. https://doi.org/10.1080/14649373.2018.1497899

Kim, T. (2020). The 5th Asian music party [Photograph].

Kim, T. (2020). A night in Taipei, Live at Kabukichō, Asian city night [Photograph].

Kishino, Y., & Hideki, Y. (Eds). (2017). *A Night in Taipei* [Cassette tape]. Helicopter Records.

McKay, G. (1998). DiY culture: Notes towards an intro. *DiY Culture: Party and protest in nineties Britain*, 2–45.

Negus, K. (2018). From creator to data: The post-record music industry and the digital conglomerates. *Media, Culture & Society, 41*(3), 367–384. https://doi.org/10.1177/0163443718799395

Reynolds, S. (2014). *Leteulomania: Gwageoe jungdogdoen daejungmunghwa 레트로마니아: 과거에 중독된 대중문화* [Retromania: Why is pop culture addicted to its own past?]. (S. Choi 최성민 옮김, Trans.). Jag-eobsil-yulyeong 작업실유령 (Original work published 2012, Faber & Faber).

Hong, S, & Shim, E. (2019, January 4). *DJ Yesyes.* VISLA Magazine. https://visla.kr/interview/85297/

Soi48. (2018). *Live at Kabukicho 歌舞伎町* [Cassette tape]. Helicopter Records.

Thornton, S. (1995). The social logic of subcultural capital. In S. Thornton (Ed.), *Club cultures: Music, media and subcultural capital* (pp. 154–164). Polity.

Wooyeong, J. (2018, April 19). *10 mixtapes, 10 perspectives.* GQ Korea. https://bit.ly/3cDxNdx

Yang, J. Y. (2010). Hip-hop and identity formations of Asian-American youth. *Korean Journal of Popular Music, 5*, 50–72. http://www.dbpia.co.kr/journal/articleDetail?nodeId=NODE02010434

Hasegawa, Y. (2015). *Go go! Korean rock travel journal.* Booknomad.

CHAPTER 26

Negotiating Musician Identities: Busking Musicians and YouTube Musicians in Hong Kong

Vicky Ho, *The Open University of Hong Kong*

Drawing on concepts of musical identity and creative identity, this chapter discusses how busking musicians and YouTube musicians negotiate the identities of being a "musician" around their music-making experiences, their expectations and understanding of musical creativity, how success is defined in a musical career, as well as how they position themselves in relation to the potential of success. The shaping of musician identities may connect or diverge in the busking scene and the YouTube scene. The analyses and discussions in this chapter are based on in-depth interviews with interviewees who create and/or perform popular music in the busking scene in Hong Kong and/or the YouTube scene (and are based on Hong Kong). They range from full-time to amateur or leisure-time music makers. Most interviewees are in their early 20s to mid-30s and belong to a young demographic.

Concepts of Musical Identity and Creative Identity

Musical identity can be approached from multiple dimensions, including technique and information, social, musical ability, physicality and emotions, and spirituality and ideals (Spychiger,

2017). Although musical identity is not identical to musician identity, the way one regards the role of music in his or her life certainly plays a part in the musician identity. According to Richard and Chin (2017), "[a] musician has been broadly defined as someone who performs, conducts or composes music" (p. 289). It is generally assumed that the musician has some level of specialised musical ability and technical skills attained through some kind of music training. Some may also expect that the musician is one who demonstrates a certain level of creativity in his or her music making. The musician identity is also a social identity when it is used to refer to one "who has a reputation as a musician, or for whom music making is their profession" (Richard & Chin, 2017, p. 289). This also illustrates Spychiger's (2017) findings that professional, amateur and leisure-time musicians vary in the levels of dimensions of musical identity. In this chapter, the focal point of discussion is how musicians interpret the identities of being a "musician".

Literature on identity issues in broader categories of creative careers may also shed some light on the making of a musician's identity. Creative practitioners tend to negotiate their creative identity around their expectations and experiences of creative work. Creative practitioners articulate their creative identity in terms of their motivations, interaction with society, external recognition, and so on (Reid et al., 2016). They tend to differentiate creative work from other job categories (Taylor & Littleton, 2012) and value the creative aspect of their work (Neff et al., 2005). Creative practitioners also negotiate their identity based on their understanding of "success" and how they measure up to that success. The external recognition and internal feelings of creative practitioners about their creative practices often create tensions for the creative identity project (Taylor, 2012). When creative workers' aspirations are troubled by unfavourable work realities, they may find their creative identities becoming relatively fragile and unstable (Morgan & Wood, 2014). When it comes to popular music careers, the conventional understanding of an overnight success might limit musicians' imagination of success (O'Dair, 2015) while the do-it-yourself (DIY) culture introduces a career pattern that is personally satisfying but not necessarily economically sustainable for young musicians (Bennett, 2018). Such tensions between internal and external factors in shaping the musician's identity will also be discussed further.

Identities as "Musician", "Busker", "Singer" and "YouTuber"

First, let us consider how the interviewees may choose to represent themselves in relation to their music-making practices. It seems that their positions are mixed identities of a "musician", "busker", "singer" and "YouTuber" as they attach different interpretations to these identity labels.

Musician

Some interviewees would identify themselves as musicians while others would not, even though they engage in similar music-making activities. Consistent with Richard and Chin's (2017) discussions, music making as a profession and the level of music creation are often used as a benchmark to define a musician. Some amateur music makers who hold other day jobs do not consider themselves musicians because music making is not their profession. For others, they think of musicians as those who "create music" and identifying themselves as musicians depends on what they count as "creating music", which could range from rearranging music and composing originals to creating derivative works. For example, in the following interview excerpt, the interviewee regards both writing and rearranging songs as forms of music creativity and these activities merit her as a musician:

> I think the reason why I could call myself a musician is because we are indeed involved in the creating process, I personally think that. I mean we keep trying to create something, be it writing or rearranging songs. (Interviewee 21, full-time YouTube musician, personal communication, May 19, 2020)

Still, there are interviewees who apply a higher standard beyond performing and creating when defining a musician. For example, the following is an interview excerpt by an interviewee who busks full-time and has engaged in creating and performing music on YouTube. When asked the question "Would you describe yourself as a musician?", the artist responds:

> I think this title sounds too big. I am someone who likes music, not a musician. I think the title musician is too big for me, because I am just trying to make a living out of music … I think a musician should have certain result, certain work so that others recognise you, that's how I would think that's a musician." (Interviewee 13, full-time busker, personal communication, April 9, 2020)

Even though this interviewee is engaged in musical performance as a profession and is involved in creating musical works including composing and lyric writing, he is still not comfortable identifying himself as a musician. Rather, he identifies as a full-time busker. To him and also some other interviewees who practise music making as a profession, the title of a "musician" is reserved for those who are more achieved and thus, more recognised. The social dimension of having the reputation as a musician (Richard & Chin, 2017) becomes important. Overall, despite the fluid definition of the title "musician" amongst the interviewees, it is clear that the title itself carries some weight.[1] It is often something yet to be attained or something that, once attained, one should try his or her very best to fulfil and live up to.

Busker/Singer

The interviewees' interpretations of the labels "busker" and "singer" are less ambivalent. For those who do not identify themselves as musicians, they are more comfortable using "busker" or "singer" as their identity labels (even though some of them also complained about the negative social perception of buskers, as will be discussed further in the chapter).

YouTuber

The interviewees so far tend to refrain from self-identifying as YouTubers. They mostly think that they do not invest as much effort in managing their YouTube channels and find it very hard to make a living out of YouTube. There are also comments about music not being a strong focus among Hong Kong-based YouTube creators. Therefore, the label "YouTuber" does not seem illustrative of their musical practices.

As we can see from the findings, there is a range of identity labels that the interviewees may or may not choose to carry. Apart from the labels, however, they also have to negotiate their identities and the value of their musical practices based on their experiences, especially as tensions rise between their subjective feelings of worth and the harsh external realities. The interviewees' experiences of internal versus external validation are what I will now expand on.

Internal Validation for the Musician Identity

The interviewees mentioned a range of sources of internal validation, including the gratification from personal expression, challenge and advancement, connection with the audience, and adventure. These factors sustain the musicians' interests and perceived worth of music making. I briefly expand on each of these internal validation factors:

Personal expression: They find an expressive value in musical performances. Performing music on the street or on YouTube is a way for them to express their ideas and feelings. Some busking musicians mentioned that they like to perform less popular songs to introduce listeners to alternative music choices. In this sense, they express their music tastes via busking.

Challenge and advancement: They consider music making on the street or on YouTube as opportunities to challenge and improve themselves musically.

Connection with the audience: This is a strong motivating force frequently mentioned by the interviewees involved in the busking scene and the YouTube scene. Connecting with the audience is typically described as ringing "resonance" with the listeners through music. For busking musicians, they tend to recognise signs of "resonance" or connection through spontaneous emotional displays from the audience. For YouTube musicians, users' comments reinforce the perception that listeners find resonance in their songs. Connecting through music also links up to a broader impact in the society, especially given the stressful urban life in Hong Kong. For example, an interviewee mentioned:

> In this place, everyone seems to be so in a rush and life seems so hard ... it seems so rough all the time, I think people in this place are like suffocating ... so I also try to soothe people through my singing ... (Interviewee 10, amateur busker, personal communication, March 21, 2020)

Consistent with Reid et al.' s (2016) study, a musician's connection to and impact on others are significant elements that sustain the perceived worth of creative careers. This factor seems to be shared by our interviewees regardless of whether they are professionally oriented or not.

Adventure: This factor is more unique to the busking scene. Buskers tend to highlight the spontaneity experienced during their busking performances. The following excerpt is an example of such a spirit:

> In fact, the best thing about [busking] is that you don't know what would happen each night, it's the most random, and that's what's unique about busking. (Interviewee 4, amateur busker, personal communication, August 26, 2019)

What this interviewee said is illustrative of how buskers treasure adventure and surprises. Some find the surprises they encounter while busking particularly fulfilling.

The Lack of External Validation for the Musician Identity

On the other hand, interviewees seem to experience a lack of external validation to uphold the musician identity. They identify precarity, the thin opportunity for success, and social stigma as setbacks to their music-making pursuits, as outlined here:

Precarity: They generally mentioned their experiences or expectations that a musical career does not come with financial stability. They or their peers tend to manage multiple jobs to financially sustain their musical pursuits.

Thin opportunity for success: Many interviewees mentioned that pursuing a musical career is or would be "very difficult". They assessed that competition is keen and that it takes more than musical skills or talent to "make it", especially in the ecology of local entertainment business. For example, they mentioned looks, networks, and knowing the game as additional criteria for success. For most interviewees, they considered the opportunity to achieve recognisable success to be rather thin.

Social stigma: They mentioned the experiences of being looked down upon or disrespected by outsiders. This is an especially common discussion among buskers. For example, they are frustrated by the misconception or accusation that busking is a means of begging. Some interviewees also thought that music making in general was not well-understood and supported by the general public. For example, one of the interviewees highlighted the kind of stereotype faced by music makers:

> People have the stereotype, like playing music has no prospect, playing music can't support [your] living ... Average people wouldn't consider [music culture] as important, wouldn't think they should support [it], or even think these [music makers] are wasting their lives, [they] don't work hard or so on, so that's why we choose to treat [music making] so seriously". (Interviewee 15, amateur busker, personal communication, April 26, 2020).

In general, they commented that the environment is not a favourable and supportive one for the development of musical or other creative pursuits.

Conclusion

This chapter addressed the question of how busking and YouTube musicians negotiate their musician identities. I have outlined some of the key patterns and themes related to the musicians' interpretations of identity labels, as well as the internal and external validation (or lack thereof) in their experiences.[2] While these musicians may experience a high level of internal satisfaction through music making, the external realities and societal discourses may make their musical identities problematic.

Acknowledgements

The work described in this chapter was fully supported by a grant from the Research Grants Council of the Hong Kong Special Administrative Region, China (UGC/FDS16/H13/18).

Notes

[1] The Chinese term representing the word "musician"（音樂人）may play a role in the interviewees' understanding of the label too.

[2] Among the general key themes outlined, there are nuances which I do not have room to fully unpack in this chapter.

References

Bennett, A. (2018). Conceptualising the relationship between youth, music and DIY careers: A critical overview. *Cultural Sociology, 12*(2), 140–155. https://doi.org/10.1177/1749975517750760

Morgan, G., & Wood, J. (2014). Creative accommodations: The fractured transitions and precarious lives of young musicians. *Journal of Cultural Economy, 7*(1), 64–78. https://doi.org/10.1080/17530350.2013.855646

Neff, G., Wissinger, E., & Zukin, S. (2005). Entrepreneurial labor among cultural producers: "Cool" jobs in "hot" industries. *Social Semiotics, 15*(3), 307–334. https://doi.org/10.1080/10350330500310111

O'Dair, M. (2015). The slow burn: Questioning the discourse surrounding popular music success and exploring opportunities for entrepreneurship in 'the long tail'. *Innovation in Music 2013, 1*(1), 247–262.

Reid, A., Petocz, P., & Bennett, D. (2016). Is creative work sustainable? Understanding identity, motivation, and worth. *Australian Journal of Career Development, 25*(1), 33–41. https://doi.org/10.1177/1038416216637089

Richard, N. S., & Chin, T. C. (2017). Defining the musical identities of "non-musicians". In D. J. Hargreaves, D. Miell, & R. MacDonald (Eds.), *Handbook of musical identities* (pp. 288–303). Oxford University Press.

Spychiger, M. B. (2017). From musical experience to musical identity: Musical self-concept as a mediating psychological structure. In R. MacDonald, D. J. Hargreaves, & D. Miell (Eds.), *Handbook of musical identities* (pp. 267–287). Oxford University Press.

Taylor, S. (2012). The meanings and problems of contemporary creative work. *Vocations and Learning, 5*(1), 41–57. https://doi.org/10.1007/s12186-011-9065-6

Taylor, S., & Littleton, K. (2012). The shape of a creative career. In *Contemporary identities of creativity and creative work* (pp. 67–87). Routledge.

CHAPTER 27

The Rise of the Godfather of Broken Hearts: The Disruption of Local Music's *Campursari* Through Didi Kempot's Music Performances

Wahyudi Akmaliah, *Centre for Society and Culture, Indonesian Institute of Sciences (PMB-LIPI)*

The emergence of new media and its diverse platforms creates an opportunity for marginalised voices, including musicians from different genres and streams, to be heard in the public sphere (Leyson, 2009; Curry, 2012; Hracs et al., 2016). Within the context of Indonesia, local musicians have been developing their craft in the provinces amidst the growth of Internet users in the post-Suharto era. New media allows local musicians to articulate, in their own mother tongue, their problems and struggles that cannot be represented by mainstream Indonesian musicians. Unlike the music produced by big music industries, who place rigid requirements for the standard and form of music that primarily appeal to a large segment of the population, the work of local musicians embraces a sense of locality by narrating their own stories and conditions without compromising the quality of music. This element of locality could not be represented by the mainstream musicians based in the capital city of Jakarta.

In West Papua with its reggae music genre, there are groups like Tropica Rasta, De Sagoo, Sulu Brothers, Papua Roots, Ulagay, and D'Joan Liberty Sky Band. In South Sumatra with its pop music genre, there are groups such as Silva Hayati, Frans and Fauna, Ovhi Firsty, Ipank, and Rayola. Their music is not only popular and well loved in South Sumatra, but also embraced by people of Minang descent who have migrated to urban areas in many Indonesian provinces. In South Sulawesi, artist Ridho Jeka successfully mixed pop music with the *dangdut* genre, interspersed with amusing local anecdotes. This music genre which incorporates anecdotal humour in songs is promoted through the YouTube channel *Musisi Jenaka Makassar* (Makassar Funny Musicians) by a group of Makassar musicians in South Sulawesi. The channel has garnered more than 75,000 subscribers at the time of writing. Focusing on the concerns of young people dealing with *cinta monyet* (puppy love), the music of another local band, NDX A.K.A., blends the local *dangdut* of *campursari* (the combination of two music elements *keroncong* and Javanese *gamelan* [Supanggah, 2003]) with rap music, and is popular primarily among the younger generation in Central Java and East Java.

Due to the strong locality factor of regional music and the different languages and dialects that exist within the Indonesian archipelago, most of these music products are only circulated and consumed by those who share the same ethnicity and language, although geographically they may live in different parts of the country, far away from their home towns. Instead of being barriers, the diversity of language expressions and local culture only serves to strengthen the primordial solidarity that could only be understood by those who share the same roots. However, this scenario remarkedly changed when singer Didi Kempot found a second wind in his career with a revival in popularity. A musician who wrote songs in his native Javanese language in the *campursari* style, Kempot was popular among the Javanese people in the 1990s for his songs on love and heartbreak. Although his popularity waned at the turn of the century, he found fame again in the 2010s, unexpectedly among younger people from diverse ethnic backgrounds. His music, once considered traditional and "uncool", has now risen to mainstream fame.

By selecting Didi Kempot as a case study, this chapter proposes three research questions: (a) What is the primary reason for the revival of Kempot's *campursari* music, a genre that combines traditional Javanese and modern music instruments? (b) What social imagination or insights are associated with the popularity of Kempot's songs among the urban youth when the lyrics are written predominantly in the Javanese language? (c) How do we define local music amidst digital technology disruption?

The presence of new digital technologies and media allows people to quickly access every information they need. However, how an event gains sufficient momentum to become viral on social media is a significant factor to be examined. The Didi Kempot revival and his new status as the hero of the youth can be attributed to social media influencers and song lyrics that resonate with young people. With the support of social networking groups who share his music videos and with Kempot's sad and touching lyrics (about people going through heartbreak or losing the love of their lives) striking a chord with the younger generation, he has been dubbed the "Godfather of Broken Hearts". This illustrates that through the impact of digital technology, many Indonesian millennials are now more appreciative of traditional forms of regional music, although his entire career as a musician and the effects of Indonesia's patriarchal society are some other factors to be considered within this explanation.

From Street to Retweet

Didi Kempot was born Dionisius Prasetyo on December 31, 1966, in Surakarta (Solo), Central Java. Since starting his career as a singer-songwriter in 1982, he had enjoyed steady popularity among the Javanese, not only in Indonesia but also in Suriname where there is a sizeable Javanese population. Kempot wrote songs only in his native Javanese language in the *campursari* style, a combination of *keroncong* and *karawitan* music blended with *dangdut*. Kempot came from a family of successful artists who helped him develop his music skills. His father Suranto (better known as Ranto Edi Gudel) was a prominent musician and comedian who often performed at *Kethoprak Tobong* (Javanese theatrical stage) and *Wayang Orang Sriwedari* (traditional dance drama company) in Central Java. His mother Umiyati Sri Nurjannah was a *keroncong* singer from Ngawi, Central Java. Meanwhile, his older brother Mamiek Prakoso was a famous comedian with the renowned Srimulat group. However, unlike other aspiring musicians with a famous artistic family, Kempot was determined to strike out on his own. He worked as a street musician in his home town Solo for three years (1982–1984) without relying on his family connections for an easier route to success (Sari & Puguh, 2020).

To pursue a music career, he moved to the capital city of Jakarta with three other friends where they lived in a small rented house in Slipi, West Jakarta. As street musicians, they frequently played at Slipi, the train station of Senen, and the nearby tourist areas. Due to his involvement with other street musician groups in Jakarta, then-Dionisius Prasetyo changed his last name to "Kempot" which is the acronym for *Kelompok Penyanyi Trotoar* (Sidewalk Singer Group). During these hard times, he saw the adversity faced by ordinary people and understood the reality of social problems affecting the working class in Jakarta. This period of hardship proved to be very productive for Kempot, as it was during this period that he wrote some of his hit songs. The opportunity to record his music came when his older brother Mamiek Prakoso introduced him to Pompi Suradimansyah, a member of the band No Koes. Didi, Pompi, Mamiek as well as support singer Dian S. formed the Batara Group together and released the comedic Javanese song "We Cen Yun" (*Kowe Pancen Ayu*/You Are So Beautiful) as a single (Sari & Puguh, 2020).

Although the song became popular with listeners, especially in Jakarta, the Batara Group did not have the wherewithal to promote it extensively. Kempot then left the group to work on a solo career, finding opportunities from different music labels amidst his popularity in Suriname following the *We Cen Yun* album. However, both his songs "Cidro" and "Bungkus Saja" that were released by other music companies also found little success at the time. In 1998, he recorded "Stasiun Balapan", written entirely in the Javanese language, with Lokananta, the first music record label ever established in Indonesia. Again, this record had no success due to a lack of promotion by Lokananta, which was facing internal business problems and suffering from the Asian financial crisis (Puguh, 2018). Kempot, however, did not to give up. His album was then offered to Musika Studio, one of the largest music companies in Indonesia. With the excellent promotion by the company and the support of many Indonesian radio stations, "Stasiun Balapan" became a huge hit and catapulted Kempot to fame in Indonesia.

As his name and popularity grew from the 2000s to 2019 after the success of "Stasiun Balapan", Kempot produced many more albums but stayed true to his Javanese roots. In total, the prolific songwriter released 80 albums with more than 700 *campursari* songs during his music career. Most of his songs have been covered by new singers, recorded into CDs and uploaded to YouTube, Spotify and other music streaming channels. His songs became hugely popular, particularly among those who shared his mother tongue. His music can often be heard on the Indonesian public transport, especially in buses, and are frequently played at various activities and events in many Javanese villages. Kempot's popularity also extends overseas among Javanese migrants who work in places such as Hong Kong, South Korea, Singapore, Middle Eastern countries, and Suriname where a third of its population comes from Javanese backgrounds (CNN Indonesia, 2020). Songs such as "Terminal Tirtonadi", "Stasiun Balapan", "Sewu Kutha", "Parangtirits", "Kuncung", "Nunut Ngiyup", "Sekonyong-konyong Koder", "Cucak Rowo", "Layanng Kangen", "Dalan Anyar", and "Suket Teki" are well known among the Javanese.

Although Kempot has gained recognition and steady popularity, his fans remain largely those of Javanese descent. For his Javanese fans abroad, his songs evoke a nostalgic imagery of life and people in home towns, and help shape the Javanese identity in a globalising world where modernity is eroding Javanese sensibilities in everyday life. Agus Mulyadi's Twitter post on June 10, 2019 revealed the influence of Kempot and his songs on the younger generation (Figure 1). Agus Mulyadi is the Executive Editor of the media and entertainment publishing website *Mojok.co* that is popular among urban young people, and is also a social media influencer with 80,700 followers at the time of writing. Through his Twitter account @AgusMagelangan, he retweeted a video post by Twitter user @trialdinoo (Keyzie, 2019) which showed a section of male fans at Didi Kempot's concert in Surakarta, Central Java. In the video, the male concert goers were singing aloud their frustrations over their own ill-fated relationships. The retweet of @trialdinoo's video quickly caught the attention of netizens and became viral, chalking up thousands of retweets, comments and likes. In the tweet, Kempot was crowned the "God Father of broken heart [sic]" and caused a massive social buzz online and offline, jump-starting the second birth of Kempot as a star-musician.

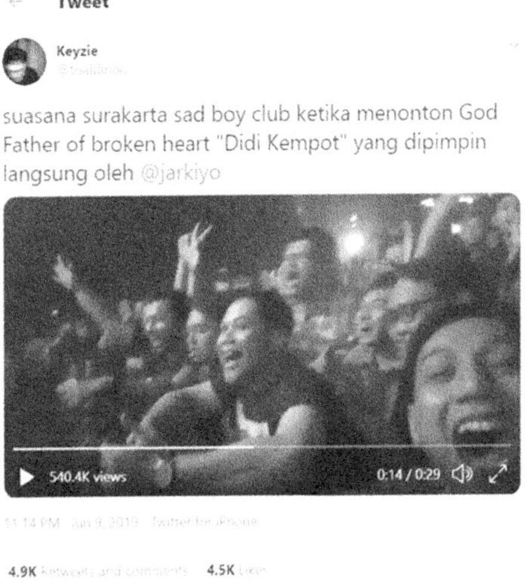

FIGURE 1 Sad boys singing their hearts out at Didi Kempot's concert
Source: Screenshot by author (Mulyadi, 2019)

Gofar Hilman, a social media influencer, urban youth trendsetter, YouTuber and Jakarta radio announcer, quickly recognised Kempot's rising popularity. One of the highly anticipated programmes which Hilman presents on his YouTube channel is NGOBAM (*Ngobrol Bareng Musisi*/Hanging out with Indonesian Musicians). When he mentioned the idea of inviting Kempot to the NGOBAM programme on his Twitter account, many people close to Kempot responded warmly. Using his personal funds, Hilman then went to a café in Solo to hang out with Kempot on July 14, 2019. Some 1,500 of Didi's loyal fans, young men and women who call themselves "Sad Boys" and "Sad Girls", were also present. After this hang-out session was uploaded to Hilman's Youtube channel on July 21, 2019, it trended for several days, and since then, it has received at least 5,870.027 views at the time of writing. After the NGOBAM appearance, Kempot's fan base expanded further. He is celebrated not only by those who speak Javanese but surprisingly also Indonesian millennials who, in the past, had no interest in his genre of music. Known affectionately as "Lord Didi, the godfather of broken hearts" by his fans, Kempot regained his waning popularity and found mainstream fame especially among younger people who identify with Kempot's sad, lovelorn lyrics about heartbreaks or loves lost, and find solace in his songs.

Crying Together with Lord Didi

Didi Kempot was soon receiving invitations to perform on national television channels such as NET TV and TransTV, and to sing at live concerts organised by various institutions and companies. He was also invited to hold solo concerts at Livespace, a large event in Jakarta, and at the Pallas, a popular club among the Indonesian upper middle class that often hosts international musicians. At these two prestigious places, Kempot was singing many of his songs that were enjoyed by young people. He has even been appointed the new ambassador to the e-commerce platform Shopee Indonesia, replacing Blackpink, a K-pop group that is famous in Asia. With his vast popularity, Kempot's concert payments have grown manifold. In the past, he was only paid Rp 25 million (USD2,300) for a concert performance. After NGOBAM, however, he received up to Rp 200 million (USD19,000) for each concert. Kempot was very thankful to Gofar Hilman for introducing him to a diverse new audience of younger people. Hilman, however, did not feel he did anything much as Kempot was a true legendary Indonesian pop musician who cleverly expressed the sadness and heartbreak of the current young people dealing with their love relationships (Kumparan, 2020).

Although both Agus Mulyadi and Gofar Hilman contributed to Kempot's rise to prominence on social media, I believe there are some other factors that lend to the popularity of his songs among the Indonesian youths of diverse ethnicities. Obviously, the momentum from going viral on social media is not enough to sustain a performing artist's career for a long time. Shinta-Jojo, Norman Kamaru and Udin Sedunia are exemplars who, after going viral on social media, had been invited to perform by many Indonesian television channels and at various music shows. However, after one or two years, their names have all but disappeared from the public sphere. Therefore, in order to explain Kempot's resurgence or revival in popularity, it is essential to understand that social media is not the only determining factor.

First, audiences are taken with the strength of Kempot's song lyrics and the blending of *dangdut* and *campursari* tunes. While other Indonesian love songs that emerged in the 1990s talked about love and despair in a direct and literal sense, such as "Hati Yang Luka" ("Broken Heart") by Betharia Sonata, most of Kempot's lovelorn lyrics would delve deep into the heartache and bitterness of love within the context of everyday life (Supriatma, 2020). For instance, in "Pamer Bojo" ("Showing off Your Lover"), he sings about someone who has been left by his or her lover:

Dudu klambi anyar neng njero lemariku
Nanging bojo anyar Sing mbok pamerke neng aku
Dudu wangi mawar sing tak sawang neng mripatku
Nanging kowe lali nglarani wong koyo aku

It is not new clothes within my wardrobe
However, the new lover that you show in front of me
This is not the fragrance of the rose that I smell
You have forgotten our love and make my heart ache

Although the lyrics are sad, the combination of *dangdut* and *campursari* music would compel listeners to dance. Therefore, in every concert, Kempot often calls out to those in the audience who are broken hearted to "dance together" (*Sakit Hati Dijogeti Wae/ If you have a broken heart, instead of crying, it is better to dance*). In addition, the words employed by Kempot in his song lyrics are mostly derived from the Javanese language used by the working class. When the lyrics are intertwined with the Indonesian language structure, young people will be able to relate and respond very well to the song (Widodo, 2020).

Second, Kempot's music challenges the patriarchal structure of Indonesian society through its depiction of soft masculinity. Javanese culture is predominantly patriarchal where a woman's place is in the kitchen, in a role subservient to her husband. The Javanese term for women, *konco wingking* (literally means "behind the scenes"), is indicative of this. Kempot's lyrics that often weave a story around a Javanese man who is bereft and crying after a broken relationship subtly challenges the existing hegemonic masculinity ideal. This proposes a kind of equality between men and women. Widjaja et al. (2020) agreed that Kempot's songs deconstruct masculinity by questioning the patriarchal structure, particularly the song "Layang Kangen" which tells the story of a woman who is living overseas as a migrant worker while her husband is at home and missing her.

Third, Kempot has had fans from the grassroots level for many years before achieving mainstream fame and becoming trendy among young people. As explained earlier, Kempot has had a long music career, beginning as a street musician in 1983. His songs have become a collective memory among the Javanese people, the largest ethnic group in Indonesia. He was invited to perform in many villages in Indonesian provinces, specifically by people of Javanese descent. Therefore, with and without the hype in social media, Kempot would still inherit the prominent "musician" moniker in the Javanese language.

Conclusion

This chapter explained the rise of Didi Kempot which culminated in the second wave of his career in Indonesian music, and the reasons why his songs are enjoyed by the Javanese diaspora in Indonesia and overseas. While social media influencers drew the attention of Indonesian youth of diverse ethnic backgrounds to Kempot's *campursari* genre of music, his rise to fame in Indonesia can be attributed to various factors: the strength of his song lyrics in expressing the sadness and bitterness of love, the ideas within his music performances and songs that challenge the patriarchal system, and his loyal and keen fans who supported him over the course his long career.

References

CNN Indonesia. (2020, May 5). Didi Kempot, 35 tahun temani Indonesia patah hati. *CNN Indonesia*. https://www.cnnindonesia.com/hiburan/20200505123741-234-500203/didi-kempot-35-tahun-temani-indonesia-patah-hati

Curry, K. L. (2012). YouTube's potential as a model for democracy exploring citizentube for "thick" democratic content. *Journal of Curriculum Theorizing. 28*(1), 141–157.

Hracs, B. J., Seman, M., & Virani, T. E. (2016). Introduction: The evolving economic geography of music. In B. J. Hracs, M. Seman, & T. E. Virani (Eds.), *The production and consumption of music in the digital age*. Routledge.

Keyzie [@trialdinoo]. (2019, June 9). *Suasana surakarta sad boy club ketika menonton God Father of broken heart "Didi Kempot" yang dipimpin langsung oleh @jarkiyo*. Twitter. https://twitter.com/trialdinoo/status/1137754956822339587

Kumparan. (2020, May 5). Didi Kempot ke Gofar Hilman: Fee naik sampai Rp 200 juta usai ngobam offair. *Kumparan.com*. https://kumparan.com/kumparanhits/didi-kempot-ke-gofar-hilman-fee-naik-sampai-rp-200-juta-usai-ngobam-offair-1tM3lxwd2Ne/full

Leyson, A. (2009). The software slump?: Digital music, the democratisation of technology, and the decline of the recording studio sector within the musical economy. *Environment and Planning A: Economy and Space, 41*, 1309–1331.

Mulyadi, A. [@AgusMagelangan]. (2019, June 9). *Di dunia ini, tak ada yang bisa menandingi Didi Kempot. Robbie Williams, Frank Sinatra, Nat King Cole, semuanya tak bisa. Sebab Didi Kempot adalah semesta yang lain*. Twitter. https://twitter.com/agusmagelangan/status/1137759995385208832

Puguh, D. R. (2018). Perusahaan rekaman lokananta, 1956–1990-an: Perkembangan produksi dan kiprahnya dalam penyebarluasan seni pertunjukan Jawa Surakarta, *SASDAYA: Gadjah Mada Journal of Humanities, 2*(2), 425–450.

Sari, A. D., & Puguh, D. R. (2020). Didi Kempot: Dari pengamen jalanan ke penyanyi terkenal, 1982–2013. *Historiografi, 1*(1), 62–70.

Supriatma, M. (2020, May 6). Didi Kempot (1966–2020): Seniman besar pop Jawa. *Tirto.id.* https://tirto.id/didi-kempot-1966-2020-seniman-besar-pop-jawa-flaJ

Widjaja, S., Santoso, M., & Widyawanti, N. (2020, May 6). Obituari Didi Kempot: Musisi campursari dengan lagu lagu yang berhasil melintasi batas dan mendobrak nilai maskulinitas. *The Conversation.com.* https://theconversation.com/obituari-didi-kempot-musisi-campursari-dengan-lagu-yang-berhasil-melintasi-batas-dan-mendobrak-nilai-maskulinitas-138004

Widodo, W. S. (2020, May 12). Didi Kempot dan bahasa Jawa yang berubah. *Kumparan.com.* https://kumparan.com/wahyu-sri-widodo/didi-kempot-dan-bahasa-jawa-yang-berubah-1tOkiMpNaiD

CHAPTER 28

Research on the "Chinese Style" Works in the Field of Popular Music: A Case Study on Jay Chou's Musical Works

Xiaodan Zhang, *Shanghai Conservatory of Music*

At the turn of the 21st century, a group of singer-songwriters represented by Jay Chou and Leehom Wang combined R&B, hip-hop and other Western popular music styles with traditional Chinese elements such as traditional instrumentation, opera singing, or lyrics containing traditionally Chinese images. This creation set off a style known as the "Chinese Style" in the Mandopop world and injected new vitality into Chinese music. The style not only became an influential way of communicating music culture, but also gave rise to a cultural phenomenon.

Although the popularity of "Chinese Style" has faded gradually since its boom, the influence remains pervasive. In this chapter, I discuss the style with the following topics: the connotations and extensions of "Chinese Style"; the development process of "Chinese Style"; the characteristics of Jay Chou's works in the evolution of "Chinese Style" music; the influence of the style within the historical background of Chinese popular music; and the stages of development in the history of Chinese popular music.

It must be noted and emphasised that "Chinese Style" was not an independent and new music genre technically. It did not have a format that can be categorised accurately, nor was it distinct from genres such as blues, soul, country, jazz, hip-hop, or rock. Unlike the aforementioned genres which were classified primarily by the composition of specific musical elements, the "Chinese Style" merely integrated traditional Chinese elements such as melodies or instrumentation into the style of Western popular music. As such, "China Style" incorporated a diverse range of genres, from R&B and hip-hop to electronic dance music (EDM), into its music. Despite the blend of styles, the "Chinese Style" sound remains distinctive due to the juxtaposition of Eastern and Western elements.

Definition of "Chinese Style"

The term "Chinese Style" discussed in this chapter can be defined in both a narrow and broad sense. In the broad sense, it refers to popular songs containing traditional Chinese elements such as Chinese classical melodies, rhythms, singing style and musical instruments. In the narrow sense, it refers to a music style or school that combines the Chinese and Western elements and was prevalent in China's popular music in the past several years (Li et al., 2010).

No consensus on the definition of "Chinese Style" has been reached. Based on existing analyses and discussions, I have summarised it as a popular music style themed around traditional Chinese culture, taking the form of modern popular music (such as R&B, hip-hop and EDM), and having Chinese connotations (Xu, 2011). It is a form of localisation of the Western popular music. There are explicit and implicit types of "Chinese Style": the former refers to works that include distinctive Chinese traditional elements (such as the use of traditional Chinese musical instruments or classical poems), while the latter refers to songs without the distinctive Chinese traditional elements but filled with Chinese traditional artistic conception. The Chinese aesthetics are a key word for

"Chinese Style"; that is a main reason why the style was most popular with the Chinese or ethnic Chinese. To sum up, there are "Chinese Style" works in form, in content, or both (Wang, 2015).

Evolution of "Chinese Style"

Before discussing the evolution of "Chinese Style", I need to give a brief summary of the development of Contemporary R&B in China. After the 1990s, some musicians from Taiwan had introduced the style to the Mandopop world. Unfortunately, it was not widely accepted by the Chinese audience due to the difference between Chinese and Western culture. Then, a young singer-songwriter called David Tao improved it by weakening the rhythm and heightening the melody, making it more acceptable to the public.

The expression "Chinese Style" had been used in popular songs in Taiwan before it became well known. For instance, Tao adapted an old favourite Taiwanese folk song called "Spring Breeze" in his first album *David Tao* (Liu, 2015). The song featured traditional Chinese music elements presented in an R&B style. Jay Chou's first "Chinese Style" single titled "Wife", was featured in his debut album released in 2000. The single failed to attract much attention for lacking the taste of China. In his second album *Fantasy* produced in 2001, he released "Nunchucks" and "Shanghai, 1943" in which he infused Chinese elements into Western music styles. The album was a huge success and shot Chou to fame. In 2002, Yanbin Hu released two "Chinese Style" songs which were markedly different from each other. Leehom Wang also reinterpreted a classic song "Legend of the Dragon" in the same year. In order to blend Chinese and Western music successfully, he used modern arrangements with the original song.

However, it was thanks to Chou's "East Wind Breaks" released in 2003 that "Chinese Style" became a well-received concept. With profound national connotations, the song went viral across China and became recognised as the first piece of "Chinese Style" music. From then on, Jay promised to present such works in his album each year, creating a unique style and diversifying popular music.

Stages of Jay Chou's "Chinese Style" Works

I. Exploratory Stage

The related albums and songs involved in the first stage of Jay Chou's "Chinese Style" works are as follows:

Published	Album	Songs
2000	*Jay*	"Wife"
2001	*Fantasy*	"Nunchucks", "Shanghai 1943"
2002	*The Eight Dimensions*	"Dragon Fist", "Grandpa's Tea"
2003	*Yeh Hui-mei*	"Double Blade", "East Wind Breaks"

"Wife" released in 2000 was Jay Chou's first "Chinese Style" work. The song, however, failed to fully express the Chinese elements within it due to complicated rhythm changes and a weak melody, limiting its impact. In contrast, the song "East Wind Breaks" released in 2003 was a groundbreaking success and was viewed as the first song of the "Chinese Style". The song marked the start of a new trend of music which fuses traditional Chinese instruments and styles with Western popular music.

At this early stage, which I call the exploratory stage, Chou was still discovering and exploring this form of music. His "Chinese Style" works were still dominated by R&B and hip-hop influences, and only appealed to a limited market (Li, 2015).

II. Mature Stage

The related albums and songs involved in this stage are as follows:

Published	Album	Songs
2005	*November's Chopin*	"Hair Like Snow"
2006	*Still Fantasy*	"Chinese Herbal Manual", "Moulin Rouge", "Far Away", "Chrysanthemum Terrace"
2007	*On the Run!*	"Incomparable", "Porcelain"

"Hair Like Snow" released in 2005 was a huge success: the classical and melancholic arrangement, the use of the Chinese traditional instrument, and the combination of popular music, rap and the "rhotic accent", were innovative and classic. "Far Away" released in 2006 combined not only popular music and rap, but also the bel canto style of operatic singing. Then, "Porcelain" in 2007 became a mega hit and was one of Chou's most well-known songs. The song combines classical Chinese lyrics and traditional instrumentation with modern sound technology. The song lyrics have been used in textbooks for high school students, and the music has been taught in music classes. In addition, Chou was invited to perform the song at the *CCTV Spring Festival Gala 2008*, an annual Chinese New Year TV Special.

At this stage of the "Chinese Style" evolution, which I dub the mature stage, the style had begun taking on a standard form. This period was also the heyday of "Chinese Style" in Chinese popular music. Traditional Chinese melodies, lyrics, singing styles, and musical instruments are standard components of songs produced during this period.

III. Deep-going Stage

The related albums and songs involved in this stage are as follows:

Published	Album	Songs
2008	*Capricorn*	"Lanting Xu"
2010	*The Era*	"Flowers Wither", "Rain Falls All Night"
2011	*Wow!*	"Shadow Play"
2012	*Opus 12*	"Eunuch With a Headache", "Worldly Tavern"
2014	*Aiyo, Not Bad*	"Passers-By"

"Lanting Xu" released in 2008 was mellower and sadder in melody compared with earlier songs. But it was the album *The Era* released in 2010 that marked a turning point in the "Chinese Style" work as employed by Chou. In this album, he experimented with different music styles and expressions. The song "Flowers Wither" from *The Era* album was particularly unique. It did not have obvious Chinese traditional musical elements, but was full of Chinese traditional artistic conception. "Passers-By" was the last standard "Chinese Style" song by Chou to date.

In general, Chou had gone beyond the standard form or pattern of "Chinese Style" songs and begun working on the connotations and profoundness of these songs. As one of the creators who led and popularised the style, Chou seemed to be a little weary of the "Chinese Style" music and tried seeking a creative change during these years. The indifference shown in "Passers-By" may be reflective of his attitude towards the standard "Chinese Style" music to some degree.

IV. Transitional Stage

The related albums and songs involved in this fourth stage include the following:

Published	Album	Song(s)
2006	*Still Fantasy*	"Moulin Rouge"
2010	*The Era*	"Rain Falls All Night"
2011	*Wow!*	"Shadow Play"
2012	*Opus 12*	"Eunuch With a Headache"
2016	*Jay Chou's Bedtime Stories*	"Now You See Mee", "Turkish Ice Cream"

There was no significant change in style between the songs released during this stage and those of the preceding stages. There were, however, marked changes in Jay Chou's creative concepts.

By the time "Chinese Style" became fashionable after 2003, many musicians were attracted to it, resulting in a plethora of similar works of mixed quality. Chou expressed his concern about excessive imitation and the lack of quality in "Chinese Style" in the song "Moulin Rouge". In "Rain Falls All Night", he tried breaking the standard "Chinese Style" pattern: the first verse of the song was an urban pop, while the second transformed to "Chinese Style". After that, the style was hardly evident in the *Jay Chou's Bedtime Stories* album released in 2016. In this album, the traditional Chinese elements in "Now You See Me" and "Turkish Ice Cream" were merely decorative elements to the EDM style music.

Chou had realised the limitations of the standard "Chinese Style" and attempted to make creative breakthroughs by limiting the traditional Chinese elements within a song, resulting in it sounding more westernised as a whole than before. Despite the seeming similarity of the new songs to those from the first "Chinese Style" stage, I think the return marks a new beginning of a higher next stage. As the first stage was an exploratory period, it was not easy to grasp the proportion between Chinese traditional elements and the Western. However, during this stage, Chou emphasised obvious Western music elements such as electronic sound effects and the loop in his works. In short, most "Chinese Style" songs were based on the R&B and hip-hop genres during the earlier stages, while EDM plays a more dominant role at the moment.

To some degree, it can be said that the evolution of Chou's music reflected the development and progression of the "Chinese Style" in Chinese popular music. The changes in Chou's music at each stage would influence the creation of other musicians, and affect the whole Mandopop music industry as well.

Localisation of Chinese Pop Music

In the broader context of the history of Chinese popular music, "Chinese Style" represented a stage in the evolution of Chinese popular music. Since popular music was introduced to Mainland China in the 1920s, some Chinese musicians had tried combining Chinese and Western music such as Li Jinhui and Chen Gexin. In the 1980s, the "Northwest Style" represented another attempt to localise disco and rock; "Zou Xi Kou", "Loessial Fields" and "My Beloved Hometown" were quite popular songs during this period. By the 1990s, songs from the "Campus Ballad" and "Urban Ballad" genre such as "My 1997", "A Letter from Home" and "A Brother Sleeps on the Top Bunk" combined ballad with the Chinese conditions. In the 21st century, "Chinese Style" as themed around R&B and hip-hop became a new form of national popular music.

When we talk about the localisation of popular music in Chinese popular music, we can find other genres such as "Lyric Song" in the 1980s and "New Folk" after 2000. The label "National Customs" in Mandopop music has also become fashionable in recent years.

Conclusion

"Chinese Style" was a popular music style at the beginning of the 21st century which themed around traditional Chinese elements and took the form of modern popular music (such as R&B, hip-hop and EDM). While it was not an independent music style or genre compared with blues, jazz or rock, it was a new form of music due to the juxtaposition of Western popular music and traditional Chinese music elements.

In fact, the development of Chinese pop music is a microcosm of the blending of Chinese and Western cultures. The expression of "Chinese Style" music can sometimes lean more heavily towards either the Chinese or the Western culture, making the process of music making more nuanced.

Therefore, no matter the attitude towards "Chinese Style" and no matter the limitations, the music style was a step forward in the Mandopop industry and in the development of Chinese-Western culture in the contemporary era.

References

Li, W., Lan L., & Guo L. (2010) A study on the definition and significance of "Chinese Style" songs. *Literature Education*, (2010.01), 111.

Li, Y. (2015) The appreciation of Jay Chou's composition in Chinese style. *Art Science and Technology*, (2015.02), 168.

Liu, Q. (2015). *Research on the phenomenon of Chinese Style in Chinese popular music* [Master's thesis, Guangxi University].

Wang, S. (2015) South Korean fad and Chinese Style. *Art of Singing*, (2015.12), 25–27.

Xu, L. (2011) *Research on songs of "Chinese Style"* [Master's thesis, Chongqing Normal University].

CHAPTER 29

Voicing the *Muhibah* Spirit Through Namewee's *Ali, AhKao dan Muthu* (2017)

Xin Ying Ch'ng, *UCSI University*

As Malaysia approached its 60th year of independence from British colonial rule on August 31, 2017, National Day celebratory events such as a re-enactment of the historic day in 1957 went on impervious to mounting frustrations against the ruling Barisan Nasional (National Front) government (Landau, 2017). The 2017 Merdeka celebration was significant as this was less than nine months before the Barisan Nasional (National Front) coalition was toppled for the first time in the 14th Malaysian General Election since the formation of Malaya. On May 9, 2018, the opposition coalition Pakatan Harapan (Alliance of Hope) won in a landslide victory, securing 113 of the 222 parliament constituencies that were contested. In a nation where political issues were frequently contested along racial, religious and ethnic lines, Namewee's music video *Ali, AhKao dan Muthu* demonstrated the celebration and idealisation of Malaysia's pluralistic and ethnically diverse identity. This chapter analyses comments recorded in the music video's official YouTube page to understand the reception and performance of Namewee's music video and how it provided an emotional response that led towards national unity.

Namewee, whose real name is Wee Meng Chee, is no stranger to the local Malaysian music scene. A versatile performer, singer, songwriter, music producer and filmmaker, Wee's work involves films, music videos and songs of various genres. Despite his recent successes from high profile collaborations with top artists in the Mandopop industry such as Wang Leehom and Jam Hsiao, the popularity of Wee's songs resides often in their unconventional lyrics, localised subjects and informal mixture of Mandarin and the vernacular. His infamous rap video *Negarakuku*, released in 2007 as a parody of Malaysia's national anthem while still a student in Taiwan, gained him a level of notoriety which led to governmental pressure that he should be prosecuted under the law. An outspoken critic, Wee's work is often seen as a social commentary on issues of racial discrimination and inequality that are strongly felt in many sectors of the Malaysian society. Apart from *Negarakuku*, Wee's film *Nasi Lemak 2.0* released in 2011 focuses on the iconic Malaysian dish as the linchpin that weaves themes of multiracial harmony and nation-building.

Ali, AhKao dan Muthu was Wee's tribute to Malaysia's 60th National Day. The music video and song demonstrate a strong patriotic spirit personified through the life journey of three title characters representing the three major races of Malay, Chinese and Indian that make up the multiracial Malaysian community. It was uploaded to YouTube on July 29, 2017. By August 3, the video had garnered close to 800,000 views and was the third highest trending video on YouTube Malaysia (Seto, 2017). According to Wee, the names Ali, AhKao and Muthu are typical names frequently associated with characters found in Malaysia's school textbooks. These names symbolically represent Malaysia's multiracial identity that is widely inculcated by and promoted through the national curricular system. Apart from highlighting the racial diversity in Malaysia, Wee made a conscious effort to include three Malaysian artists from different generations in the recording of the song and filming of the music video. The song features the vocals of 11-year-old Malay artist Aniq, 67-year-old local pop music veteran David

Arumugam of the band Alleycats, and Wee himself (Figure 1). The strong demonstration of the *muhibah* spirit, symbolised by the interracial and intergenerational selection of artists in *Ali, Ahkao dan Muthu,* elicits an emotional response among Malaysians collectively identified as national.

FIGURE 1 Still from the music video of *Ali, AhKao dan Muthu* featuring (from left to right) Aniq, David Arumugam and Wee Meng Chee
Source: Screenshot by author (Namewee, 2017)

Interracial Community Imagined as National

Riding on the overwhelming response of *Ali, AhKao dan Muthu,* Wee launched a music video competition on August 3, 2017, stipulating that performers must include all three major races of Malay, Indian and Chinese singing to the same song. The competition allowed for creative renditions of the new song and a total cash prize of RM20,000 from the organisers for the best three entries. The music of *Ali, AhKao dan Muthu* is straightforward with singable melodic lines and clear harmony. With a strong introduction of electric guitar riffs with bass and drums, each artist in the trio ensemble takes turns singing a single melodic line before coming together at the chorus. The lyrics were penned by Wee himself in simple Malay, coupled with a strong narrative portraying the unchanging friendship of the three title characters and their journey to adulthood. Wee's competition provided an opportunity for an actualisation of racial integration which is iterated in textbooks but not often realised. By focusing on the song and music video, the competition presented participants a part to play in fostering interracial harmony through the performative act of singing.

Wee's *Ali, AhKao dan Muthu* is significant on two accounts. First, the music video provides a new methodological framework on *voice*, especially in the discussion of national identity and racial unity imagined and highlighted in the song. Second, the YouTube comments for this song provide a particularly pertinent barometer in documenting the political climate of the nation especially in response to the general election in 2018. In relation to the first aspect, I draw on theoretical concepts of voice that focuses on music as a performative, instead of a compositional, centred act. According to Dunn and Jones (1994), the aspect of voice is utilised as a term that signals the interrelationship between vocal expression and its accompanying cultural constructions.[1] Voice represents a myriad of meanings in relation to cultural issues and popular expression, including—but not limited to—issues of identity, empowerment, authority and autonomy. My envisioning of voice and the performative act of voicing in the singing of Wee's song realise aspects of interracial harmony, expressed not only vocally through the lyrics but also visually through the music video.

Given that the transient quality of Aniq, Arumugam and Wee's singing voices makes for difficult pinning down, I also analysed the reception of *Ali, AhKao dan Muthu* as documented on Wee's official YouTube channel. Using responses generated from the YouTube comments, I mapped the responses onto discourses of identity politics, more specifically those that collectively highlight issues of nationhood and national belonging in relation to Malaysia. Given the overwhelming response to Wee's song, I only documented and analysed the first 500 of 6,910 comments (as documented on June 24, 2020) that were posted since the upload of the official YouTube video on July 29, 2017 at 8:00 p.m. (Namewee, 2017). The comments found on YouTube document first-hand responses to Wee's music, effectively making the video sharing site a platform for cultural mediation. This is significant as potential sites of reception are no longer confined or fixed to printed or literary material, but located on the fluid digital and online platform of YouTube.[2] In a way, I analysed how *Ali, AhKao dan Muthu*'s performance allows for emotional engagement that taps into wider national concerns and issues of race and identity in Malaysia.

Muhibah as Basis of Unity

As clearly explained by author David CL Lim, the prevailing notion of race and belonging in Malaysia in the dealings of everyday life is unmissable and "half-grasped in the essentialist sense as something real, heritable and more important than other categories of difference like class and gender" (Lim, 2008, pp. 155–156). Hence, the realisation of a united Malaysia regardless of the delineations and divisions of race, ethnicity and religion has been promoted repeatedly under different governmental initiatives from previous prime ministers such as Mahathir Muhammad's Vision 2020 and Najib Tun Razak's 1Malaysia. Through this, the Malay term *muhibah*, broadly translated as attributes of friendship, goodwill and mutual tolerance, has been echoed and reiterated extensively from speeches to print and digital media in the idealisation of the interracial harmonious spirit to which Malaysians are called to adhere.[3] The conceptualisation of *muhibah* capitalises on aspects of similarities that unite, as opposed to differences that divide, for the purpose of nation-building. The concept of camaraderie is clearly demonstrated in *Ali, AhKao dan Muthu*, where Wee's music and the corresponding YouTube comments not only resonate with Malaysian citizens but also voice a strong identification for a nation united by the spirit of *muhibah*.

Among the 500 comments collected from the music video on YouTube, a theme focusing on national unity and interracial harmony clearly emerged. Due to Wee's wide international fan base, the comments posted were not solely from Malaysians. There were comments from fans and listeners from neighbouring Southeast Asian countries such as Indonesia and Thailand, and also Taiwan. Despite being the first Malay song written by Wee, listeners identified strongly with the qualities of an enduring friendship that transcends racial, religious, linguistic and cultural limitations often perceived as barriers to establishing relationships. Such means of identification were seen clearly through the strong emotional responses expressed in the comments, as at least 30 listeners reported to have been "moved to tears". The ability of music to move listeners emotionally could be explained as emanating from the music's structural elements of rhythm, melody, tempo, mode and dynamics (Rühlig, 2016, p. 60). However, Frith's explanation on popular music as predominantly "an experience of identity … [where] we are drawn, haphazardly into emotional alliances with the performers and the performers' other fans" is significant (2011, p. 121). Upon identifying with the lyrics, the narrative and the message behind *Ali, AhKao dan Muthu*, Wee's listeners projected an idealised version of Malaysia that has been socially mediated and collectively imagined as real.

The YouTube comments equally pointed to several accounts of discrepancies where patriotic zeal and pride for the nation were in direct conflict with expressions of condemnation and frustrations towards the ruling government. Comments such as "Government teach Ali Ahkao Dan Muthu to hate each other" (Tony LK, July 29, 2017, 9:09:57 p.m.) and "Tbh [to be honest] Malaysian is a harmony family [sic] but the government make us hate each other. Yes all the politics party make use hate and separate each other" (Izal, July 29, 2017, 8:57:32 p.m.) are among two of the many comments that encapsulate the feelings of citizens towards perceived governmental failures in the projects of nation-building. This is exemplified by the supposed politicisation of issues by authorities whose practices can be presumed to be symptomatic of institutionalised racial discrimination and race-based affirmative policies appropriated as national. Despite the active promotion of policies representing national solidarity and unity, the comments on YouTube highlight actual sentiments felt among citizens. Alleged mismanagement of state investment funds, such as the controversial 1MDB scandal, ultimately renders nation-building efforts hollow. Additionally, mounting dissatisfaction against perceived manipulation of the electoral system culminated in four large-scale protests held between 2007 and 2015 in Kuala Lumpur (Fernandez & Hookway, 2015).

Conclusion

Amidst social unrest and political distrust, Wee's music video in celebration of the 60th National Day provides a reference point where interracial friendships are promoted despite inherent cultural and religious differences. This is demonstrated by many YouTube comments which suggest that *Ali, AhKao dan Muthu* should be sung as a national anthem, in collective acknowledgment of its message of interracial harmony and national solidarity. To Wee's fans, Ali, AhKao and Muthu are not only figurative characters in what Frith called "an imaginative cultural narrative" (Frith, 2011, p. 124). They represent tangible glimpses of what an idealised Malaysia would look like in the actual realisation of the *muhibah* spirit. As Ali, AhKao and Muthu sang at the top of their lungs, "*Kawan selama-lamanya, satu hati, satu jiwa. Kita semua rakyat Malaysia, tak kira darah dan warna, hanya satu impian, satu negara*", they dreamt of a Malaysia where its people are united regardless of race and colour in aspiration for one heart, soul, dream and nation.

Notes

[1] For more information on concepts of voice and the accompanying theoretical constructs in relation to music studies, see Dunsby (2009) and Feldman et al. (2015).

[2] For more information on the area of reception and how that correlates with interpretations and readings of musical works that shift away from a single theological approach to a more inclusivist one, see Samson's entry in Grove Music Online (Samson, 2001).

[3] The Malay definition of *muhibah* is taken from the online Malay dictionary moderated by Pusat Rujukan Persuratan Melayu under Dewan Bahasa dan Pustaka (Kamus Bahasa Melayu Dewan Bahasa dan Pustaka Malaysia, n.d.). Examples and accounts on the wide-ranging uses of *muhibah* can be found from *New Straits Times* ("What makes us bangsa Malaysia?", 2003), Sennyah (2004), and Gomez and Harinderan (2008) to more recent ones from Zahiid (2019) and Lee (2019).

References

Dunn, L. C. & Jones, N. A. (Eds.). (1994). *Embodied voices: Representing female vocality in Western culture*. Cambridge University Press.

Dunsby, J. (2009). Roland Barthes and the grain of Panzera's voice. *Journal of the Royal Musical Association, 134*(1), 113–132.

Feldman, M., Wilbourne, E., Rings, S., Kane, B., & Davies, J. Q. (2015). Why voice now?. *Journal of the American Musicological Society, 68*(3), 653–685.

Fernandez, C., & Hookway, J. (2015, August 30). Malaysia protesters face uphill battle to dislodge Prime Minister Najib Razak. *Wall Street Journal.* https://www.wsj.com/articles/malaysia-protesters-face-uphill-battle-to-dislodge-prime-minister-najib-razak-1440929869

Frith, S. (2011). Music and identity. In S. Hall & P. du Gay (Eds.), *Questions of cultural identity*. (pp. 108–127). http://dx.doi.org/10.4135/9781446221907

Gomez, J., & Harinderan, K. (2008, February 11). PM: Muhibah spirit must continue: [Main/Lifestyle edition]. *New Straits Times.*

Izal. (2017, July 29). *Merdeka 60th Theme (Ali AhKao Dan Muthu) Namewee/Dato' David Arumugam/Aniq @亞洲通吃 2018 All Eat Asia.* [Video]. Youtube. https://www.youtube.com/watch?v=nVjvTJ6sEEc

Kamus Bahasa Melayu Dewan Bahasa dan Pustaka Malaysia. (n.d.). Muhibah. In *Pusat Rujukan Persuratan Melayu*. http://prpm.dbp.gov.my/cari1?keyword=muhibah

Landau, E. (2017, July 29). All geared-up for the 60th Merdeka celebrations. *New Straits Times.* https://www.nst.com.my/news/nation/2017/08/274024/all-geared-60th-merdeka-celebrations

Lee, L. T. (2019, September 10). Uphold spirit of muhibah. *New Straits Times.* https://www.nst.com.my/opinion/letters/2019/09/520408/uphold-spirit-muhibbah

Lim, D. C. L. (Ed.). (2008). "Your memories are our memories": Remembering culture as race in Malaysia and K.S. Maniam's Between Lives. In D.C.L. Lim (Ed.), *Overcoming passion for race in Malaysia cultural studies*. (pp. 153–166). Brill.

Namewee. (2017, July 29). *Merdeka 60th Theme (Ali AhKao Dan Muthu) Namewee/Dato' David Arumugam/Aniq @亞洲通吃 2018 All Eat Asia.* [Video]. Youtube. https://www.youtube.com/watch?v=nVjvTJ6sEEc

Rühlig, T. (2016) "Do you hear the people sing" "Lift Your Umbrella"?: Understanding Hong Kong's pro-democratic umbrella movement through YouTube music videos. *China Perspectives, 4*, 59–68.

Samson, J. (2001). Reception. *Grove Music Online*. https://doi.org/10.1093/gmo/9781561592630.article.40600

Sennyah, P. (2004, May 9). Priority for racial understanding, tolerance programmes: [New Sunday Times, 2nd edition]. *New Straits Times.*

Seto, K. Y. (2017, August 3). 'Ali, Ahkao dan Muthu' goes viral on Youtube. *New Straits Times.* https://www.thestar.com.my/news/nation/2017/08/03/ali-ahkao-dan-muthu-goes-viral-on-youtube/

Tony LK. (2017, July 29). *Merdeka 60th Theme (Ali AhKao Dan Muthu) Namewee/Dato' David Arumugam/Aniq @亞洲通吃 2018 All Eat Asia.* [Video]. Youtube. https://www.youtube.com/watch?v=nVjvTJ6sEEc

What makes us bangsa Malaysia? (2003, September 3). *New Straits Times.*

Zahiid, S. J. (2019, January 22). Promote 'muhibah' with open houses for Raya, Deepavali too, commerce group told. *Malay Mail.* https://www.malaymail.com/news/malaysia/2019/01/22/promote-muhibah-with-open-houses-for-raya-deepavali-too-commerce-group-told/1715220

INDEX

H

I

J

K

L

M

N

O

P

Printed and bound by CPI Group (UK) Ltd, Croydon, CR0 4YY

05/05/2026

14871572-0002